HARD TO SWALLOW

HARD TO SWALLOW
Hard-core Pornography on Screen

edited by
Claire Hines & Darren Kerr

WALLFLOWER PRESS
LONDON & NEW YORK

A Wallflower Press Book
Published by
Columbia University Press
Publishers Since 1893
New York • Chichester, West Sussex
cup.columbia.edu

Copyright © Clare Hines & Darren Kerr 2012
All rights reserved.
Wallflower Press® is a registered trademark of Columbia University Press.

A complete CIP record is available from the Library of Congress

ISBN 978-0-231-16210-4 (cloth)
ISBN 978-0-231-16213-5 (pbk.)
ISBN 978-0-231-85015-5 (e-book)

Design by Elsa Mathern

CONTENTS

Notes on Contributors — ix

Introduction: Is Hard-core Hard to Swallow? — 1
Claire Hines and Darren Kerr

Part One
Turned On: Hard-core Screen Cultures

1. Pornography in the Multiplex — 11
   Brian McNair

2. The Dark Side of Hard-core:
   Critical Documentaries on the Sex Industry — 27
   Karen Boyle

3. Art School Sluts: Authenticity and the Aesthetics of Altporn — 42
   Feona Attwood

4. Pornogogy: Teaching the Titillating — 57
   Mark Jones and Gerry Carlin

Part Two
Come Again? Hard-core in History

5. 'White Slavery', Or the Ethnography of 'Sexworkers':
   Women in Stag Films at the Kinsey Archive — 81
   Linda Williams

6. Lost in Damnation:
   The Progressive Potential of *Behind the Green Door* — 101
   Darren Kerr

7. The Limits of Pleasure? Max Hardcore and Extreme Porn — 113
   Stephen Maddison

8. Playmates of the Caribbean: Taking Hollywood, Making Hard-core — 126
   Claire Hines

Part Three
Fluid Exchanges: Hard-core Forms and Aesthetics

9. Fashionably Laid: The Styling of Hard-core   147
   Pamela Church Gibson and Neil Kirkham

10. *Shortbus*: Highbrow Hard-core   163
    Beth Johnson

11. Homespun: Finnporn and the Meanings of the Local   177
    Susanna Paasonen

12. Reel Intercourse: Doing Sex on Camera   194
    Clarissa Smith

13. Power Bottom:
    Performativity in Commercial Gay Pornographic Video   215
    John Mercer

14. Interrogating Lesbian Pornography:
    Gender, Sexual Iconography and Spectatorship   229
    Rebecca Beirne

    Selected filmography   244

    Index   247

ACKNOWLEDGEMENTS

We would like to thank the Faculty of the Creative Industries and Society and our colleagues, past and present, at Southampton Solent University for their support throughout the writing of this book. In particular we would like to thank Jacqueline Furby, David Lusted, Karen Randell, Steven Peacock, Donna Peberdy, Tony Steyger, Mark Aldridge and Mark de Valk for their generosity, suggestions, sense of humour and sometimes just for listening. To this list we must add Scott Anderson and Robin Jones for putting up with our endless porn-talk in JM227. We would also like to acknowledge a debt of gratitude to the enthusiasm and commitment of the 'Sex on Screen' students and especially Dr Wendy Leeks for supporting the course. Thanks also to Yoram Allon and Jodie Taylor at Wallflower Press for their cooperation and assistance throughout the project.

Finally, special thanks to our respective family and friends for their encouragement, confidence and patience in our work, especially Jackie and Sue.

This book is dedicated to Jason and Stephen.
And to J.

NOTES ON CONTRIBUTORS

Feona Attwood is Professor of Sex, Communication and Culture at Sheffield Hallam University, UK. She is the editor of *Mainstreaming Sex: The Sexualization of Western Culture* (2009) and *porn.com: Making Sense of Online Pornography* (2010), and the co-editor of journal special issues on Controversial Images (in *Popular Communication*, 2009), Researching and Teaching Sexually Explicit Media (in *Sexualities*, 2009), and Investigating Young People's Sexual Cultures (in *Sex Education*, 2011).

Rebecca Beirne is Lecturer in Film, Media and Cultural Studies at the University of Newcastle, Australia. She has published journal articles and book chapters on queer representation in popular culture, and is a founding executive member of PopCAANZ: the Popular Culture Association of Australia and New Zealand. She is the author of *Lesbians in Television and Text after the Millennium* (2008), the editor of *Televising Queer Women* (2008) and co-editor of *Making Film and Television Histories: Australia and New Zealand* (2012).

Karen Boyle is Senior Lecturer in Film and Television at the University of Glasgow, UK. She is the author of *Media Violence: Gendering the Debates* (2005) and editor of *Everyday Pornography* (2010) and has published articles on related issues in journals including *Feminist Media Studies*, *Women's Studies International Forum* and the *New Review of Film and Television Studies*.

Gerry Carlin is Senior Lecturer in English at the University of Wolverhampton, UK. He has published articles on British Modernism and critical theory, and is currently researching 1960s culture.

Pamela Church Gibson is Reader in Cultural and Historical Studies at the University of the Arts, London, UK. She has published extensively on film, fashion, fandom, gender and 'heritage' and is the author of *Fashion and Celebrity Culture* (2011) and the editor or co-editor of four anthologies, including *The Oxford Guide to Film Studies* (1998) and *More Dirty Looks: Gender, Pornography and Power* (2004).

Claire Hines is Senior Lecturer in Film and Television Studies at Southampton Solent University, UK. Her research and publications focus on sexuality, gender, fantasy and 007. She is the co-author of *Fantasy* (2011) and is currently writing a book that explores the relationship between James Bond and *Playboy*.

Beth Johnson is Lecturer in Film and Visual Theory at Keele University, UK. Her recent publications include work on masochism, perversion, real sex and experimental film. She has just completed a book about the works of television auteur Paul Abbott (2012) and is the co-editor of *Television, Sex and Society: Analyzing Contemporary Representations* (2012).

Mark Jones is Senior Lecturer in English and Film Studies at the University of Wolverhampton, UK. He has published articles on science fiction, horror and popular music. He is currently researching 1960s exploitation fiction and film.

Darren Kerr is Senior Lecturer in Film and Television at Southampton Solent University, UK. He has published articles on screen violence, adaptation and sex on screen. He is currently researching contemporary British horror across film and television and is co-editing a forthcoming collection entitled *Tainted Love: Screening Sexual Perversities*.

Neil Kirkham is Lecturer in Cultural and Historical Studies at the University of the Arts, London, UK. He has recently completed his PhD, entitled 'Simple Pornographers? The Marquis de Sade and the Evolution of the Hard-Core Pornographic Film Narrative', and is preparing a series of journal articles based on his doctoral research.

Stephen Maddison is Principal Lecturer in Cultural Studies at the University of East London and co-runs the website opengender.org.uk. He is the author of *Fags, Hags and Queer Sisters: Gender Dissent and Heterosocial Bonds in*

Gay Culture (2000). His work on pornography has appeared in the journals New Formations and Topia, and in the recent collections Mainstreaming Sex (2009) and porn.com: Making Sense of Online Pornography (2010).

Brian McNair is Professor of Journalism, Media and Communication at the Creative Industries Faculty, Queensland University of Technology, Australia. His books include Mediated Sex: Pornography and Postmodern Culture (1996), Striptease Culture: Sex, Media and the Democratisation of Desire (2002) and Porno? Chic! How Pornography Changed the World and Made it a Better Place (2012).

John Mercer is Lecturer in Media and Cultural Theory at Birmingham City University, UK. He is the co-author of Melodrama: Genre, Style and Sensibility (2004), and has published articles on gay pornography that have appeared in Paragraph, The Journal of Homosexuality and the anthology Framing Celebrity (2005).

Susanna Paasonen is Professor of Media Studies at University of Turku, Finland. Most recently, she is the author of Carnal Resonance: Affect and Online Pornography (2011) and co-editor of Working with Affect in Feminist Readings: Disturbing Differences (2010).

Clarissa Smith is Reader in Sexual Cultures at the University of Sunderland, UK. Her published work includes studies of softcore pornography, sexualisation and young people, sex toy retailing, British sexual culture and masochist fiction, and the book One for the Girls! The Pleasures and Practices of Reading Women's Porn (2007).

Linda Williams is Professor of Film and Media, and Rhetoric at the University of California, Berkley. She has published widely on the subject of sex and cinema. Her books include Hard Core: Power, Pleasure and the 'Frenzy of the Visible' (1989/1999) and the anthology Porn Studies (2004). Her most recent book is Screening Sex (2008).

INTRODUCTION

IS HARD-CORE HARD TO SWALLOW?

Claire Hines and Darren Kerr

Hard-core is hard to swallow. Obvious puns aside, it does seem apt to use this popular idiom to introduce a collection of essays focused on what in contemporary culture remains one of the most problematic of screen genres, pornography. But perhaps, given the collection's remit to critically analyse screen representations of hard-core porn, this particular opening, and even the book's title, might be more accurately phrased as a question rather than a statement. So, why is hard-core hard to swallow?

Certainly, this is a question that we as editors had at the forefront of our minds while we worked on putting this collection together. Some answers to this question emerged during a trip to New York, when in addition to taking in Manhattan's usual iconic sights such as the Empire State Building, Statue of Liberty and Central Park, we also elected to visit the city's Museum of Sex (or MoSex as it likes to be called). Our visit to MoSex can serve as a useful metaphor for the way that this collection thinks about sex and contributes to the way that we study sex on screen.

Located on Fifth Avenue, the Museum is just a few blocks away from the towering Empire State Building in a section of New York that – rather fittingly – used to be known as the 'Tenderloin', a district notorious for its many brothels, dance halls and bars. But even though the building that MoSex is now housed in is alleged to have once been a brothel (a claim which can of course be linked to porn's familiar discourse of authenticity, discussed here by some of our contributors), in keeping with the Museum's careful approach to its sexual subject matter, the design of its new façade treads that all-important line between sexy and sleazy, legitimate and illicit.

From the outside, the building's blacked-out lower windows advertise its current (and often most sensational) exhibitions, tempting visitors in. At the same time, the Museum's furtive side entrance is a reminder that, for many people, a curatorial approach to sex and sexuality is at best strange and incongruous and at worst unethical, damaging, or quite simply wrong. The difficulties its curators have experienced since the institution opened in 2002 can help us to identify some of the most obvious reasons why, as one of the most graphic visualisations of sex on screen, hard-core pornography is still so hard to swallow.

Firstly, it is significant that when MoSex was founded as a museum it was denied non-profit status by New York State. The result of this decision is that, unlike the city's other notable museums, such as the Metropolitan Museum of Art, the Museum of Modern Art (often shortened to MoMA – MoSex is a tongue-in-cheek reference to the Museum of Sex's more distinguished counterpart) or the Guggenheim, which are all non-profit institutions, the Museum of Sex is forced to rely almost exclusively on ticket sales in order to run. This denial of non-profit status can be thought of as symbolic of the low cultural/artistic status of a museum/visit or a book/student devoted solely to the subject of sex. Furthermore the fact that visitors must be over the age of 18 and pay a set fee in order to enter this museum is also symbolic of the reputation, function and value of pornography as a commodity where money is exchanged for sex.

Secondly, from its inception in 2002, MoSex's commitment to 'being an institution unlike any other, one wholly dedicated to the exploration of the history, evolution and cultural significance of human sexuality', and mission to advocate 'open discourse surrounding sex and sexuality', have been viewed as inherently problematic tasks considering its graphic subject matter (Museum of Sex 2008a). After all, can a museum setting really contain sex? And do the (paying) public want it to? In an article for *Time* following MoSex's opening, journalist Joel Stein (2002) gave his verdict on the experience of visiting it as one 'heavy on the museum and light on the sex [...] Even the good stuff is shown in that museum way that kills the fun' (incidentally, the 'good stuff' that he is referring to here includes 'S/M paraphernalia' and stag films). Although debatable, his is an opinion that neatly summarises the tensions that also frame many of the contributions to this collection – between public and private, curatorial and voyeuristic, intellectual and venereal, aesthetic erotica and hard-core porn. Much like the Museum of Sex and the other influential academic works on the hard-core screen discussed below, the contributors to this collection continue to negotiate and debate these boundaries, while also challenging them.

The final point for us to consider is the actual exhibitions and installations that MoSex contains. From its inaugural and award-winning exhibition 'NYCSEX: How New York Transformed Sex in America', to the exhibition on 'Sex in Design/Design in Sex' we saw during our trip, MoSex supplements its permanent collection of over 15,000 artefacts with temporary exhibitions that focus on different aspects of sex and sexuality, including sex in art, kink, technology, pin-up photography and even 'The Sex Lives of Animals'. However, when we looked round the Museum, it was the exhibition 'Action: Sex and the Moving Image' that, for obvious reasons, caught our attention. Not only were we interested in the moving images featured in the exhibition, we were also attentive to the ways in which these images were presented by MoSex and how our fellow visitors responded to them.

In line with the Museum's stated aim to stimulate thought and discussion, 'Action: Sex and the Moving Image' surveys the history of sex on screen – ranging from early stag films to sexploitation, and 1970s porno-chic to contemporary celebrity sex tapes – in order that visitors 'become literate in the barrage of sexual driven images in our society' (Museum of Sex 2008b). Of course, as readers of this collection are no doubt aware, this objective comes with its own complications since education and information necessitate exposure and literacy necessitates familiarity – the implication therefore is that the visitor/viewer becomes complicit with the material that is either viewed (at a safe distance?) or consumed (the connotation here is of dangerous proximity). To some extent however MoSex does appear to acknowledge and even embrace the voyeuristic pleasures that the films it exhibits might arouse. For example, the Museum illuminates its typically bright white exhibition space with low-key blue lighting, images are projected onto blocks on both the floor and walls, and at the edge of the room there are some 'peepshow-style booths' (Walters 2008) that show video/clips on a loop. 'In other words', as film critic Ben Walters writes following his own visit to the exhibition, 'the experience is not short on moving images, nor on moans, pants and gasps for that matter'.

It is unlikely though that the 'moans, pants and gasps' that might be heard in the 'Action' exhibition or indeed elsewhere in the Museum of Sex actually come from any of its patrons. For while we sat down in a booth to watch an explicit sex video in its entirety, most visitors did not really linger at the exhibits, or if they did they were more liable to giggle than groan. MoSex's good-natured warning – 'Please do not touch, lick, stroke or mount the exhibits' – is also a clever marketing ploy (and is printed on postcards, posters and fridge magnets that can be purchased from the museum shop) that plays on the potential for arousal, so that visiting the Museum becomes, amongst other things, a form of intellectual foreplay.

Fig. 1 Forewarning and foreplay: marketing MoSex. Courtesy of the Museum of Sex.

For us, 'Action' was a particularly fascinating (if fairly heterosexual) exhibition about sex on screen that charts many of the key social, cultural, technological and theoretical debates and developments that also provide the discursive frameworks for this book. Moreover, the issues raised by a visit to a museum that is about sex (and for some people the issue is that such an institution exists in any case) are very similar to those raised by an academic book that is about hard-core pornography: the desire to study and analyse all aspects of human sexuality, including hard-core, can be hard to swallow, because with this desire also comes a fundamental challenge.

To follow Michel Foucault (1987), this challenge is then, in part, to continually interrogate the ways in which sex is spoken about, and for this collection it is via the hard-core screen. As a result of its controversial history pornography is now seemingly defined and readily explained before it is even looked at. Between the anaesthetised reappropriation in modern porno-chic and continued legislative action that restricts its availability, pornography is no longer descriptive but indicative. So indicative has this term become, mostly of unwanted and unwelcome excess, that it is now a short-hand for the sensational vernacular of journalese in its use of 'torture-porn', 'poverty-porn' and 'gun-porn'. It is, by design, habitually contained within moral, ethical and political discourses on public health and cultural well-being.[1] This reductive and provocative use of the word, as inherently objectionable, defines it as being *known* and yet this supposed knowing has emerged over a time when a growing body of critical and academic research – in conjunction with new institutions like the Museum of Sex and more established institutions like the Kinsey Institute – has drawn attention to just how *unknown* the hard-core screen really is.

This scholarship has sought to move beyond the hyperbole of moral campaigners' arguments about screen pornography and its effects. Endlessly cited in the recent critical history of pornography, Linda Williams' breakthrough study from 1989, *Hard Core: Power, Pleasure and the 'Frenzy of the Visible'*, has now come to be recognised as an indispensable account of the subject and the need to address matters of *on/scenity*. Edited collections from Williams (2004), Pamela Church Gibson (2004) and Peter Lehman (2006) have further illustrated how the hard-core screen is eclectic, expressive and needs to be historicised and theorised. These frameworks for understanding have been the focus of work from Laura Kipnis (1996), Laurence O'Toole (1999) and Brian McNair (2002), who collectively investigate the very terms of debating pornography, hard-core's relation to history and technology, and links between sex and modern culture.

The contradictory state of hard-core, as both known and unknown, drives the demand for new critical readings, understandings and approaches that, by necessity, returns us to the screen as a *text*, which is the primary focus of this collection. *Hard to Swallow* looks closely at screen representations of pornography and explicit sex alongside hard-core's relationship with history, culture and sexuality. Part One, 'Turned On: Hard-core Screen Cultures', offers a timely account of pornography and the screen coming together. This section considers the effects of hard-core's relationship to vision technologies and particularly how hard-core in the mainstream is frequently less exploitation and more exploited. Brian McNair's 'Pornography in the Multiplex' expands on his own critical work on the *pornographication* of culture by tracing the relationship between hard-core and the big screen. McNair reflects on the desire of cinema to harness the 'sexually transgressive power of porn' while trying to avoid its objectionable status in the mainstream. In contrast Karen Boyle focuses on the small screen to consider the ways in which documentaries on porn blur the boundaries between factual television broadcasting and the pornographic. What is at stake here is the questionable means by which docuporn, such as Channel 4's *Hardcore* strand (25–28 April 2005; 10–19 April 2006), critiques its 'dark' subject matter.

Whilst film and television have been staple sites for the study of hard-core, Feona Attwood discusses the emergence of alternative online pornographies produced by 'new porn professionals' such as Bella Vendetta and the Suicide Girls. This analysis of online screen representation, art and politics in altporn serves to further question matters of authenticity and sexual self-expression in pornography. The need to interrogate these hard-core screen cultures converges on the academy in Mark Jones' and Gerry Carlin's chapter on the relationship between higher education and the pornographic. The 'secure' critical investigation of hard-core in higher education is challenged by Jones and Carlin to address the complexities of taking porn into pedagogy.

Part Two, 'Come Again?: Hard-core in History', reflects on the necessity to continually engage with hard-core heritage and its relationship to contemporary critical understanding. This section deals with the problematic past of the hard-core screen, whilst acknowledging its challenging future as a subject of study. Linda Williams reflects on the talk she gave on the occasion of the Kinsey Institute's first public screening of material from its stag collection. The resulting account is published here, examining a collection of stag films curated under the theme of 'women-in-charge'. Williams not only addresses matters of female agency and the intricacies of representing women in the stag film, but also calls for the preservation and dissemination of hard-core's heritage in anthologies to further understand the impact of pornography on culture. Like Williams, Darren Kerr considers the issue of female agency in a controversial hard-core classic. Often overlooked as a result of the 'porn wars' critical debates, *Behind the Green Door* (1972) is re-evaluated as a progressive moment in porn history with its reflective awareness of how fantasy is produced, sexual performance is exhibited and hard-core porn is consumed.

Pornographic film criticism has continually sought to engage with contentious developments in the history of hard-core which has, as Stephen Maddison notes, become increasingly explicit. The notorious work of 'Max Hardcore' forms the basis of Maddison's analysis which explores the limits of pleasure in the highly controversial realm of 'extreme porn'. The final chapter in this section registers a significant historical moment in hard-core porn's aspirational return to big screen production style, effects and marketing. In a comparative study, Claire Hines examines parallels between Hollywood and hard-core, and looks at the ways in which the porn film phenomenon of *Pirates* (2005) achieves crossover status.

Part Three, 'Fluid Exchanges: Hard-core Forms and Aesthetics', offers case-studies which consider the various intersections between porn, culture and identity. Collectively they explore the indelible relationship that the iconography of hard-core has on the politics of representation in a variety of porn film forms. Pamela Church Gibson and Neil Kirkham explore the previously neglected function of fashion and style in hard-core. Their investigation takes into account not only the further fragmentation of hard/soft-core in 'clothed pornography', but also explores a famous example of such engagement in the 2002 hard-core opus *The Fashionistas*. Church Gibson and Kirkham demonstrate how the film brings together the iconography of the fashion world with hard-core, to unsettle the conventions of heterosexual pornography. In the next chapter very different connections are made when hard-core meets high-brow in John Cameron Mitchell's *Shortbus* (2006). Beth Johnson interrogates the challenges posed by a 'real sex' film that repositions hard-core aesthetics to consider the relationship between physical and intellectual arousal against the backdrop of New York City.

Attention to iconography and aesthetics also loom large in Susanna Paasonen's analysis, but to a rather different effect. This account of Finnish porn considers the ways in which certain images of Finland's national culture and heritage 'author' the hard-core 'homespun' films in Finnporn, or *suomiporno*. Paasonen's concern is how the regional and the national can impact on matters of realism, authenticity and familiarity and the viewer's relationship to what is depicted on screen. Familiarity also informs Clarissa Smith's question of whether porn stars act during moments of hard-core sex. This offers a clear challenge to the idea that sex in porn is 'interchangeable', as evidenced by Smith's close analysis of not only sexual performance for the camera, but also women's agency and 'the specific social world which constitutes pornographic production'.

The expressive qualities of hard-core performance are taken up by John Mercer to argue how performativity in gay pornographic films 'inflects gay culture'. Of particular relevance here are the discursive positions of top and bottom that have emerged specifically in line with the generic expectations of gay male porn. The final chapter in this section further explores queer identity in hard-core as Rebecca Beirne investigates contemporary lesbian pornographic films. The films in question, produced by lesbians for lesbians, continue to 'educate' the viewer whilst, as Beirne argues, drawing attention to authenticity and re-evaluating the gaze.

Finally, editing this book, we feel privileged to have worked with academics who share our enthusiasm and commitment to the study of the hard-core screen. In the spirit of MoSex's caveat, we might preface this volume with some similarly playful advice to our readers about what not to do with the collection of essays. Instead, like us, we hope that you will find them interesting, enlightening and provocative and that they stimulate further critical engagement, making the hard-core screen a little less hard to swallow.

NOTES

1   Still evident in the UK Government's 2007 Department of Health Rapid Evidence Assessment on viewing extreme pornographic material.

WORKS CITED

Church Gibson, P. (2004) *More Dirty Looks: Gender, Pornography and Power*. London: BFI.
Department of Health (2007) *The evidence of harm to adults relating to exposure to extreme pornographic material: a rapid evidence assessment (REA)*. London: Stationary Office.
Foucault, M. (1987) *The History of Sexuality Vol. 2: The Use of Pleasure*, trans. R. Hurley. London: Penguin.
Kipnis, L. (1996) *Bound and Gagged: Pornography and the Politics of Fantasy in America*. Durham, NC: Duke University Press.
Lehman, P. (ed.) (2006) *Pornography: Film and Culture*. New Jersey and London: Rutgers University Press.
McNair, B. (2002) *Striptease Culture: Sex, Media and the Democratisation of Desire*. London: Routledge.
Museum of Sex (2008a) 'Our Mission and History', *Museum of Sex*. On-line. Available: http://www.museumofsex.com/inside/our-mission-and-history/ (accessed 15 April 2009).
____ (2008b) 'Action: Sex and the Moving Image', *Museum of Sex*. On-line. Available: http://www.museumofsex.com/exhibit/action (accessed 15 April 2009).
O'Toole, L. (1999) *Pornocopia: Porn, Sex, Technology and Desire*. London: Serpent's Tail.
Stein, J. (2002) 'Having Sex, Museum-Style', *Time*, 15 October. On-line. Available: http://www.time.com/time/columnist/stein/article/0,9565,365016,00.html (accessed 15 April 2009).
Walters, B. (2008) 'We can all be voyeurs at the Sex Museum's film exhibition', *Guardian* [Film Blog], 31 December. On-line. Available: http://www.guardian.co.uk/film/filmblog/2008/dec/31/new-york-sex-museum-film-exhibition (accessed 15 April 2009).
Williams, L. (1989) *Hardcore: Power, Pleasure and the 'Frenzy of the Visible'*. London: University of California Press.
____ (ed.) (2004) *Porn Studies*. Durham, N.C.: Duke University Press.

TURNED ON
Hard-core Screen Cultures

CHAPTER ONE

PORNOGRAPHY IN THE MULTIPLEX

Brian McNair

Moving image pornography is as old as cinema itself. As has been the case with other media technologies before and since (print, photography, video tape, internet), the pornographic potential of film was an important factor driving its development – a killer application, indeed. Short pornographic films were being circulated in America in the 1910s and in France even earlier. Film made an enhanced voyeurism possible – watching others having sex, without the inconvenience of having to be present. In her discussion of the origins of moving image pornography Linda Williams (1990) links it to the 'Animal Motion' experiments of Eadweard Muybridge, and what she characterises as their fetishisation of the body. Pornography, she argues, takes fetishisation of the human form a stage further, for the purpose of sexual arousal, and in film finds an ideal carrier medium.

The illusion of reality permitted by the technology of the moving image was quickly spotted by early pornographers, and the first stag reels appeared in the late nineteenth century. The French 'cinema of attractions', 'obsessed with exploring the mechanisms of looking made possible by the movies', was visible in 1896 (Matlock 2004). These short films were made for exclusively male audiences, gathered together in brothels or at stag parties, at a time when female sexuality was suppressed or prohibited from free expression. The consumption of moving image pornography in early 'cinemas' is paradigmatic of the gendered nature of such consumption ever since. It began as a men-only pursuit, and if that male-ness has been diluted in recent years, porn has continued to be perceived – and critiqued – as an essentially male cultural form.

The content of the early stag reels was remarkably similar to that of later generations of pornographic movie – the graphic representation of sexual activity, unadorned by professional quality scripts, acting or production techniques; moving images of people fucking, in all the ways that were possible (and a few that were not, or only with great difficulty, but were tried anyway; *The Good Old Naughty Days* (2002), a compilation of French reels made in the 1920s, includes scenes of, as the *Sight & Sound* review puts it, 'spanking, cunnilingus, fellatio, group sex, voyeurism, urination, masturbation, anal and vaginal intercourse, ejaculation and bestiality' (Williams 2004)). To the extent that they had narratives, these were merely structuring devices for guiding the viewer from one climactic scene to another. The point of porn then, as now, was to turn the viewer on, to induce an erection, to bring him to the point of masturbatory orgasm by granting access to transgressive representations of otherwise hidden, private activities.

Because they were transgressive, early porn movies existed on the fringes of legality, if they were not outlawed entirely. Western societies policed porn with vigour in the early twentieth century, with grand gestures such as the throwing of 25 kilometres of 'obscene' film into the river Seine by the Parisian police in 1912. The desires porn stimulated were generally regarded as unseemly and shameful, their indulgence a private act of transgression, to be shared if at all only with other like-minded males. Like prostitution and gambling the consumption of pornography was not something one would wish to do in polite company, but was ritualised within male bonding contexts in which groups of men together had licence to look, whoop and holler.

Here again, the early history of moving image pornography is paradigmatic of what came later with the invention first of sound, then colour photography. Pornography was liberalised in the Western world in the 1960s, as is well known. But if it was no longer a criminal offence to view pornography in most countries (and rules about what could be shown in cinemas varied between, for example, the more liberalised regimes of Sweden and Germany, and the highly restricted environment of the UK), it remained a leisure activity steeped in shame. After the sexual revolution pornographic films were shown in cinemas for the first time, but only in specially designated 'adult' theatres, to audiences comprised largely of solitary men who sat and did what they had to do in the anonymity provided by darkness. Even after the sexual revolution the consumption of pornography remained a private, solitary practice, geared to masturbation, and not to the shared, public space of the mainstream cinema. If pornography was the pariah of representational practice, these X-rated venues were on the shadowy, shameful margins of cinema culture. They were legal, but hardly mainstream. In most cities they were located in the red light urban zones, often alongside sex shops, brothels and peep shows, removed from the sight of decent folk. Teenage boys, such as this author in the early 1970s, would sneak into places like the Classic Grand in Glasgow, to see porn films with titles such as *Teenage Jailbait* (1973), *Erotic Dreams* (1974) and *Do You Believe in Swedish Sin?*(1972) (see McNair 2002). The films were soft-core, reflecting the state of sexual censorship in the UK at that time, but the furtive nature of their consumption in these dark palaces of sin made them powerfully erotic.

For a brief period only can it be said that pornography became part of mainstream cinema culture, part of the popcorn and hotdog business. This was the first wave of porno-chic, taking in the early to late 1970s with films such as *Deep Throat* (1972) and *Behind the Green Door* (1972). The story of *Deep Throat* is well known, and features in a documentary made by Fenton Bailey and Randy Barbato (*Inside Deep Throat*, 2005) and which was itself screened in cinemas as part of the trend towards porno-chic in the multiplex (see below). To summarise: the liberalisation and sexualisation of Western culture in the 1960s permitted pornography to become more explicit, more acceptable, and more ambitious in its aesthetic qualities. Films became longer, their scripts more developed, their production values more luxurious. They were still a long way from winning any awards (except those eventually established by the porn industry itself), but their makers aspired to artistic seriousness. P. T. Anderson's *Boogie Nights* (1997) dramatises this phase of porn's history, as we see Dirk Diggler (Mark Wahlberg) and his colleagues act out 'proper' narratives in which sexually explicit scenes are 'contextualised' by the action, rather than merely gratuitous. *Boogie Nights* pokes affectionate fun at the absurdity of this ambition, but it was sincerely held, and full-length feature films such as *Deep Throat* were the result. This 90-minute long film told the story of a woman who discovers that she has her clitoris in her throat. As a result, she can achieve orgasm only by 'deep throating' a succession of erect penises, a novel form of sex therapy which is shown in its full splendour.

Made for less than $200,000, *Deep Throat* appeared at a moment in US cultural history when sexual liberalisation had progressed sufficiently to permit exhibition in a mainstream cinema in New York. Ordinary people, as opposed to the raincoat-adorned brigade of sleazy perves who in the public imagination frequented adult cinemas, were curious about pornography, by then emerging into public view on a number of fronts. The stigma associated with the form was in decline, and anti-porn feminism was yet to unite with born-again evangelism to reinforce its pariah status. Thus, the queues which formed to see *Deep Throat* as the buzz around the movie spread included young and old, men and women, couples and grannies. For the first time, pornography crossed over from the underground of adult entertainment to that of mainstream cinema.

The huge success of the film at the box office encouraged similarly ambitious works, such as *Behind the Green Door* and *The Devil in Miss Jones* (1973) – sexually explicit, hard-core pornography (i.e. depicting penetrative sex), but framed with a degree of narrative sophistication and at least the aspiration to aesthetic worth. In less liberal regimes, such as the UK, this first wave of porno-chic produced less explicit soft-core films such as the *Confessions...* series, beginning in 1974 (see Hunt 1998). The same year also saw the first of the *Emmanuelle* films reach multiplex audiences, marketed not as pornography but high-class erotica for discerning liberals. Though less explicit, these films had the same significance in their respective markets as *Deep Throat* had in the US – they expressed the growing social acceptability of images which had previously been forbidden in public by legislation, or marginalised to the periphery of cinema culture.

This liberalism did not last. The rise of second-wave feminism in the 1970s brought with it an anti-porn discourse centred on the alleged contribution of the form to the maintenance of patriarchal culture. Moving image pornography, like advertising, was subsumed within the feminist critique of patriarchal culture's general objectification of women. Its graphic representations of sexual activity were defined as oppressive, violatory, exploitative and degrading. As the women's movement grew, the consumption of pornography became again a shameful activity, at least for those men who viewed feminism with empathy and solidarity.

As the 1970s gave way to the 1980s, the Reagan presidency saw a resurgence of born-again religious extremism in the US, and the emergence at the heights of government of another set of arguments against porn, this time premised on theological views of the sacred nature of human sexuality. Porn was demonic and sinful, in this reading, because it encouraged and championed sexual activity outside of the sanctified realm of marriage and family. In the mid-1980s anti-porn feminism fused with Christian evangelism, leading to the Minneapolis Ordinance and other gestures designed to criminalise or marginalise pornography (see McNair 1996). Pornography remained legal in the US, thanks largely to the protections on free expression and speech offered by the first amendment to the constitution, but it re-acquired pariah status, since viewing it branded one either as a sinner damned to eternal hellfire, or a misogynist only one step away from committing rape. The naive curiosity and excitement generated by the appearance of *Deep Throat* in 1972 was a thing of the past. As Linda Ruth Williams puts it in a review essay on *Inside Deep Throat*, 'after a heady, anything-is-possible moment of "porno chic", when the world and her husband queued up outside theatres and hard-core became the darling of the embryonic "couples audience", came the shaky years when feminists joined hands with moral enforcers to censure the new form' (2005b: 25).

The *pornographication* of mainstream Western culture (see McNair 2002) which occurred from the late 1980s brought a second wave of porno-chic, as we shall see below, and *Deep Throat* would later be revived, even canonised, in the re-evaluation of all things retro – including 1970s porn – which characterised the 1990s and 2000s. But pornography did not, and has not moved back into mainstream cinema, even momentarily, for one simple reason (I suggest). In the early 1970s and the era of *Deep Throat*, there was no video technology and no internet. Home computers did not exist. Moving image pornography could be viewed only on celluloid, either on home projectors or in cinemas. For most people, the latter was the most convenient means of accessing moving image porn.

In the 1980s and 1990s, as the production and consumption of pornography expanded in the liberal capitalist world, it did so not in the form of films made for cinema, but on video tape, disc, and then online, using personal computers. The consumption of pornography, to repeat, is an essentially private past time, indulged in as an accompaniment or prelude to masturbation. It is thus best suited to media platforms which allow solitude and privacy – the very opposite of cinematic exhibition. The dramatic expansion of what I have elsewhere called the *pornosphere* (McNair 2002) occurred, therefore, not in the cinema, but in the domestic environment, where it has remained. This is probably just as well, since pornography has never inspired what anyone could call great movies, even when accessing decent production budgets and artistic talent. Notwithstanding occasional attempts to demonstrate otherwise, pornography is stubbornly antithetical to art, whatever medium is employed to distribute it, and thus difficult to present in any context other than the immediate sexual self-gratification which has always been its distinctive aim. The challenge to make pornography which is at the same time aesthetically valid remains unfulfilled.

PORNO-CHIC IN THE MULTIPLEX

The expansion of pornography since the 1980s, then, has not occurred in the public sphere of the cinema, but in the private realm of the living room, on the back of technologies which decentralise, diversify and democratise the communication system, and which also make it much harder to control than ever before. Pornography has been globalised, through websites such as YouPorn.com which make what would once have been called 'stag reels' accessible to consumers all over the world, including countries in which traditional platforms for distributing porn, such as magazines and video tapes, were tightly policed. In the process porn has retained its transgressive essence, and thus its allure in markets where it was hitherto banned or restricted. Although it has never been more available, nor the legal and moral constraints on its consumption fewer, pornography remains a cultural form on the periphery of the mainstream. Why go to see porn in a cinema, when it can be accessed in the privacy of one's own home?

There *is* a public, cinematic dimension to the expansion of pornography, however – part of the pornographication of mainstream culture which is at least as significant as the changing patterns of pornographic consumption permitted by new technologies. Pornography has become the *subject* of public discourse, as well as the *object* of transgressive desire, in all forms of popular media, from TV soap operas to style magazines and fashion (see McNair 2002). The term of convenience for this trend is porno-chic, capturing the fact that in many of these popular cultural contexts, the pornographic has been viewed as fashionable, desirable, aesthetically significant, and politically relevant. As the prohibitions on sexual culture loosened in the latter years of the twentieth century pornography emerged as a source of near universal fascination, proving the adage that what is forbidden is, for that very reason, more desirable than that which is permitted. As it became easier to access pornography, it also became more acceptable to talk about it, to treat it seriously in books such as this, to acknowledge the legitimacy of its transgressive pleasures.

A PRELUDE – THE CINEMA OF PORNO-FEAR

Cinema, like other media, found pornography a rich subject for exploration in a variety of contexts which fit with the broad label of porno-chic. Before considering those, however, we note that the period before the pornographication of Western societies was one in which porno-fear dominated public discourse on the pornographic. Whatever people did in private, or in the sleazy surroundings of the peep show and the adult cinema, public engagement with porn had to be premised on its condemnation, and to endorse D. H. Lawrence's 1936 definition of porn as the attempt to defile sex, or 'do dirt' on it.

This mood I have previously referred to as *porno-fear*, in deliberate contrast to the less condemnatory notion of porno-chic. In the texts of porno-fear, pornography is something of which we should be afraid, very afraid, lest it corrupt our morals, destroy our marriages and relationships, violate our young, or contaminate our urban centres with vice. All of these elements are present in a classic of cinematic porno-fear, Paul Schrader's *Hardcore* (1979). In this film, starring Rod Steiger, a morally upright evangelical preacher pursues his daughter when she runs away to the decadent west coast of the US, only to turn up in a porn movie. The plot takes us on a journey through the LA porn industry, in which all those he encounters are either damaged, or despicable, and wholly deserving of the beatings Steiger's character dishes out. Pornography threatens the American family, literally and symbolically.

The plot of *Hardcore* was reprised by Joel Schumacher in *8mm* (1999). Twenty years after Schrader's film, and at the height of porno-chic (see below), Steiger's father-in-search-of-daughter is replaced by Nicolas Cage's private-eye-in-search-of-someone-else's-daughter (a private eye, played by Peter Boyle, features in *Hardcore* too, but having located the missing daughter, he then withdraws from the narrative). To find her, he too must travel to Los Angeles and become involved in the porn industry, in particular its more extreme and violent sectors. While Cage's daughter is not at risk, the search for her, and his mounting disgust at what he learns of the porn business, threatens the peace and sanctity of his own family, which narrowly avoids collapsing under the strain. In *8mm*, the stakes are higher, the fear even greater than in *Hardcore*, since the missing girl is suspected of having been involved in a 'snuff' movie, i.e. a film in which someone is actually killed for the sexual pleasure of the viewer. Such is the depravity and squalor of the porn industry as depicted by Schumacher that the viewer welcomes the successive dispatching of the baddies as an increasingly enraged Cage makes his way towards the conclusion of his search. Both *Hardcore* and *8mm* exemplify what I mean by porno-fear – a view of pornography as distasteful, deviant, dangerous, destructive, toxic to the family and individual morality. Both Steiger and Cage are, if not tempted by the porn to which they are exposed in the course of their quests, gripped by ambivalent sexual desires.

A more subtle, though substantially similar approach to the subject of pornography and its impact is taken in Schrader's 2002 film, *Auto Focus*. Based on the true story of Hogan's Hero TV star Bob Crane (Greg Kinnear), who was murdered by persons unknown in 1978, the film portrays a man brought down by sexual obsession, facilitated by the arrival in the late 1960s of video technology permitting him to make home-made pornography. The subject of this film is not the porn industry, but the deviant desires which fuel it. It is these which compel him to make his own pornography, and thus destroy Crane's marriage, his career, and in the end his life. As one online reviewer described it, the film is 'a tale of sexual compulsion and moral dissolution' (Morrison 2002).

PORNO-CHIC IN THE MOVIES

It would be misleading to suggest that porno-fear has inspired a large number of mainstream films, or that the three titles discussed above represent a major trend in cinema. They do, however, reflect a prevalent attitude to the pornographic in public culture which until quite recently one would find also in journalism, political discourse, art and popular culture in general – a queasiness rooted in the combination of danger and desire surrounding the consumption of pornographic texts, and which links D. H. Lawrence's literary denunciations to Schrader's and Schumacher's morality tales. The appearance of *8mm* and *Auto Focus* in 1999 and 2002 respectively came, however, in the midst of a period of unprecedented mainstream receptiveness to all things pornographic (except, that is, pornography itself, which remained in the private sphere, for the reasons described above). They may thus be viewed as reactions to porno-chic.

If the 1972 screening of *Deep Throat* opened the first era of porno-chic, and was the only time when pornography crossed over into the mainstream cinema, the second can be traced to the late 1980s and the emergence of cultural products which expressed interest in and fascination with the pornographic. In the second era of porno-chic, which continues to the present day, pornography became destigmatised, fashionable. Jeff Koons' *Made in Heaven* photographs from 1987, shot with his then-wife and Italian porn star Cicciolina, represent a key moment in the emergence of porno-chic in high art (see McNair 1996). One could also cite Madonna's late 1980s and early 1990s work, particularly the *Sex* book (1992); advertisements such as Dunlop's S/M-themed promo for TV and cinema, featuring on its soundtrack the Velvet Underground's 'Venus in Furs'; the UK Channel 4's *Red Light Zone* (1995) documentary strand on sexual taboo and transgression as examples of the gradual mainstreaming of pornography, not in the sense that porn itself became part of mainstream TV or cinema or pop music culture, but that talking about and referring to porn, in terms which were not condemnatory, became routine in these non-pornographic contexts.

In cinema we can identify two categories of porno-chic. First, dramas by auteur directors such as Milos Forman (*The People vs. Larry Flynt*, 1996) and P. T. Anderson (*Boogie Nights*) have addressed the nature of the pornography business, and the fortunes of the people who worked in it. Where porno-fear presented porn as the province of the depraved and the demonic, its performers as sick and damaged children, Forman and Anderson tried to understand the human dimension of the industry, to demystify and normalise it. Forman's film focused on the issues raised by pornography for freedom of speech in the US, and was not a celebration of Larry Flynt's *Hustler* magazine, but it portrayed Flynt (Woody Harrelson), his wife and their colleagues and supporters as business people first and foremost, making and selling a legal product for which there was a demand. It used the story of Flynt as a vehicle for a discussion of what freedom of speech means in the US. Forman's film was not 'pro-porn', and the drug-fuelled downfalls of Flynt and his wife (played by Courtney Love in a much-praised role) are not sanitised. His point was that freedom of speech, if it has any value, must include the freedom to produce

Fig. 2 *Boogie Nights*. Courtesy of the BFI.

and consume sexually explicit material of the type contained in Flynt's porn magazines. The film is anti-censorship, rather than pro-porn.

Anderson's *Boogie Nights* is less ambivalent, being less apologetic and at times even celebratory. The film depicts the porn industry as a welcoming, surrogate family for those lost souls who enter its ranks, a place of safety where eccentric individuals such as Roller Girl (Heather Graham) can be themselves and have a role. In so far as Dirk Diggler becomes a cocaine-addicted liability to himself and his employers, this is portrayed as an occupational hazard not of porn in particular, but the Los Angeles entertainment industry in general. And in the end, he returns to the fold, like the prodigal son. *Boogie Nights* presents a world which can sometimes be sleazy and exploitative, but which also has validity and meaning for those who work within it. The porno worlds of *Hardcore* and *8mm*, by contrast, are portrayed as totally without merit, deserving only of annihilation.

A similarly non-judgemental tone informs Marry Harron's *The Notorious Bettie Page* (2005). This bio-pic of the iconic 1950s porn star (played by Gretchen Mol), who specialised in sadomasochistic imagery, also peered beneath the veil of notoriety to examine her life and motivations. Bettie's normalness is stressed, as is that of the people who view her pictures and films. As with *Boogie Nights* and its representation of the 1970s/1980s LA porn industry, in *The Notorious Bettie Page* 'the world of fetish producers comes across as a haven of support and camaraderie (Williams 2006: 58).

In the 2000s porno-chic made its way into mainstream film comedy, with films such as Luke Greenfield's *The Girl Next Door* (2004), Michael Traeger's

The Moguls aka The Amateurs (2005) and Kevin Smith's *Zack and Miri Make a Porno* (2008) having fun with the new-found normality of the pornographic. *The Girl Next Door* plays into teen fantasies (male, at least) of proximity and access to a porn star, having one move in next door to its central character. The dramatic tension and humour in the story arises from the clash of two worlds. In contrast to the era of porno-fear, however, it is the porn star who is portrayed as being the most rounded and interesting character, whose role in the narrative is to loosen up the tight-assed college boy (see Lawrenson 2004).

In *The Moguls*, the residents of a small US town decide to make a porn movie as a way of putting their community back on the map. Though not well-reviewed, the film records a moment in US culture when the idea of 'ordinary' people – i.e. people who are not depraved or damaged – making pornography is still unusual and transgressive enough to be funny, though entirely believable. Smith's *Zack and Miri Make a Porno* works on the same principle – two quite average individuals do porn to make some money. In the process, they discover that they are in love. Like *Boogie Nights*, the making of a porn movie provides a surrogate family for a cast of likeable, vulnerable, needy misfits. Ten years after Forman and Anderson led the way, the most mainstream of movie genres was embracing the pornographication of popular culture.

A darker take on pornography, though still in the category of porno-chic as I have defined it above, informs Swedish director Lukas Moodysson's *A Hole in My Heart* (2004) (see Gilbey 2005). Far removed from the light-hearted approach of *Zack and Miri Make a Porno*, Moodysson presents the story of the making of an amateur porn film in an anonymous Swedish suburban apartment. Two men – Rickard (Thorsten Flinck) and Geko (Goran Marjanovic) – enlist 21-year-old Tess (Sanna Bråding) to perform with them in a series of increasingly graphic sexual episodes, culminating in a scene where Geko vomits into Tess' mouth. The film is shot like a documentary, on video, with most of the dialogue and action improvised by the actors. Scenes inside the apartment are interspersed with bloody footage of cosmetic genital surgery (Tess, we learn, has had breast and labial surgery), and scenes involving Eric (Björn Almroth), Rikard's teenage son, who is an increasingly disturbed onlooker as the action proceeds.

The film is difficult to watch, and does not flinch in its re-enactment of the more extreme forms of pornography. Like *Boogie Nights* and the other mainstream movies noted above, however, Moodysson focuses on the motivations and back stories of the characters, seeking reasons for their interest in porn, and what they might gain from it. Rickard, we learn, has lost his wife and is bringing Eric up alone. Moreover, as a child he was sexually abused by his father. Geko is less obviously damaged, but still in need of friendship and love. Tess has had early sexual experience, possibly abusive, and in her early twenties seeks celebrity (she wants to be on *Big Brother*, but has failed the audition, we learn). She enjoys sex, but also seeks pain. By the end, the viewer has reached some understanding of what it is about these lives which lead them to find making pornography an acceptable, even desirable activity. They are sad characters, but sympathetic too, searching for something which life has otherwise denied them. In an explicit justification of their behaviour, Rickard says at one point:

> Some people say that what we're doing is fucking dirty and ugly. But if that's the case, the whole of mankind has a problem. We're just giving people what they want.

Moodysson himself states that 'the film is an attack [on porn], but also a defence. And it is not the story of four damaged people. It is the story of four wonderful people ... It defends pornography, or at least it defends the people working in pornography.'[1]

Although devoid of the narrative gloss and production values of *Boogie Nights*, *A Hole in My Heart* is still porno-chic, in so far as it humanises the industry and those who work in it, and seeks to enlist understanding rather than revulsion. Moodysson's film challenges us to have sympathy with and empathy for the downbeat and depressed characters it features. While taking care not to make the making of a porn movie look sexy, like his earlier *Lilya 4-ever* (2002) the film proclaims that there are greater evils in this world than the fact that some people are prepared to fuck for money, or even for companionship. Making porn is far from being the worst thing that can happen to a person, he says.

PORNO-DOCS

A second category of cinematic porno-chic is the documentary. A notable feature of film culture in the late 1990s and early 2000s was the appearance in cinemas, including multiplexes, of small-budget, independently produced documentaries. These documentaries sometimes had a political, polemical motivation (*Super Size Me*, 2004; *Fahrenheit 9/11*, 2004). Sometimes they engaged with sensitive subject matter such as child sexual abuse (*Capturing the Friedmans*, 2003). Sometimes they depicted, using docu-dramatic techniques, remarkable human achievements (*Touching the Void*, 2003; *Man on Wire*, 2008). Sometimes they explored the mechanics of particular industries and life styles, including the porn industry. These films were often successful at the box office, a trend confirmed in many countries, including the UK, the US and Australia. They often contained confessional elements, and were therapeutic in intent, as their subjects revealed to the cinema-going public aspects of their lives which in a previous time would have been regarded as deeply private.

On television, as part of the broader trend for porno-chic, auteur documentary makers such as Louis Theroux made films about the pornography industry in the late 1990s (e.g. *Porn* in 1998), and Nick Broomfield made *Fetishes* for the cinema in 1996, about the motivations of the women who worked in an upmarket S/M salon in New York, and also their clients. In 1999 Gough Lewis made *Sex: The Annabelle Chong Story*, which was screened to some critical acclaim at the Sundance Film Festival before receiving a wider release in cinemas across the world. *Sex* told the story of Singapore-born porn star Grace Quek, and her marathon sex session with 251 men in ten hours, an ostensibly record-breaking event which was, in addition to the presence of a documentary-maker on set, filmed for a porno video release.

Sex was a film about the making of pornography, and the emotional and psychological state of one particular woman in the industry. While the marketing of the film played up the promise of explicit sexual content, it also presented a disturbing picture of how one young woman's emotional problems found expression in the performance of sexual excess. The film was not in the porno-fear category, preferring to adopt a non-judgemental position on the porn industry, its performers and producers, but presented the viewer with difficult questions – is Chong a post-feminist symbol of female sexual autonomy, as she herself is heard to argue in the film, or a victim of past sexual trauma, self-destructively sacrificing herself to a misogynistic industry? And if the latter, what does that make the consumer of the films in which she appears, including that featuring the 251-man gang bang?[2]

As mentioned above, *Inside Deep Throat*, made for the cinema in 2005 by Bailey and Barbato, documentarised the story of the original porno-chic text, *Deep Throat* (see Williams 2005b). More than thirty years after *Deep Throat*'s release, this documentary marks its canonisation as a classic, and its historic significance as a cultural milestone.[3]

THE CINEMA OF SEXUAL TRANSGRESSION

Lukas Moodysson's *A Hole in My Heart* may be viewed as porno-chic, for the reasons I have given. It also belongs to a movement in European art-house cinema towards the much more explicit treatment of sex in the context of works which eschew eroticism and resist the label of 'pornography'. Filmmakers, including mainstream directors such as Paul Verhoeven, have always pushed at the boundaries of what is possible in sexual representation, albeit within the constraints imposed by commercial markets. But *A Hole in My Heart*, and films such as *Destricted* (2006), a compilation of short films by seven artists, including Sam Taylor-Wood, Gaspar Noé and Matthew Barney, 'representing their views on sex and pornography' (DVD back cover), engage with the sexually transgressive in an altogether more direct way than mainstream cinema has allowed.

These films have exploited more liberal public and official attitudes to sexually explicit material, often referring to the pornographic, or appropriating its codes and conventions, while insisting on their status as not-pornography. These are films which contain elements of the pornographic, deliberately or not, but which are neither marketed as porn, or as being about porn, i.e. as porno-chic. Lars von Trier's *The Idiots* (1998) was an early example of this trend, with its explicit scenes of group sex involving characters who are pretending to be disabled ('spassing'). This was the first Dogme 95 film, transgressive in its production techniques as much as its subject matter. The film was not about porn, but its content, and the explicit nature of its sexual representation would not have been possible in a non-pornographic context were it not for the trend towards public acceptance of, and interest in, the pornographic which fuelled porno-chic.

In 1999 Catherine Breillat released *Romance*, the first of three films in which she addresses female sexuality in unprecedentedly explicit terms. The structure of *Romance*, in which a young woman engages in a sexual odyssey involving sadomasochism, rape fantasy, public fellatio and other acts, all enacted 'for real', reminds one of pornography, but this is not a porn movie. Breillat's interest, as a woman and a feminist, is in female sexuality, and she uses the liberal environment of the late 1990s to explore her subject in ways which would not have been possible a decade earlier. Her *Anatomy of Hell* (2002) has a similar focus, and refers obliquely to pornography with its casting of Italian porn star Rocco Siffredi as the man chosen by the plot's female protagonist to guide her through a journey of sexual self-exploration (although one would not pick up on the reference unless one were familiar with Siffredi's output). The film was criticised by one reviewer thus: 'Without taboos her films would be redundant, their pornography crude rather than polemical' (Bickerton 2005: 42). But none of Breillat's films can fairly be described as pornography. Rather, they use a cultural environment of unprecedented sexual openness to explore hitherto taboo themes.

Breillat's work forms part of a broader movement of what has been termed 'New French Extremism', which 'has seen auteurs of the *jeune cinema francais* continue to push the limits of acceptable sexual and violent representation in an art-cinema format' (Vincendeau 2005: 62). Alongside Breillat's films in this movement we can place Gaspar Noé's *Irreversible* (2002), with its distressing rape scene, and Virginie Despentes and Coralie Trinh Thi's *Baise-Moi* (2000). The latter achieved notoriety for its gleefully nihilistic account of two women who, after enduring rape and other sexual humiliations, embark on a revenge killing spree. *Baise-Moi* is not pornography either, although it features real-life porn actors in its central roles, and contains explicit sex scenes which, in content and style, would not look out of place in a porn movie (see Mühleisen 2004). It is, like *Romance* or *A Hole in My Heart*, a film which would make no sense without the viewer's assumed knowledge of what porn is, and what it looks like. Anne Gjelsvik and Rikke Schubart, in their introduction to *Femme Fatalities: Representations of Strong Women in the Media*, describe the film as an example of that 'aesthetic strategy' in which

> female directors criticise patriarchy by employing male genres such as pornography. A sexualisation of people, lifestyles and everyday surroundings is central in mainstream entertainment and *Baise-Moi* forces such sexualisation to the extreme by using porno-actors, hard-core pornographic aesthetic, and the point-of-view of the female protagonists. (2004: 12)

FROM EXTREME TO MAINSTREAM

Baise-Moi was released in 2000 in the UK, just as the classification regime of the British Board of Film Classification was being relaxed under the pressure brought by 1990s pornographication. It was shown, therefore, in British cinemas. Relaxation of the rules in the arena of sexual representation also allowed British directors to be more direct and explicit, as tested in Michael Winterbottom's *9 Songs* (2004).

The story of a love affair told in sexual episodes punctuated by live music performances, *9 Songs* avoided the anger and nihilism of 'New French Extremism', to represent sex-as-love. Like *Baise-Moi* and *Romance*, however, the film refers to pornography in its structure – a succession of sex scenes in which the degree of intimacy escalates, from straight sex to oral, then to bondage and so on. There is a 'money shot' (male ejaculation), but this is no porn movie. Rather, it is an attempt to utilise the conventions of pornography in a non-pornographic context (see Williams 2005a). The same can be said of the US production *Shortbus* (2006), made by John Cameron Mitchell. Described by one reviewer as 'a graphic sex comedy with plenty of action and a smattering of orgasms, all claimed by the director to be real' (Wilson 2006: 74), *Shortbus* contains scenes as explicit as those of many porn movies, but in a comedic context.

Although *9 Songs* and *Shortbus* were both shown in multiplexes, they are both less than mainstream. My final example is a film by a firmly mainstream director, made for an international multiplex market. Ang Lee's *Lust, Caution* (2007) is a spy thriller set in wartime Shanghai, but with sex scenes which are

Fig. 3 *9 Songs*. Courtesy of the BFI.

both more explicit, and more deviant than anything previously made for this market. In interviews given to publicise the film's release the director was concerned to stress that *Lust, Caution* was not a pornographic movie. Philip Kemp, however, wrote that 'if the much debated sex scenes are anything to go by, Lee could well become the finest porno director of all time. The scenes are not only totally credible in their context, but carry a fiercely erotic charge rarely seen in mainstream cinema' (2008: 72). We note that the tone here is far from condemnatory. To be regarded as a 'porno director' is no longer shameful.

CONCLUSION

The attempt to make films which harness the sexually transgressive power of the pornographic, while avoiding the latter's pariah status and being received as art – or at least as 'not-porn' – continues. As Lee's film shows, this porn-to-art aesthetic has now moved from the art-house margins to the big-budget mainstream. The commercial success of *Zack and Miri Make a Porno*, at the same time, shows the continuing appeal of porno-chic at the very heart of the mainstream market. As for pornography itself, to which all of these films refer in one way or another, it seems likely to remain the province of the private, domestic sphere, where online technology has made it more accessible than ever before. A remake of *Deep Throat* for the twenty-first century is not impossible, especially if clothed in postmodern irony (who would have thought there was mileage in a *Starsky & Hutch* (2004) remake?) but one wonders what the point would be for an audience able to access all and any type of pornography in the comfort of its own home. We will see.

NOTES

1. From Moodysson's comments on extra features, *Lukas Moodysson Presents* (2005) 4 Disc Boxset.
2. Chuck Palahniuk's novel *Snuff* (2008) presents a similar, though fictionalised scenario, with six hundred men having sex with one suicidal porn star.
3. While these documentaries were screening in cinemas, TV was broadcasting documentaries such as *Pornography: A Secret History of Civilisation* (1999, Channel 4) (also involving Fenton Bailey) and *Pornography: The Musical* (2003, Channel 4).

WORKS CITED

Bickerton, E. (2005) 'Anatomy of Hell', *Sight & Sound*, 15, 1, 40–2.
Gilbey, R. (2005) 'A Hole in My Heart', *Sight & Sound*, 15, 7, 52–3.
Gjelsvik, A. and R. Schubart (eds) (2004) *Femme Fatalities: Representations of Strong Women in the Media*. Göteborg: Nordicom, Göteborg University.
Hunt, L. (1998) *British Low Culture: From Safari Suits to Sexploitation*. London: Routledge.
Kemp, P. (2008) 'Lust, Caution', *Sight & Sound*, 18, 2, 72.
Lawrence, D. H. (1936) *Pornography and So On*. London: Lawrence and Wishart.
Lawrenson, E. (2004) 'The Girl Next Door', *Sight & Sound*, 14, 4, 49–50.
Matlock, J. (2004), 'Keeping Up Appearances', *Sight & Sound*, 14, 4, 28–30.
McNair, B. (1996) *Mediated Sex: Pornography and Postmodern Culture*. London: Arnold.
_____ (2002) *Striptease Culture: Sex, Media and the Democratisation of Desire*. London: Routledge.
Morrison, J. (2002) 'The Prerecorded Fetish'. On-line. Available: http://www.indyweek.com/gyrobase/Content?oid=oid%3A18520 (accessed 31 March 2009).
Mühleisen, W. (2004) 'Baise-Moi and Feminism's Filmic Intercourse with the Aesthetics of Pornography', in A. Gjelsvik and R. Schubart (eds) *Femme Fatalities: Representations of Strong Women in the Media*. Göteborg: Nordicom, Göteborg University, 21–38.
Vincendeau, G. (2005) 'Ma mére', *Sight & Sound*, 15, 3, 62.
Williams, L. (1990) *Hard Core: Power, Pleasure and the 'Frenzy of the Visible'*. London: Pandora.
Williams, L. R. (2004) 'The Good Old Naughty Days', *Sight & Sound*, 14, 4, 50–1.
_____ (2005a) 'The girl can't help it', *Sight & Sound*, 15, 4, 42–3.
_____ (2005b) 'Anatomy of a skin flick', *Sight & Sound*, 15, 6, 24–6.
_____ (2006) 'An innocent broad', *Sight & Sound*, 16, 8, 58–59.
Wilson, V. (2006) 'Shortbus', *Sight & Sound*, 16, 12, 74.

CHAPTER TWO

THE DARK SIDE OF HARD-CORE: CRITICAL DOCUMENTARIES ON THE SEX INDUSTRY

Karen Boyle

Since the late 1990s, a documentary-pornography hybrid – or docuporn – has become a regular feature of late-night television scheduling in Britain. Although docuporn is not always about pornography, it borrows the conventions both of reality TV formats and of soft-core pornography to offer (hetero)sexual arousal with an alibi in an 'infotainment' context. Whilst cable channels are most associated with docuporn, this hybrid form has also found a home on Britain's terrestrial channels: most notably on Channel 4 and five. Indeed, Jane Arthurs (2008) – one of the few academics to have studied these programmes – found that by 1999 the majority of 'factual' broadcasting about sex on Britain's five terrestrial channels could be characterised as 'sex industry docuporn'. Arthurs' work does, however, take a broader view, situating docuporn in the context of sex documentaries more generally. In 1999 alone, she identified a total of 230 sex documentaries on terrestrial television in Britain (2004: 156). Clearly, this is a relatively small proportion of the schedule, but the domination of docuporn within fact-based broadcasting about sex raises some serious questions both about the mainstreaming of the aesthetics, narratives and politics of pornography and about the marginalisation of non-pornified sexual content.

However, it would be misleading to suggest that *all* documentaries about sex – or, indeed, about the sex *industry* – are uncritical docuporn. For example, in 2005 and 2006 Channel 4 offered two seasons of documentaries focusing on the 'dark side of pornography' (25–28 April 2005; 10–19 April 2006). I have proposed elsewhere that even documentaries critical of the sex industry find it difficult to maintain a critical tone as the conventions of 'sexually-arousing' docuporn have become widely accepted and the overall scheduling context is increasingly sexualised (Boyle 2008). In this chapter, I want to investigate these claims in detail, first through an analysis of sex documentaries more generally across the television schedules for 2006, and second through a more detailed discussion of *The Dark Side of Pornography* seasons.

Whilst this chapter focuses on television documentary in Britain the patterns observed here may be of broader significance. In North America and in Europe, many writers – both popular and academic – have referred to the 'pornification' of mainstream culture (for example, Paul 2006; Paasonen *et al*. 2007) and recent academic writing on pornography has often mirrored this process by questioning the boundaries of the pornographic (such as Williams 2004). An examination of television documentaries about pornography speaks to many of the same concerns. Certainly, docuporn deliberately blurs the boundaries of television and pornography, yet its existence *on television* in some ways depends upon maintaining the distinction. Staying on the television side of the boundary legitimates docuporn and provides an alibi for its viewers (it is not pornography but television), whilst also encouraging viewers to become consumers of featured products and advertised services which offer the sexual content and contact that these programmes cannot themselves deliver (see Boyle 2008). An examination of these programmes offers another useful intervention in academic debates about pornography more generally. As I have argued elsewhere, there has in recent years been a textual turn in academic studies on pornography, meaning that questions about production and consumption contexts have been lost (Boyle 2006). Yet television documentaries about the sex industry – both celebratory docuporn and the more critical documentaries that are the focus of this chapter – are almost obsessively interested in precisely those questions about production and, to a lesser extent, regulation that academic study of pornography has moved away from. A discussion of television documentaries therefore contributes to recent scholarly debates about pornographic encounters with the mainstream but, at the same time, as the objects of study are themselves meta-textual (soft-core pornographic commentaries on pornography), it offers an opportunity to consider how pornography talks about itself, not simply as a textual category but as an industrial practice.

SCHEDULING SEX

An analysis of television schedules can provide a useful background for textual analyses of television, establishing a sense of the broader context in which individual programmes are situated. With the rapid growth in delivery platforms, the television schedule is clearly only one possible unit of analysis but it is, I think, a useful one in this context precisely because situating programmes about sex and the sex industry *on television* provides a sense of legitimacy and distinguishes the texts from pornography 'proper'. Arthurs' work – which includes an analysis of the 1999 schedules based on the listings magazine *Radio Times* – provides a model for this kind of analysis, although the rapid proliferation of channels makes a direct replication of her study less meaningful. In analysing the schedules for 2006 (the year of Channel 4's second *Dark Side* season), I have focused on Freeview channels in order to establish what is available on British television *without* subscription, and I have restricted my study to the night-time (from 9pm-close) in light of Arthurs' finding that 95 per cent of sex documentaries were scheduled after the watershed (2004: 94).

So how much 'real' sex is there on television? Listing only those programmes focusing explicitly on human sex, sexual behaviour, sexual display and the sex industry,[1] I identified a total of 647 programmes in one twelve-month period. With 286 programmes – 44 per cent of the total – the now defunct Ftn screened more sex documentaries than any other channel, with an emphasis on docuporn series (*Sin Cities*; *Inside Spearmint Rhino*; *3001: A Sex Oddity*) typically sandwiched between quiz shows and sensational documentaries on crime and the supernatural in the early hours of the morning.[2] Of the terrestrial channels, five had the greatest number of sex documentaries with 67, almost double its 1999 figure (Arthurs 2004: 156). Docuporn series account for much of this content with titles such as *Real Wife Swaps*, a six-part series about Britain's swingers (from 10 April); *Burlesque Girls* (four-part, from 19 April) and *Going Down in the Valley* (six-part, from 17 July), two US-set series focusing on aspects of the sex-industry; and *Naked in New Zealand*, a five-part series focusing on Australian strippers on tour (from 17 July). Screening from midnight, these series – like their Ftn counterparts – seem to target docuporn's traditional 'male post-pub audience' (McLean 2001: 22). Programmes scheduled earlier in the night seem to be more circumspect about their relationship to pornography: dressing up titillation as sex education (*A Girl's Guide to 21st Century Sex*, eight parts from 30 October); promising to 'shock' rather than arouse;[3] offering intimate confessions from ordinary people,[4] or, alternatively, making claims to global significance.[5] While Arthurs (2004: 95) suggests that the legitimacy of documentaries about the sex industry can never be assumed but has to be achieved, five's 2006 schedules suggest that this may apply more broadly to documentaries about *sex* screening before midnight. After midnight, the (soft) pornographic appeal of these programmes seems to be more straightforwardly stated and docuporn dominates.

Whilst five's sex output is up, the number of sex documentaries on Channel 4 in 2006 is less than half what it was in 1999 with only 44 sex documentaries screening in the period studied. With BBC2 showing two sex documentaries and both BBC1 and ITV showing *none*, the total of sex documentaries on these five channels in 2006 (at 113) is less than half the figure identified by Arthurs in 1999 (2004: 156). These figures can, in part, be accounted for by the development of 'families' of channels, with E4 (launched in January 2001) and More 4 (from October 2005) picking up much of the post-midnight sex traffic and contributing 136 sex documentaries between them in 2006. When the 4 'family' of channels are taken collectively, then, they account for 28 per cent of sex documentaries on Freeview. Similarly, BBC and ITV sex documentaries are now more likely to appear on BBC3, BBC4, ITV2, ITV3 and ITV4, though the numbers are small compared to the 4 family and five (see Table 1).[6] It is also worth noting that most of the sex documentaries on the terrestrial channels are repeats (or are later repeated, on the original channel or their sister digital channels). Interestingly, however, this does *not* always apply to the more critical documentaries.

Channel 4's sex documentaries are now concentrated in the 11pm–midnight slot and – unlike E4 where the celebratory *Porn: A Family Business* had endless re-runs – Channel 4 works hard to package its content as legitimate documentary. The grouping of many of these documentaries in seasons or strands (*The Penis*; *The Dark Side of Pornography*; *Tainted Love*; *Sex and Religion*; *Sex in the 80s*; *Sex in the 90s*) provides a sense of gravitas and it is notable that in this context the sex industry is frequently branded as an aspect of sexual practice. For instance, both the *Sex in the 80s* and *Sex in the 90s* seasons begin with considerations of the sex industry – *Madam Cyn's Home Movies* (31 May) and *Lap Dance War* (28 June) respectively – while the *Sex and Religion* strand opens with *The Real Blue Nuns* (16 October), a documentary focusing on the nun as a figment of erotic entertainment. Clearly this has implications for the kind of stories about commercial sex that can be told in these spaces, encouraging an emphasis on sex in relation to business, entertainment and social mores, and marginalising questions about demand, harm and inequality.

Although the listings magazine does not provide detail on every programme, it is nevertheless possible to use an analysis of the schedules to

BBC1	0
BBC2	2
ITV	0
CHANNEL 4	44
FIVE	67
BBC3	21
BBC4	10
ITV2	5
ITV3	2
ITV4	6
E4	107
MORE 4	29
SKY 3	4
UKTV HISTORY	64
FTN	286

Table 1 Number of sex documentaries by channel, 9pm-close, 2006 (Source: *Radio Times*).

observe some general trends and these point to the ways in which fact-based television's representation of sex and the sex industry mirrors aspects of pornography. First, whilst there is an interest in both women's and men's sexual experiences, these experiences are framed rather differently. It is the freakish, the excessive and the dysfunctional which is of interest in relation to women's bodies. Women seem to be controlled by, and defined by, their bodies. For example, female bodies are too fat (*Larger Than Life*, five, 8 May), too orgasmic (*A Hundred Orgasms A Day*, five, 16 February) and inappropriate (*The Trouble With My Breasts*, five, 17 November). In contrast, documentaries focused on the male body emphasise either the unique – as in *The World's Biggest Penis* (Channel 4, 1 February) – or the everyday (*My Penis and I*, BBC3, 3 January; *Me and My Balls*, ITV2, 18 October). The few programmes focusing on male sexual dysfunction are less about bodies out of bounds than psychological problems,[7] meaning that men's bodies are rarely policed in the same way as women's. Even when their sexual practices are constructed as extreme or freakish – as in *Guys and Dolls* (five, 18 September and 10 October), a programme focusing on men who have 'relationships' with life-size dolls – men are the subjects of the documentaries and are usually treated as individuals within them.

Second, the sex *industry* is largely equated with the women within it. This is most obvious in docuporn series such as *Burlesque Girls* (five), *The Brothel* (BBC3), *Inside Spearmint Rhino* (Ftn) or *Porn: A Family Business* (E4), which typically follow a number of women in, or breaking into, the sex industry. Elsewhere (Boyle 2008), I have analysed the stories about commercial sex that emerge in these programmes to argue that docuporn relentlessly equates commercial sex with women, using 'on set' interviews with women involved in the sex industry to detail their motivations, the specific sexual 'services' they perform for money and how much they earn in the process. This not only replicates pornography's obsessive focus on the female body but – importantly – renders the demand side of the equation invisible so that the sex industry exists because there are horny women willing to perform sexually for money, and not because there are 'johns' willing to pay to sexually possess another human being. When men are associated with the sex industry it is, in contrast, as featured stars (*The Real Dirk Diggler: The Life and Times of John Holmes*, five, 29 June), or, more often, as entrepreneurs and visionaries, pushing the boundaries of the permissible, defending freedom of speech and expanding pleasure (e.g. *Sex in the 70s: The King of Soho* on Paul Raymond, More 4, 31 July or *Porn: A Family Business*, E4).

Third, sex documentaries are frequently documentaries about the 'other', offering insights into lives that are private, hidden, glamorous, dangerous or freakish. It is hardly surprising, then, that a significant majority of these programmes focus on people and places outside of the UK: in my examination of the Freeview schedules for 2006, of the 531 sex documentaries with a recognisable location 428 (over 80 per cent) were set outside the UK in whole or part. As one reviewer comments in relation to a Channel 4 documentary about murder, internet sex and swinging in Australia: 'I'm surprised Channel 4 hasn't introduced a strand called "Foreigners Do the Strangest Things"' (Graham 2006: 84). 'Foreigners do the strangest things' would work equally well as the tagline for 4's *Eurotrash*, five's *Real Sex* ('hedonism and the pursuit of pleasure in a variety of exotic locations around the world'), or Ftn/Bravo's long-running *Sin Cities* which takes a quintessentially English presenter around the world in search of perverse sexuality. Yet, despite the globe-trotting pretensions of *Sin Cities* and the hyperbolic claims made by some five documentaries, the 'world' of sex documentaries is largely a Euro-American one. For British viewers, Euro-American locations typically offer both the reassurance of the familiar and the excitement of the foreign. Where anti-porn feminist Susan Cole (1989) once demanded that we ask who the men and women in pornography are, how they got there, and what our relationship to them is, these documentaries allow the British viewer to indulge their curiosity on the first two points whilst placing sex 'workers' at a safe remove so that questions about safety, harm and regulation – if they emerge at all – are always someone else's problem or responsibility. With this in mind, it is striking that in the 2006 schedules trafficking and issues of migration were not tackled in any obvious way in fact-based formats.[8] Yet, even when such issues are tackled, Arthurs' work suggests that there is a reluctance to consider this a *British* problem, focusing instead on the various kinds of threat or risks of contamination *from* the other (2004: 104–5).

Finally, it is worth noting that the same films, themes, people and places crop up time and time again across different programmes and channels – you could be forgiven for thinking that the entire history of pornography (itself a recurring theme) could be boiled down to Hugh Hefner, *Deep Throat* (1972) and *Emmanuelle* (1974). More mainstream 'stars' are certainly not neglected with 'celebrity sex tapes' the subject of documentaries for both Channel 4 and five,[9] whilst the legalised brothels of Nevada – in particular, the Moonlite Bunny Ranch with features in both BBC3's *The Brothel* (from 12 June) and five's *Cathouse* (1 December) – must have struggled to find space for punters in among all the camera crews. Similarly, it seems like there is barely a porn-shoot in LA that is not itself being filmed for the likes of *Going Down in the Valley*, *Porn: A Family Business*, *Sin Cities*, or the numerous one-off documentaries that promise access to this most visible 'hidden' industry. Outside of the sex industry, swinging, bigamy, polygamy and sado-masochism are all recurring objects of fascination, as, perhaps surprisingly in the context of British television, is the penis.[10] In short, a few sensational topics, individuals and locations largely define fact-based programming on sex and the sex industry on British television. Unsurprisingly perhaps, less 'sexy' but salient themes – the reform of British prostitution laws; work challenging the demand from men to buy sex; the links between drug ab/use and the sex industry; 'extreme' pornography and recent moves to regulate it in Britain; sexually transmitted diseases; child pornography and prostitution – are rarely touched upon. One could argue that sex on television has become so synonymous with the light-hearted 'infotainment' approach of docuporn that we lack a televisual language for representing these issues critically. It is this argument I want to develop in the remainder of this chapter through a discussion of a series of programmes which – on the surface – appear to offer a more critical stance.

THE DARK SIDE

Channel 4's two *Dark Side of Pornography* seasons comprised of nine individual documentaries, each an hour in length and typically beginning at 11.05pm. The first season, showing in April 2005, consisted of *Porn Shutdown* (25 April), focusing on a recent HIV outbreak in the LA-based porn industry; *Diary of a Porn Virgin* (26 April), following two British women, and one British man, embarking on careers in porn; *Debbie Does Dallas Uncovered* (27 April), an account of the successful 1970s US-porn film told largely by the men who made it, but with a particular emphasis on trying to locate its female star; and *Death of a Porn Star* (28 April), an investigation of the death (and life) of *Eurotrash* regular Lolo Ferrari (Eve Valois), the woman with the world's biggest breasts. The second season, in April 2006, kicked off with *Amateur Porn* (10 April), which, like *Diary of a Porn Virgin*, focused on the domestic porn-industry. It was followed by *Me and My Slaves* (11 April), a portrait of 'Rick', a sado-masochist slave master, now a Christian yearning to escape his former life; *Hunting Emmanuelle* (12 April), an account of the production and influence of the *Emmanuelle* films; the self-explanatory *Does Snuff Exist?* (18 April); and concluded with *The Search for Animal Farm* (19 April), an investigation into a notorious bestiality film and its female 'star', Bodil Joensen.

The positioning of the programmes in a season focusing on the dark side of pornography appears to offer something different to the celebratory docuporn that otherwise dominates the night-time schedules. Here, the look at pornography is legitimated by the apparent seriousness of subject matter and this is reinforced by the ident which 'brands' the programmes. Showing a naked white woman in profile, sitting alone on the end of a bed with her head downcast and surrounded by recording equipment, this ident conveys a sense of (her) isolation and desolation, whilst the continuity announcer solemnly promises programmes which 'expose' hidden truths. If this branding helps to assure the legitimacy of the programmes (and, hence, of the viewers' interest), and establishes a somewhat sombre tone, nonetheless, there is an indication that the content may not vary too widely from other sex documentaries in that timeslot. Whatever 'side' it is approached from, it would appear that pornography is about women and whilst individual women may be emotionally affected, there is no-one behind the camera or in front of the screen to hold accountable. Whilst the ident-woman is undoubtedly downcast, otherwise she looks healthy and even somewhat idealised: naked rather than nude, perhaps. She is slender (no eating disorders or breast implants here), her pale skin is even in tone and blemish-free (no bruises or track-marks) and she is not wearing obvious make-up nor accentuating her body with pornographic accoutrements. Her environment may be somewhat clinical but it is clean and expensive-looking, the recording equipment the only indication that this is about pornography and not, for instance, infidelity or infertility.

Fig. 4 *The Dark Side of Porn's* sombre ident.

Despite the distinctive branding, it is notable that both the 'darkness' and the 'pornography' of the title are fairly elastically defined. Programmes like *Debbie Does Dallas Uncovered* or *Hunting Emmanuelle* would sit comfortably outside of this strand: both documentaries present the films they focus on as light-hearted, quirky and ground-breaking. In both these cases, the female stars are portrayed as succumbing to the 'dark side' (drug use and addiction) *after* the making of the film because of other people's moral judgements and their own character flaws. As the narrator of *Debbie Does Dallas Uncovered* puts it: 'the porn industry has its share of victims, mainly self-inflicted'. The overall scheduling context also encourages a reading of these stories as individual aberrations: *Debbie Does Dallas Uncovered* is followed in the schedule by *Cathouse*, a straightforwardly celebratory docuporn where the women loudly and repetitively extol the virtues of their profession and the sexual pleasures on offer.

Programmes entitled *Death of a Porn Star* and *Does Snuff Exist?* may be more obviously at home on the dark side, but in neither case is it obvious that these are stories about *pornography*, at least if we define pornography as sexually explicit material intended for sexual arousal. According to her husband, Lolo Ferrari rejected the label 'porn star' in life, having only ever spent one afternoon on a porn set during desperate times. In the documentary, Ferrari – best known in Britain through her appearances on *Eurotrash* – is referred to as a 'porn star' and an 'international sex icon'. These labels – which, despite

Ferrari's rejection of them, confer a certain status and celebrity – position Ferrari in relation to sex. However, the repeated, decontextualised images of her ever-increasing breasts and the detailed discussion of the surgery behind them, suggest that this is pornography-as-freakshow: Ferrari is not a figure to desire but a figure to despise, to laugh at, to feel superior to. Predictably, *Death of a Porn Star* can offer no broader critique of the culture but is rooted in personal trauma and guilt: why did Ferrari do this to herself, why did those around her let her, or encourage her to? It is hardly surprising that the programme does not interrogate the commercial, popular appeal of her image: it is followed in the schedule by a double-helping of *Eurotrash*, offered in tribute to Ferrari. Regardless of the star's death, the 'light-side' triumphs.

Does Snuff Exist? offers no such 'lightness' but it does similarly manage to evade uncomfortable questions about the nature of the sexual and the desires of consumers. It is a curious programme, structured – like other programmes in the *Dark Side* seasons such as *Debbie Does Dallas Uncovered*, *Hunting Emmanuelle* and *The Search for Animal Farm* – around a search or quest. The object of investigation – snuff movies – is defined at the outset in relation to its supposed sexual appeal. However, as the programme progresses, the sexual slips almost entirely from view as a gallery of talking heads discuss various instances of filmed death, real (fatal accidents caught on camera; filmed murders, including state executions; war footage) and elaborate fakes (from *Snuff* (1976) and *Cannibal Holocaust* (1979) to more mainstream, contemporary horror). Whilst there is clearly an argument for linking these texts to commercially-produced pornography, the programme shies away from this to focus on what does or does not *exist* with no analysis of who might want to watch it or why. As in docuporn, then, snuff is here represented as a supply-led industry. Across the *Dark Side* this emphasis is apparent in programmes focused on the people (mainly, but not exclusively women) who make and star in pornography, whether professional or amateur.

Moreover, the search for snuff is constructed, at least in part, around the search for exceptional individuals prepared to go that step further. It is in this context that Al Qaeda can be described as 'innovators' in filming death whilst the narrator anticipates that 'an amateur filmmaker could be *the one* to make a real snuff film'. I have already argued that, in television documentaries at least, men's roles in the sex industry are as entrepreneurs or visionaries and it is striking that such patterns persist, even at the extremes. *Me and My Slaves*, with its portrait of sado-masochist slave master 'Rick', offers a partial exception to this, yet it is notable that – unlike the other programmes in the *Dark Side* – this documentary is devoted to *one* individual. *The Search for Animal Farm*, in contrast, although fascinated with the 'queen of bestiality', provides an account of her films in the context of both Danish porn of the late 1960s and British censorship of the 1970s. This leads the filmmakers to Copenhagen and another visionary: Ole Ege, a professional pornographer 'at the forefront' of Copenhagen's 'burgeoning' sex industry after the abolition of censorship there in 1969. Whilst the search for the female star of the notorious bestiality films seems to revolve around questions of *her* sexual pleasure and experience – and so to legitimate the repetition of just-legal images of her extracted from the bestiality films – the men who committed those images to film are not questioned about their own sexuality or motivation. A less extreme example can be found in *Diary of a Porn Virgin*: here, the two women (Frankie and Sahara) talk at length about their motivations, their lives before porn and their families' responses to their change of career. They are followed over a period of weeks and are shown both preparing for, and during, their pornographic performances: travelling to the set; putting on make up and costume; masturbating, urinating and having intercourse on set, with strategic camera positioning rendering the hard-core reality soft-core for television. Although the male 'porn virgin' Lee is certainly not in the entrepreneurial or visionary mode, like his professional male counterparts in other documentaries there is assumed to be no complexity to his involvement in porn. He is filmed only on the day of his audition and the key question for Lee and the other anonymous male hopefuls is simply whether they will achieve and maintain an erection – an erection which will not, of course, be shown on British television. Instead, the visual focus in nearly all of these critical documentaries – as in docuporn – is women's bodies.

To illustrate and expand on these points, I want to turn now to *Porn Shutdown*, the first of the *Dark Side* programmes, and the only one to explicitly deal with disease and physical injury to porn-performers.[11] Nevertheless, an analysis of just the first ninety seconds of this programme facilitates a discussion of the season's debt to docuporn in various ways. The programme is introduced with a voice-over, provided by English actor Christopher Eccleston whose association with quality, popular television lends a legitimacy to proceedings:[12] 'On April 13th last year, HIV came to pornoland.' During his introduction, a rapidly edited series of nine decontextualised clips of and about pornography fill the screen, accompanied by upbeat, frenetic music. The visuals – like the *Dark Side* ident – equate pornography with women's bodies: all of these women are anonymous and will remain so throughout the programme. In docuporn, such as *Porn: A Family Business*, montage sequences like this provide fleeting glimpses of what television cannot offer in any detail and are frequently used after ad breaks where other genres would typically use a location shot. In the context of *Porn Shutdown*, then, these women are 'pornoland'. The only man appearing in this montage is Max Hardcore and although he is also a porn performer it is notable that he is fully dressed here and not filmed on set. Again, this is a common device across the documentaries studied: women are interviewed in the places and costumes of pornography; male performers are rarely interviewed and, when they are, it is usually not on the porn set.

The montage sequence is followed by four brief interview extracts with people who will all be identified later in the film. First up is a dishevelled and angry Meriesa Arroyo, filmed in the parking lot of a health clinic expressing her outrage at the failures of the STD screening system. Later in the programme, we realise that this was filmed just after Arroyo had received her positive test result, but, even without this knowledge, the editing here identifies Arroyo with the arrival of the virus, cutting straight from Eccleston's 'HIV came to pornoland' to Arroyo's outburst. After the clip of Arroyo, Eccleston picks up the story: 'and one woman brought the $9billion porn industry to a standstill'. The woman is Dr Sharon Mitchell who is here shown in her clinic, taking blood from a young woman's arm: if Dr Mitchell is identified as the woman who brought the industry to a standstill, then the anonymous young woman in her clinic represents that industry. Although we later learn that the outbreak was, in fact, traced to a *male* performer (Darren James), the film focuses on the women infected by him, including Arroyo, and on how the industry-wide health screening system – initiated by Dr Mitchell – worked in practice. Not only is James absent from this opening sequence, he is an insubstantial figure throughout the documentary. Shown only in still photographs where he is fully clothed, there is nothing in the visuals to identify James as a porn star and very little information is provided about him: we are not told if he is still in the industry or even if he is still living. Assuming James (who, according to IMDb, is now working as a porn director) had declined to participate in the film, other documentaries in the series – *Debbie Does Dallas Uncovered*, *The Search for Animal Farm* – do not shy away from representing the absent, enigmatic *female* porn stars through their films, and with more than 160 porn-credits to his name such images of James would not have been difficult to come by. That *Porn Shutdown*, in contrast, simply sidesteps James suggests once more that there is no complexity to men's involvement in porn, nothing enigmatic – or, for that matter, visually interesting – about the male porn-performer.

In a brief interview extract, Dr Mitchell outlines how she dealt with the outbreak ('how many people can I alert, how fast, I've got to make a quarantine list immediately and I've got to maybe shut the industry down') before we cut to a clip from a pornographic film in which a naked woman is being strangled until she passes out, her assailant barely visible at the edges of the frame. Over this clip, Eccleston continues 'But amid the clamour to control an epidemic, the dark underbelly of the porn industry was exposed'. According to the third featured interviewee in this opening sequence – gonzo porn producer-performer Max Hardcore – that dark underbelly is female sexuality, and, again, the editing supports this view. As Hardcore claims that it is a fantasy of a lot of women to be completely and utterly dominated, choked, slapped and humiliated, his claims are punctuated with extremely brief clips from pornographic films which show women being treated in exactly the ways he describes. In television interviews – as in industry publications and events (see Jensen 2007; Tyler 2007) – sex industry insiders are remarkably candid about the abuses of their industry. Male producers describe time and time again how dirty, filthy, disgusting women are degraded, abused, humiliated and hurt in their films: but they call it sex. This pornographic doublespeak makes critiques of the industry extremely difficult as there is no language that has not been colonised and rebranded as sex. When Dr Mitchell links the abuses of pornography to real-life torture and degradation by US soldiers in Iraq later in the programme, for instance, her language is virtually indistinguishable from the language of gonzo porn as represented here by Hardcore.

Max Hardcore's claims about women are lent weight by the final interview extract in this sequence, with gonzo porn-performer Kami Andrews. Andrews predicts, 'eventually my ass is going to fall out. Eventually, I'm going to be hurt and it won't be able to be fixed'. Yet she delivers this prediction in matter-of-fact tones as she is being made-up for a porn shoot, her hair in rollers and make-up under her eyes. The implicit question posed here is not who profits from gonzo, or even who enjoys it, but why women *choose* to perform, to keep going until, as Andrews puts it, their asses 'fall out'. Although the emphasis here is on Andrews' face, a cut to another porn clip puts another woman's ass literally centre-screen: women in pornography are virtually interchangeable. This naked woman is attacked by a man who, predictably, remains on the edges of the frame. It is, however, clear that he is supposed to be an Islamic terrorist: bearded, armed, underground. Eccleston resumes: 'This is the story of how porn got out of control.'

In addition to setting up the problem of pornography as the problem of women, then, this brief opening sequence establishes a safely distanced position for the British television viewer. This is a story about 'pornoland', which, although quickly identified as a real place, sounds more like a theme park or holiday destination. Even when the location is closer to home – as in *Amateur Porn* – the function of the voice-over seems to be to bring the viewer into the pornified space ('Welcome to ... the pleasure and pain of amateur porn'). In *Porn Shutdown*, the location itself is both familiar from numerous other programmes in or about the area and 'foreign' to a British audience: the skies are too blue, the trees too green, the freeways too vast. In the opening minutes of the programme, shots of the geographical location – typically long-shots with the fast-moving freeway in the foreground, sunny skies and the Hollywood hills in the rear – are intercut with shots from the porn set, sexualising the landscape and locating the pornography. The facts and figures detailed in the accompanying voice-over are excessive:

This is pornoland, the San Fernando Valley just north of Los Angeles. Over four thousand porn films are shot here each year, more than one thousand porn stars ply their trade, often having sex up to forty times a month. Sixty gallons of semen are ejaculated for the camera each year. Everyone has sex with everyone else every few months. The vast majority of movies are shot without condoms. All it took was one man and one rogue porn shoot to bring the industry to its knees.

Whilst the entire population of pornoland is implicated, it is – unsurprisingly – a woman who visually enacts the industry-wide crisis at the conclusion of this voice-over (on her knees on the porn set). Moreover, the description here is of a supply-led business, and so our narrator – who, with his strong regional accent is himself quite clearly not *of* this world – can take us on the guided tour without implicating us in the bizarre and abusive practices on display. Other documentaries in the *Dark Side* seasons also feature narrators as tour-guides, often using the language of travel and exploration to describe the programme's quest to uncover hidden, lost or remote worlds. Shots that travel over the landscape, follow or look out from cars, trains and planes, are also frequently used, underlining this idea that pornography – even in British contexts – occupies a distinct, distant location that must be journeyed to. In *Porn Shutdown*, the use of pseudo-terrorist porn to demonstrate how porn 'got out of control' further underlines this sense of distance: this is about pornography from 'over there', about people who are not 'like us'.

The overall argument I am developing about these programmes, then, is that even though some take an explicitly critical approach to specific aspects of pornography, they struggle to maintain that tone. The extent to which this struggle may in itself be a result of Channel 4's need to balance public service regulations on the one hand with the need to sell advertising space and secure an audience on the other, is an issue considered in some detail in Arthurs' work (2004). What has concerned me in this chapter, however, is the extent to which this unevenness in tone may undercut critique and, more seriously, replicate and naturalise pornographic modes. The narrative and visual focus of the programmes in the *Dark Side* seasons is – as in docuporn and pornography itself – largely on women: men's sexuality and the demand for pornography are thus naturalised. What is 'dark' about pornography seems to be what is 'dark' about women's lives and the 'choices' that they make: choices which are presented in largely sexual terms with little consideration of the broader social context that facilitates and sometimes necessitates women's entry into the sex industry. The ambivalence of this 'darkness' – and the suggestion that it is *chosen* by the women involved – is underlined by the lack of a critical language to describe women's experiences as the language of abuse is repackaged as sexual. In this context, women's testimonies of pleasure and pain become formulaic distractions from the visual attractions these programmes offer: the showy editing; exotic locations or familiar locations made strange; and, of course, women's bodies on and off-set. Whilst these programmes do not straight-forwardly position their viewers as would-be 'johns' as docuporn typically does (Boyle 2008), their emphasis on the 'other' (the foreign, the freaky, the 'star'), their use of interrogatory (male) voice-over and their foregrounding of movement and travel, works against any meaningful identification with the women in pornography and makes it easy to dismiss any critical comments they do make as an uncomfortable blip in porn's fun exterior. Taken in the context of sex documentaries across the television schedules as a whole, these critiques are limited at best.

NOTES

1 Programmes focusing on sexual violence (such as *Panorama: Sex Crimes and the Vatican*, BBC1, 1 October), gender and sexual identity (*Return to Gender*, five, 2 February), or romantic relationships (*Sex, Love and War*, UKTV History, from 29 December) were excluded, as were long-running reality series focused on dating (*Test Drive My Girlfriend*, ITV2) or where sex was a recurring theme but not the ostensible focus of the series (*Club Reps: The Workers*, ITV). As such, the figures presented here are a deliberately conservative estimate of the sex content on British television during the period studied.
2 Ftn was replaced by Virgin 1 on 1 October 2007.
3 See *The Sex Tapes That Shocked the World* (22 February and 22 September) or the films in the *Shock Docs* series, including *Paying For Love in Paradise* (15 November) and *My 100,000 Lovers* (13 December).
4 See, for instance, the three programmes in the *Private Parts* series: *The Trouble With My Breasts* (17 November), *The Trouble With My Vagina* (24 November) and *The Trouble With My Penis* (29 December).
5 In typically hyperbolic titles, five promises to reveal *The Sex Tapes That Shocked the World* as well as *How Nudity* (2 August), *Porn* (9 August) and *Fetish* (22 December) *Conquered the World*.
6 Although five's sister channels, five US and five live, both launched during the period of study, neither included sex documentaries at this time.
7 *Mindshock: Sex on the Brain* (Channel 4, 10 July) is billed as a 'factual series shedding light on the human mind', whilst the only programme to focus critically on pornography-use questions its possible psychological effects on a serial-killer (*Ted Bundy: Natural Porn Killer*, Channel 4, 16 August).
8 These issues were, however, taken up in drama. Channel 4's award-winning *Sex Traffic* was repeated on More 4 (19 and 26 August); the *True Voice of Prostitution* (More 4, 20 April; Channel 4, 11 December) included a monologue from a migrant woman trapped in the sex industry in Britain; and re-runs of *The Vice* on ITV3 (from 18 February) also

tackled trafficking.
9 *Celebrity Sex Tapes Unwound* (Channel 4, 24 October) and *The Sex Tapes That Shocked the World*.
10 On swinging see the series *Real Wife Swaps* and 4's *A Swinging Murder* (2 August). Bigamy and polygamy documentaries include: *Philip and His Seven Wives* (BBC4, 25 April); *The Bigamists* (SKY3, 4 and 6 May), *The Man With 80 Wives* (Channel 4, 19 July), *I Love You. And You. And You* (Channel 4, 26 July). Sado-masochism is the theme of *Fetishes* (More 4, 3 March, 3 June, 25 August), *How Fetish Conquered The World*, *Me and My Slaves*, a number of *Sin Cities* and *Sin Cities Unleashed* episodes and an episode in *A Girl's Guide to 21st Century Sex* (11 December). Penis documentaries include: *My Penis & I* (BBC3, 3 January, 25 February); Channel 4's 'penis season' *The Perfect Penis* (30 January), *Chopped Off: The Man Who Lost His Penis* (31 January), *The World's Biggest Penis* (1 February) – all of which were repeated on More 4; and *Private Parts: The Trouble With My Penis* (five, 29 May, 29 December).
11 *Porn Shutdown* was repeated in 2006 and was the only programme in my study of the schedules from that year to deal with sexually-transmitted disease.
12 At the time of *Porn Shutdown*, Eccleston was appearing in BBC1's *Doctor Who* (March–June 2005) and has more recently been seen in NBC's *Heroes* (2007–).

WORKS CITED

Arthurs, J. (2004) *Television and Sexuality: Regulation and the Politics of Taste*. Maidenhead: Open University Press.
Boyle, K. (2006) 'The Boundaries of Porn Studies', *New Review of Film & Television Studies*, 4, 1, 1–16.
____ (2008) 'Courting Consumers and Legitimating Exploitation: The Representation of Commercial Sex in Television Documentaries', *Feminist Media Studies*, 8, 1, 35–50.
Cole, S. (1989) *Pornography and the Sex Crisis*. Amanita: Toronto.
Graham, A. (2006) 'A Swinging Murder', *Radio Times*, 29 July–4 August, 84.
Jensen, R. (2007) *Getting Off: Pornography and the End of Masculinity*. Cambridge, MA: South End Press.
McLean, G. (2001) 'We've Seen it all Before', *Guardian*, G2 Supplement, 17 April, 22.
Paasonen, S., K. Nikunen and L. Saarenmaa (eds) (2007) *Pornification: Sex and Sexuality in Media Culture*. Oxford: Berg.
Paul, P. (2006) *Pornified: How Pornography is Damaging Our Lives, Our Relationships, and Our Families*. New York: Owl Books.
Tyler, M. (2007) Unpublished paper presented at Feminism and Popular Culture, the Feminist and Women's Studies Network Association Conference, University of Newcastle, June 2007.
Williams, L. (ed.) (2004) *Porn Studies*. Durham N.C.: Duke University Press.

CHAPTER THREE

ART SCHOOL SLUTS: AUTHENTICITY AND THE AESTHETICS OF ALTPORN

Feona Attwood

The emergence of alternative online pornographies offers an important new focus for discussions about the current diversity of pornography as a genre and about its significance for those who produce and consume it, especially as the internet becomes an increasingly important 'screen' for representation. This chapter discusses the emergence of online altporn[1] – 'the pornography of this decade, if not of the whole century' (Cramer & Home 2007: 164). It examines the sites' reconfiguration of the 'porn body' through retro glamour, alternative style and a contemporary ideal of sexual authenticity. This altporn aesthetic has recently been picked up and recirculated in the porn industry, most notably in the *Hustler*-backed 'Vivid Alt' imprint and Eon McKai's film, *Art School Sluts* (2004), acclaimed for its high production values and its 'indie' ethos.

Sex educator and columnist, Violet Blue, in an interview with McKai, notes the association of the 'alt' aesthetic with a young, hip generation of media consumers, previously neglected by mainstream porn producers. For this generation, it has become important to see porn performers who represent their social group, 'like the girls you'd see in a coffee shop and boys at the record store posing'. The appearance of a new style of performer has been accompanied by the emergence of a group of new porn professionals – 'porn intellectuals, directors, performers and bloggers' who are 'younger, paler, decidedly less straight' than the norm (Blue 2007). This focus on 'real people' in porn, combined with the production of a 'hip' porn aesthetic characterises altporn generally. In this chapter I want to ask how we might interpret the significance of this new style and its particular take on sexual aesthetics.

As Katrien Jacobs (2004) has noted, alternative porn is produced in a range of cultural locations such as art performances, films and magazines, but is most often found in digital media, and especially, since the late 1990s, online. It is generally associated with small groups of independent 'savvy media practitioners' (Jacobs 2004), and latterly with experiments in which porn becomes 'appropriated and reinterpreted by alternative producers and activist sex workers, younger pro-porn feminists, queer porn networks, aesthetic-technical vanguards, p2p traders, radical sex/perv cultures, and free-speech activists' (Jacobs 2007: 3). The altporn scene is documented at altporn.net, 'a guide to altporn and subculture erotica', which lists a variety of sites. Most confine themselves to still imagery, though a few are involved in independent film production. They range from the relatively mainstream and commercial *Suicide Girls* – 'the Wal-mart of altporn' (Ray 2007a: 163) – to alternative fetish sites like *Bella Vendetta* which focuses on 'REAL underground kink' such as asphyxiation, age play, blood sex, body modification, clown porn, gender fucking, menstrual art, tickling and weapons, and the queer 'hot radical porn' at *No Fauxxx*. *Suicide Girls* was launched in 2001 by 'Spooky' (Sean Suhl) and 'Missy Suicide' (Selena Mooney), *No Fauxxx* was launched in 2003 by Courtney Trouble and *Bella Vendetta* was launched by Bella Vendetta in 2004.

Fig. 5 'Black Metal Bitch' photo of Bella Vendetta by Dark Wolf Photography. Courtesy of Bella Vendetta.

Although very different from one another in some respects, altporn sites share a set of characteristics; they feature 'models who are real people' and frequently 'men and women of subculture', and they are 'considered woman-friendly and sex-positive' (Ray 2007a: 160). In some instances they also function as communities of one kind or another. Porn is combined with non-sexual content such as interviews and news items while the sites' links work to locate sex in a much broader cultural context alongside music, art, counterculture and politics.

The combination of sexually explicit images with non-sexual interests and with the features of non-sexual online communities such as blogs, discussion groups and message boards, camsites and chat rooms distinguishes altporn from other more established forms of porn production. In this respect altporn can be understood as part of a broader participatory culture which is focused on social networking, self-imaging and user-generated content. It also draws on a performance ethos amongst some web users which involves a 'sharing of porn as personal-social activities and developing mediated work and play practices' (Jacobs 2007: 50). Here 'media production' is understood as a form of communication with like-minded people.

Whilst emerging from the ethos of online amateur gift economies where material is shared freely, many altporn sites, including *Suicide Girls*, *No Fauxxx* and *Bella Vendetta*, are now organised as pay sites. Subscription rates at the time of writing are for *Suicide Girls* $4 per month, for *Bella Vendetta* $8.45 per month and for *No Fauxx* $13.99 per month. Altporn sites are also taste cultures where individual identity and group membership is expressed through discrimination about a range of pursuits, including sex. Aesthetically, they appear quite different to much online porn, not only in terms of their deployment of subcultural style, but because of their foregrounding of technical and artistic qualities. This is often emphasised by the site producers and reproduced in discussions of altporn. For example, *Wired* magazine contrasts mainstream sites which feature 'ugly web design, annoying pop-up ads, and badly-lit pictures of big-haired breast-implanted blondes' with 'stylish subculture sites' which have 'artful nude photos of women who are more likely to be purple-haired, pale and pierced' (Barron 2002). Similarly, McKai characterises his altporn films as 'tasteful and hip enough to leave out on the coffee table' (in Blue 2007).

TRANSGRESSIONS

The attempt to define porn has a long and frustrated history, often expressed around notions of 'common decency' and 'offensiveness' which depend on a series of judgements about aesthetics and authenticity. These judgements have been explored in a number of academic accounts. It has been argued that porn is seen as debasing because its viewing practices appear to violate the distance between subject and object (see Falk 1993), promoting 'promiscuity and commodification' (Nead 1992: 89), whilst its content violates social norms about what should be seen and what is obscene. For some, these violations – the transgressions of porn – are a claim to authenticity. Porn is a refusal of artifice; an upending of bourgeois conventions, and, like other forms of carnivalesque low culture, overturns civilised values and celebrates the body as 'insistently material, defiantly vulgar, corporeal' (Kipnis 1996: 132). From this perspective, the authenticity of porn depends on its down-to-earth lack of pretension and the challenge it offers to social norms of class, sex and gender.

An opposing view sees porn as having a 'debased, merely instrumental role' (Sontag 1969: 39) and an 'inbuilt reactionary mechanism' (Carter 1992: 11). Here, authenticity is explicitly linked to attempts at ideological subversion which is achievable only through the adoption of an artistic sensibility. For Angela Carter, the more porn 'acquires the techniques of real literature, of real art, the more deeply subversive it is likely to be' (1992: 19). But the emergence of obscene content in the high-brow formats of literature and art can also be understood as the development of a new form of cultural capital bound up with 'shocking the bourgeois' (Bourdieu 1984: 47). As Mark Jancovich (2001) argues, it has become one way in which an emerging section of the bourgeoisie has distinguished itself from other class factions, in the process marking itself as cool, edgy and hedonistic – a very contemporary form of 'real'.

Aestheticised forms of sex media can go where pornography cannot. Erotica travels much more easily and widely than hard-core video, 'especially in a bag adorned with the face of Virginia Woolf' (Juffer 2005: 74), and as Barbara de Genevieve (2004) notes, even content that is considered obscene – fisting, squirting, transsexuals, blindfolds and coffins – is regularly found in contemporary 'performance, film, video, photography, painting, sculpture, and writing'. As Jane Juffer shows, discourses of aesthetic and psychological value were largely responsible for the deregulation of sexually explicit texts in the twentieth century, providing they were not, as Supreme Court Justice William Brennan, ruled, 'utterly without redeeming social importance' (2005: 67). Their new accessibility lent them new kinds of authenticity, marking them as psychologically beneficial, socially important, aesthetically and intellectually challenging. However, this shift has also lead to charges of artificiality. The aestheticised texts that Brian McNair characterises as 'porno-chic' are, from some viewpoints, less authentic than 'proper' porn. Where hard-core porn is anonymous, 'real', sexually intense, dirty and unrefined, porno-chic texts are celebrity-led, staged and sanitised, knowing and ironic, sophisticated, glossy and technically proficient (see 2002: 64–8). Yet although they are apparently much 'safer' than other porn texts, they encourage new kinds of transgression, in the literal sense of 'going beyond' and crossing boundaries (Juffer 1998: 233).

These kinds of transgression have had particular repercussions for women's access to sex media. A range of cultural texts – couples pornography, erotica, sex advice, lingerie advertising and sex toys have, as a result, become much more available to women, both geographically and conceptually. Erotica can be purchased in mainstream bookstores. Ann Summers parties locate sex in the context of the home and present it in the form of a healthy and heterosexual 'fun' femininity (see Storr 2003). In the process sex is linked to a range of acceptable codes drawn from art, literature, health and fashion. These forms of 'domesticated' porn gain their authenticity from a claim to reflect their consumers' identity (see Juffer 1998: 113), from their appeal to a feminine sensibility and from their location of sex in a recognisably female landscape. Thus, femininity, the 'everyday and the erotic' are reconciled through 'a much more *located* sense of sexual practice' than is found in the 'sexual numbers' of hard-core porn (Juffer 1998: 107).

As this brief survey shows, porn, aesthetics and authenticity are repeatedly linked with notions of transgression, though in quite different ways. Porn's transgressiveness need not depend on a 'dirty' style; indeed, as Juffer shows, 'domesticated' forms of porn may cross many more boundaries than their smuttier counterparts. Nor need it be sexually explicit – the magazines that Laura Kipnis examines in her discussion of transvestite porn include many images which feature fully-clothed men who are not engaged in sexual activity. Kipnis notes that the personal ads included in these magazines can also be seen as 'amateur self-portraits' (1996: 71), which, like the work of artist Cindy Sherman, 'put categories of identity into question by using the genre of the self-portrait to document an invented "self"' and investigate 'the question of femininity and its masquerades' (1996: 75). These images signify both as advert and portrait and they perform and deconstruct sexual identity.

Like the ambiguous images of Kipnis' transvestite magazines, altporn privileges the amateur self-portrait and re-presents the feminine self. It has simultaneously been claimed as art and porn and there is some ambivalence about its relation to both of these. According to altporn.net, altporn is 'perhaps an unfortunate moniker' and 'nudity or graphic sexuality are not requirements for inclusion' on the site. Some altporn sites, notably *Suicide Girls*, reject the 'porn' label, preferring to see themselves as producing a form of modern pin-up. Others have embraced the term, often as part of a strategy of re-appropriation. This is especially true of those sites which perceive themselves as transgressive; not necessarily because of their dirty style, but, for example, because of their presentation of fetishes like bloodplay or their unsettling of straight modes of representation. This deviance in terms of sexual practice and diversity is accompanied by new claims to authenticity and quality – to be arty, revolutionary and real – and these are also part of the sites' transgressive impact. Thus, *No Fauxxx*'s mission is to produce 'Punk Rock Porn' which is 'politically exceptional, fully inclusive, revolutionary and art-heavy', while *Bella Vendetta* is concerned with taking revenge on the porn industry by documenting an 'underground sexual culture' of 'sexy tattooed boys' and 'empowered women' who are 'sexy in REAL life'.

STRIKE A POSE

The aesthetic of altporn is best understood within the context of a broader sexualisation of mainstream culture which has, on the one hand, thrown up a stylish and sophisticated model of femininity exemplified by the 'bourgeois bohemian' figures of *Sex and the City* (Arthurs 2003: 86), and, on the other, mainstreamed a porn star look often referred to as 'cookie-cutter' by altporn practitioners to denote its plastic, unoriginal and genericised appearance. Altporn also produces a version of sexy femininity derived in part from glamour and pin-up style. Like the figure of the bourgeois bohemian, and indeed, Kipnis' lonely-heart transvestite figure, this negotiates 'a space that oscillates between portraiture and pornography' (Buszek 2006: 11), foregrounding the expression of self through image and linking glamour with the expression of 'personality'.

The use of sexiness and style to indicate personality is increasingly evident elsewhere in popular culture, most notably in the phenomenon of celebrity nudity which has taken a variety of forms including the celebrifying of some hard-core porn stars such as Jenna Jameson and Ron Jeremy, the mainstreaming of glamour girls such as Jordan and the sexualising of mainstream performers such as Christina Aguilera. Here, as in altporn, the recycling of representational codes associated with celebrity works to glamorise sex and to resist the charge that sexual display inevitably objectifies and depersonalises its subjects. As Alan McKee (2006) shows, contemporary porn audiences also draw on these ideas when they discuss the aesthetics of pornography, regardless of whether they prefer texts which privilege fantasy and ideal bodies, or realism and ordinary bodies. In both cases, the notion of quality porn depends on a perceived authenticity of performance demonstrated through its performers' 'real enjoyment', 'genuine interest', 'enthusiasm' and 'chemistry'.

This figuring of self through sexiness is also picked up in the practice of boudoir photography described by Ruth Barcan, whereby ordinary people imitate 'the images of perfection associated with stars' (2004: 249), commissioning their own sexy and glamorous images. This idea that sexy and sophisticated image-work can be an expression of individuality is also found in altporn sites such as *Suicide Girls* where it is claimed that 'creativity, personality and intelligence are not incompatible with sexy, compelling entertainment'. All of these developments are part of a broader shift in which media have become increasingly central to the presentation of experiences and identities. Public and private, celebrity and ordinary, media and daily life have become blurred and everything has become 'a potential media object' (Kitzmann 2004: 81).

In some instances an engagement with sexy images can be understood as a part of the development of a form of cultural capital in which 'hipness is rendered varyingly as authenticity, quality, creativity or individuality' (Epley 2007: 53). As Nathan Scott Epley points out, the resurgence of hipster interest in 1940s and 1950s pin-ups may represent a form of ironic and even cynical consumption, giving hipster consumers permission to consume sexist representations (2007: 55). Yet cynicism is not inevitable – feminist appropriations of the pin-up are based on a more passionate relationship in which 'the pastiche of familiar conventions of female beauty [is] combined with elements taboo to dominant ideologies of gender and sexuality' (2007: 57).

This passionate form of relationship is also found in practices of alternative femininity where women mix conventionally attractive signs of femininity with other more subversive elements. Here women 'make a spectacle of themselves', yet conversely this provides them with a protective layer which allows them to 'hold the gaze' of potentially hostile observers (Holland 2004: 150). The image of active female sexuality constructed in much altporn is similarly complex, drawing on but also away from the figures of bourgeois bohemian and cookie-cutter pornstar. It emphasises youth, outsider status and subcultural membership, mixing sexual signifiers with the codes and conventions of retro and contemporary subcultural imagery. Thus, a more widespread tendency towards self-expression through sexual display and media participation is inflected by the use of styles which originate in taste and/or sexual subcultures. As Shoshana Magnet (2007) writes, even the blander sites such as *Suicide Girls* eroticise 'deviant' and 'cyborg' femininity, using tattoos and piercings to disrupt conventional beauty ideals. While some sites focus on quite specific sets of signs – for example, 'nerd porn' favours glasses and computers to indicate androgyny, intelligence and a passion for technology – elements such as piercings and tattoos, fishnets, knee socks and fetish shoes, short fringes and dyed hair appear across many altporn sites.

Missy Suicide, one of the founders of *Suicide Girls*, has described how the site was inspired by post-punk and the retro style of pin-up photographs of 1950s models like Bettie Page who she saw as 'self-confident, elegant and upbeat' (2004: 7). Missy's vision combined post-punk and retro style in order to showcase 'new Pin-Up girls, each with their own ferociously unique style and outlook' (2004: 8). Page is particularly significant for altporn because of the way she combines girl-next-door appeal with mainstream glossy allure (she was a *Playboy* centrefold in 1955) *and* notoriety as a fetish model (she worked extensively with photographer, Irving Klaw, to produce pin-ups and film loops of bondage and domination scenarios). This combination of ordinariness, mainstream success and kinkiness makes her a particularly apt model for a cool and late-modern sexual sensibility because of the way it signifies the mundane, the spectacular and the deviant. Page's popularity might also be attributed to characteristics of her self-presentation which distance her from connotations of sleaze. For example, photographs of Page often emphasise her exuberance and happiness, and in the 'darker' images produced by Klaw, the 'hammy gusto' of her exaggerated expressions of shock or dominance work to highlight her sexual activity as a form of play and performance (see Buszek 2006: 247). At the same time they appear expressive of personality rather than of the anonymity often attributed to the fragmented and interchangeable bodies of pornography. Her collaboration with the celebrated female photographer, Bunny Yeager, the various mysteries over her disappearance in 1960, her subsequent life as a recluse and the development of a Bettie Page cult in the late 1980s have all worked to elevate her further as a personality.[2]

Maria Buszek has argued that pin-up style has been a recurring object of fascination for a range of audiences because it acts as 'a kind of visual shorthand for the desirable female', yet represents contradictory elements in which women are shown as 'self-aware, assertive, strong, and independent' (2006: 343; 8). The association of pin-ups with a sex-positive approach has assumed increasing importance in a context where sexual self-creation, self-expression and plurality are foregrounded in a range of forms, from mainstream music where performers like Madonna have encouraged women to 'construct and control their lives according to their own fantasies', to the lesbian porn imagery in *On Our Backs* (1984–2006) and subcultural media such as riot grrrl zines which have 'recycled and recontextualized imagery' to construct a form of girl-focused and sometimes 'girlie' feminism (2006: 314–27; 345).

The case of riot grrrl is particularly interesting here because of the way it foregrounds ordinary women's presentation of their bodies and sexual personae as a site of importance and complexity. Drawing on a DIY ethic of countercultural production apparent in a range of radical movements and subcultures, riot grrrl made bodily display a means of debating and reappropriating female sexuality. It 'gave a name, a face, a sound to feminist frustration' (Ditto 2007: 8), speaking with a 'youth-centred voice that was felt to be missing from forms of feminism available in the 1990s' (Downes 2007: 26). This heritage is drawn on explicitly by Missy Suicide in her discussion of the origins of *Suicide Girls* in the cultural milieu of Portland, Oregon 'where everyone was an artist and everyone created something' (2004: 7). The creativity of real people expressing themselves through display is also evident at altporn sites such as *No Fauxxx* which is concerned with representing authenticity through the diversity of 'normal people interested in expressing their sexualities ... all sizes, all genders, all sexual orientations, all races, and from all sorts of places, doing all sorts of things'.

'PORN THAT DOESN'T FAKE IT!'

The claim of *No Fauxxx* to produce 'porn that doesn't fake it!' is more particularly a determination to go beyond a singular 'fake' presentation of sex, replacing this with a plurality of authentic expressions. There is a diversity of subgenres; 'Soft core, pin-up girls, black and white erotica, sensual shots' and a range of sexual practices are depicted; 'masturbation, role-playing, kink, and fetish ... BDSM, bondage, S/M, shown as a positive thing as opposed to scary, dangerous, or perverted. And also maybe some really dark creepy stuff too...' Sex and gender are also plural categories. The site welcomes models who are 'Straight, lesbian, gay, queer, and bisexual couples and groups', as well as 'Girls, Boys, Transgender, transsexual, genderqueer, or gender-bending models'. In addition, *No Fauxxx* seeks 'Models of all races, taken out of the stereotypical context models of color are usually assigned in the sex industry', along with 'Able-bodied models as well as Not-so-abled bodies' and 'Punks, goths, emo kids, hipsters, hippies, and other "alternative" models'. Finally, the site seeks to disrupt conventional body ideals by seeking to showcase 'Fat, thin, chubby, curvaceous, zaftig, short, tall, and athletic models'. All this, for *No Fauxxx*, equates to 'HOT HOT HOT HOT PORN'.

Claims to the authenticity of altporn rest particularly heavily on the presentation of altporn producers and models. Altporn models are envisaged, not as the passive object of a gaze when they display their bodies, but as actors and artistic producers who are expressing what has been described as a form of 'empowered eroticism' (van der Graf 2004). This is possible, according to Missy Suicide, because they are represented, as 'whole people' rather than 'just bodies' (in Phillips 2005). Cultural forms which deal with the outside – the portrait or pin-up – and those that deal with the inside – diaries and other autobiographical forms – are combined to indicate this, and at *No Fauxxx*, the process is further emphasised through the inclusion of a 'candids' section featuring photographs of models' 'non-pornographic selves'. Here, 'the rhetoric of artificiality in classical mainstream pornography – artificial body parts, sterile studios, wooden acting' is replaced with 'a rhetoric of the authentic' which depends on 'personalization and psychologization' (Cramer 2007: 174).

The self-presentation of the founders of *Suicide Girls* and *Bella Vendetta* is also interesting in this respect. In the early 2000s Missy Suicide was probably the most visible figure to be associated with altporn. A series of struggles over the *Suicide Girls* site which has included claims that models are exploited[3] has undoubtedly damaged her reputation as a spokesperson and she is much less visible now. This is underscored in her site profile which is located amongst numerous profiles of other *Suicide Girls* staff, downplaying her importance as a personality and motivating force. In addition, the three headshots featured in the profile at the time of writing shift attention away from the altporn body as a site of deviant display, drawing on much more conventional feminine codes; in one she sports a bow in her hair and red lipstick and in the other wears peach coloured satin and pearls.

In contrast, Bella Vendetta appears both as artist and model. Bella describes herself as 'CEO, founder, brain power, designer and Goddess' and documents a wide range of her projects in the arts, including film production, direction and performance, poetry writing and performance, performance art, modelling, erotic writing and zine writing and editing. Her company, MyOwnBrainProductions, also makes clothes for 'people with multiple personalities' and her multi-dimensionality is further highlighted in her use of different names (Kristen DeLuca for writing, Bumble DeLuca for poetry and Bumblina DeLuca for acting and poetry) and in the three quite different images of herself in the profile, used to illustrate 'Bella Herself' and her work in film and modelling.

The first of these is a colour image which emphasises her red lips and eye make up, vest top and necklace and her green Mohican hairstyle. Her stance – side on, head cheekily cocked, tongue poked out, eyebrows raised, coupled with 'alt' signifiers – piercings, tattoo and glasses – stress her irreverence and disdain for 'respectable' femininity. The other two are more restrained black and white images, one which reproduces a 'Cabaret' style pose with corset, trilby and stockings, and the second a more conventionally pretty close-up of her face, lit up and gamine. In her model profile, her image is different again. Bella puts both bare breasts and tattoos on show and manages an unsmiling come-on look over the top of her glasses.

The profile combines information about Bella's professional life where she is 'Godmother, model, photographer, writer, artist, fashion designer, stylist, enabler, gangsta, Lady Pimp, Hustla and overall GODDESS' with more personal details – her astrological sign, favourite bands, books, clothes, food and drink, things to do, fiancé and pets. In addition the profile details her sexual tastes – best sex toy, favourite kink ('weapons ... blood, violence and cars'), turn-ons, current crush, turn-offs and guilty pleasures. Thus, taste, lifestyle, personality and sexual identity are foregrounded while cultural production becomes a key marker of agency and self-expression.

For altporn producers such as Bella Vendetta the sexual, the personal, the cultural and the political are intimately linked. Bella's site is 'a celebration of sex' and it is also 'set up to make you question your ethics, question your ideals, question your sexuality and question what it is that turns you on'. The pleasures of sexual display are not in conflict with feminism, nor do they indicate that she is a 'slut'. The 'beautiful revenge' of the website name refers both to a revenge on the porn industry and on an individual man who cheated on her. Describing how she beat him till she broke her hand, and how the name 'Bella Vendetta' later came to her 'out of the clear blue sky', Bella shows how the personal and political are rolled into one. Her act of retaliation, her work as a model, and the website itself all become her 'direct response to the world at large'. Drawing together these strands – the pleasures of display, subcultural representation, individual entrepreneurialism and sexual politics – Bella summarises her motives for contributing to the porn industry like this:

> Because if a sexual revolution is to occur then change and honesty must be taught, learned and recognized. Because it is necessary to accurately portray my sexual subculture. Because not all girls look like Barbie and want cum on their face. Because I couldn't find the porn I wanted to look at so I made my own.
>
> And because I'm a horny kinky bitch and I get off knowing that strangers are jerking off to photos of me. Because I really like the concept of making money with my cunt.

ARTIST AS MODEL

Susanna Paasonen has argued that in the 2000s, there has been a move to contrast the recycling of 'commercial, predictable and dull' porn online with new forms of 'netporn' which are characterised as 'networked, interactive, novel, intellectually and aesthetically challenging' (2007: 164). This contrast has been useful in marking the features of production, style and distribution which some new pornographies employ. However, an overemphasis on this distinction works to erase the movement of style and content between 'old' and 'new', 'online' and 'offline' pornographies and threatens to reproduce the structure of earlier porn debates which fixated on positions 'of either for or against' porn. As she notes, if we are to understand the specificity of particular pornographies, 'we need to remain dedicated to contextualization' (2007: 170).

Critiques of altporn frequently focus on the extent to which major altporn figures such as Missy Suicide can be considered radical and whether the style they purvey can be properly seen as 'alternative'. *Suicide Girls* remains the target of most altporn criticism; critics argue that the site offers a limited view of alternative practices, identities and bodies (see Magnet 2007), represents a selling out of alternative ideals for profit and encourages passive and standardised exchanges between site members (see Jacobs 2007). For Florian Cramer and Stuart Home, sites such as *Suicide Girls* simply represent the commercialisation of alternative porn. They are 'no different from the popular genre of industrial pseudo amateur pornography', whilst also rapidly becoming 'the research and development arm of the porn industry' (Cramer & Home 2007: 165). Although some of these criticisms may be justified, the danger of this kind of focus is its tendency to raise questions about how radical altporn is and whether we should be 'either for or against' it. This is likely to lead us away from understanding the specificity and complexity of new online pornographies.

More work is needed to tell us how altporn sites are experienced by the different groups who use them – casual browsers, altporn aficionados, community members, model-performers and webmistress/producers. However, what seems to be clear is the way that for some producers and performers at least, porn is taking on different meanings in contexts like this where performers are socially and economically mobile and relatively autonomous and where there appears to be some equivalence between performer and audience. Altporn locates sex, sexual representation and sexual display in relation to other aspects of culture, as part of a mix of media, lifestyle and sexual practice through which the self is expressed and community is created, transgressing existing boundaries in the process.

Alternative pornographies of all kinds are now feeding back 'into the imageries of commercial pornography that they seem to subvert' (Paasonen 2007: 163), as the movement of she-male and hentai pornographies from the margins to the mainstream, and the development of the Vivid Alt imprint itself indicates. Yet the use of an altporn aesthetic – personalised and politicised, kinky and glossy – is also part of a move towards defining a particular identity and status for the 'new porn professionals' that Violet Blue describes. In this context, the altporn aesthetic and the kind of cultural and identity production it articulates is able to indicate a contemporary form of authenticity which is hip-but-real. As Audacia Ray notes of the *Bella Vendetta* site, many women who have worked in sectors of the commercial sex industry choose to model for free here because they perceive a match between their sexuality and the forms of self-presentation that *Bella Vendetta* showcases (2007a: 169). There is also some overlap between these altporn models and the body modification community to which *Bella Vendetta* also belongs. Similarly, *No Fauxxx* includes a range of artists and underground heroes amongst its models – 'Madison Young, feminist art gallery owner and famous bondage model, Biscuit, incredible filmmaker, cello player, photographer, Anna Logue, internet porn star... Scream Club, Oly queer hiphop sensations!' As with Bella Vendetta, they pose as 'an expression of their personal and real sexuality' (Ray 2007b). Ray herself, a porn director, blogger, editor of sexworker magazine *$pread*, curator, critic and author, models at both sites. It is perhaps unsurprising that in these new arenas of 'porn professionalism' where the display of modified, queer and artistic bodies is celebrated, the site founders are simultaneously artists and models and that their sites are 'arty and porny without being snobby about either' (Ray 2007b). This may be part of a more general shift in which some forms of creative labour and commercial forms of sexuality are beginning 'to mix in a complex way with beauty, ego and non-commercial sexuality' (Ray 2007a: 173). How these new mixes develop remains to be seen. For now, in some altporn sites at least, art, porn, sexual self-expression and politics are being brought together in new and interesting formations.

ACKNOWLEDGEMENT

I would like to acknowledge the support of the AHRC in funding a period of study leave which enabled me to research women's online sexual self-presentation.

NOTES

1. I have adopted the term altporn rather than 'indieporn' which is used by other writers such as Katrien Jacobs (2007) and Florian Cramer (2007) to indicate an aesthetic which is now found in both independent and more mainstream pornography.
2. More recently, interest in Page, who died in 2008, expanded beyond the particular subcultures and scenes in which retro – particularly 1950s' – style has been important, producing a 'craze of Betty Page memorabilia: trading cards, dolls, mugs, posters, T-shirts, a play, Bunny Yeager photo collectibles, and every conceivable kind of merchandising likeness of the Betty Page pinup' (Corwin & Yeager 1994: 29). The Bettie Page craze coincided with the revival of a burlesque scene which also draws heavily on retro styles of fashion and performance. The appearance of a feature film, *The Notorious Bettie Page* in 2005 and the rise to prominence of neo-burlesque star, Dita von Teese, marked a further stage in which retro styles circulating within subcultures were themselves mainstreamed. Media interest in von Teese, and former husband, Marilyn Manson, a performer whose stage persona draws heavily on gothic and 'satanic' imagery, neatly drew together a mainstream fascination with retro and subcultural styles, fetish imagery and an overriding concern with sexual display and performance.
3. See for example, Randy Dotinga (2005). A more recent dispute between *Suicide Girls* and photographer, Lithium Picnic, was settled in 2008; see Amelia G. (2008).

WORKS CITED

Arthurs, J. (2003) '*Sex and the City* and Consumer Culture: Remediating Postfeminist

Drama', *Feminist Media Studies*, 3, 1, 83–98.
Barcan, R. (2004) *Nudity: A Cultural Anatomy*. Oxford and New York: Berg.
Barron, J. (2002) 'When Sub-Pop Meets Porn'. On-line. Available: http://www.wired.com/news/culture/0,1284,53034,00.html (accessed 23 October 2006).
Blue, V. (2007) 'Eon McKai's Altporn Liberation Army'. On-line. Available: http://sfgate.com/cgi-bin/article.cgi?file=/gate/archive/2007/02/08/violetblue.DTL (accessed 8 February 2007).
Bourdieu, P. (1984) *Distinction: A Social Critique of the Judgment of Taste*. Cambridge, MA: Harvard University Press.
Buszek, M. E. (2006) *Pin-Up Grrrls: Feminism, Sexuality, Popular Culture*. Durham and London: Duke University Press.
Carter, A. (1992) *The Sadeian Woman: An Exercise in Cultural History*. London: Virago.
Corwin, S. and B. Yeager (1994) *Betty Page Confidential*. New York: St. Martin's Press.
Cramer, F. (2007) 'Sodom Blogging: Alternative Porn and Aesthetic Sensibility', in K. Jacobs, M. Pasquinelli and M. Janssen (eds) *C'Lick Me: A Netporn Studies Reader*. Amsterdam: Institute of Network Cultures, 171–5.
Cramer, F. and S. Home (2007) 'Pornographic Coding', in K. Jacobs, M. Pasquinelli and M. Janssen (eds) *C'Lick Me: A Netporn Studies Reader*. Amsterdam: Institute of Network Cultures, 159–70.
de Genevieve, B. (2004) 'No Fisting, No Squirting, No Coffins'. On-line. Available: http://www.degenevieve.com/ (accessed 23 February 2007).
Ditto, B. (2007) 'Foreword', in N. Modem (ed.) *Riot Grrrl: Revolution Girl Style Now!* London: Black Dog Publishing, 8.
Dotinga, R. (2005) 'Suicide Girls Gone AWOL'. On-line. Available: http://www.wired.com/culture/lifestyle/news/2005/09/69006 (accessed 23 February 2007).
Downes, J. (2007) 'Riot Grrrl: The Legacy and Contemporary Landscape of DIY Feminist Cultural Activism', in N. Monem (ed.) *Riot Grrrl: Revolution Girl Style Now!* London: Black Dog Publishing, 12–49.
Epley, N. S. (2007) 'Pin-ups, Retro-chic and the Consumption of Irony', in S. Paasonen, K. Nikunen and L. Saarenmaa (eds) *Pornification: Sex and Sexuality in Media Culture*. Oxford: Berg, 45–57.
Falk, P. (1993) 'The Representation of Presence: Outlining the Anti-aesthetics of Pornography', *Theory, Culture & Society*, 10, 1–42.
G., A. (2008) 'SuicideGirls vs Lithium Picnic Lawsuit Settled'. On-line. Available: http://www.blueblood.net/2008/06/suicidegirls-vs-lithium-picnic-lawsuit-settled/ (accessed 26 March 2009).
Holland, S. (2004) *Alternative Femininities: Body, Age and Identity*. Oxford and New York: Berg.
Jacobs, K. (2004) 'The New Media Schooling of the Amateur Pornographer: Negotiating Contracts and Singing Orgasm', *Spectator*, 24, 1. On-line. Available: http://www.libidot.org/katrien/tester/articles/negotiating-print.html (accessed 16 December 2007).
____ (2007) *Netporn: DIY Web Culture and Sexual Politics*. Lanham, MD: Rowman and Littlefield.
Jancovich, M. (2001) 'Naked Ambitions: Pornography, Taste and the Problem of the Middlebrow', *Scope*. On-line. Available: http://www.nottingham.ac.uk/film/journal/

articles/naked-ambition.html (accessed 22 May 2001).

Juffer, J. (1998) *At Home With Pornography: Women, Sex and Everyday Life*. New York and London: New York University Press.

_____ (2005) 'Excessive Practices: Aesthetics, Erotica and Cultural Studies', in M. Berube (ed.) *The Aesthetics of Cultural Studies*. Malden, MA: Blackwell, 58–79.

Kipnis, L. (1996) *Bound and Gagged: Pornography and the Politics of Fantasy in America*. New York: Grove Press.

Kitzmann, A. (2004) *Saved From Oblivion: Documenting the Daily from Diaries to Web Cams*. New York: Peter Lang.

Magnet, S. (2007) 'Feminist sexualities, race and the internet: an investigation of suicidegirls. com', *New Media & Society*, 9, 577–602.

McKee, A. (2006) 'The aesthetics of pornography: the insights of consumers', *Continuum: Journal of Media and Cultural Studies*, 20, 523–39.

McNair, B. (2002) *Striptease Culture: Sex, Media and the Democratisation of Desire*. London & New York: Routledge.

Nead, L. (1992) *The Female Nude: Art, Obscenity and Sexuality*. London and New York: Routledge.

Paasonen, S. (2007) 'Porn Futures', in S. Paasonen, K. Nikunen and L. Saarenmaa (eds) *Pornification: Sex and Sexuality in Media Culture*. Oxford: Berg, 161–70.

Phillips, N. (2005) 'Cynical, Bitter, Jaded As Hell. Also Naked', On-line. Available: http://www.citypages.com/databank/23/1147/article10895.asp (accessed 13 May 2005).

Ray, A. (2007a) *Naked on the Internet: Hookups, Downloads and Cashing in on Internet Sexploration*. Emeryville CA: Seal Press.

_____ (2007b) 'Rated: Alt Porn' Kunsetbeeld. English version. On-line. Available: http://docs.google.com/View?docid=ah95q5gc8qv9_193ck8rhsf6 (accessed 17 January 2008).

Sontag, S. (1969) 'The Pornographic Imagination', *Styles of Radical Will*. New York: Dell, 35–73.

Storr, M. (2003) *Latex & Lingerie: Shopping for Pleasure at Ann Summers Parties*. Oxford and New York: Berg.

Suicide, M. (2004) *SuicideGirls*. Los Angeles: Feral House.

van der Graf, S. (2004) 'Blogging Business: SuicideGirls.com', *M/C Journal* 7(4). On-line. Available: http://journal.media-culture.org.au/0410/07_suicide.php (accessed 2 April 2005).

CHAPTER FOUR

PORNOGOGY: TEACHING THE TITILLATING

Mark Jones and Gerry Carlin

In 1966, the same year that the Supreme Court's decision allowing the publication of *Fanny Hill* effectively marked the end of literary censorship in the United States, the National Council of Teachers of English published a slim volume on pornography (Frank and Hogan 1966).[1] John P. Frank contributed an experiment in which four professors of literature and two psychologists read and responded to a number of allegedly obscene works, including *Fanny Hill* (written in 1748). Determining whether the texts were 'pornographic' seems to have been relatively simple (all except Henry Miller's *Tropic of Cancer* (first published in 1934) were), but the subjects' application of tests of literary merit or social value, and therefore the legal test of obscenity, were vague and contradictory. Still, Frank concluded optimistically that 'if the determination of obscenity is to be attempted on any rational, as distinguished from a merely instinctive, basis, the experts can help the community to solve this problem as well as it is likely to be solved' (1966: 47). In the same volume, Robert F. Hogan (1966) took a more activist stance, accepting that as the existence of pornography was inevitable it should be addressed by teachers of English in the classroom, so that its potential effects might be mitigated through education.

Frank's and Hogan's papers are informed by, and examples of, the substantial surge in scholarly engagement with pornography which occurred in the early 1960s. However, this application of intellectual endeavour by 'legal scholars, philosophers, theologians, and other thinkers' (Soble 1986: 3) served merely to complicate, rather than clarify, definitions of the obscene, to the point where in 1964 Supreme Court Justice Potter Stewart famously evaded the issue, asserting 'I know it when I see it' (*Jacobellis v. Ohio*, 378 US 184, 197). Over forty years later, as pornography becomes culturally pervasive, we see a lot more of it, but whether we know it any better is open to question. In the intervening period, pornography has moved from the object of courtroom debate, through criminological and psychological studies, moralistic and feminist political campaigns, to a point where the most common fields in which it is considered are likely to be technological or economic. Academic research continues, though the concentration now is typically on textual properties, and the role of pornography in identity formation. But as the academic, journalistic and policy discourses move further away from questions of moral value and definitions of obscenity, the percolation of pornography through society has reached the higher education classroom, revitalising some traditional aspects of the debate, and generating new controversies. This chapter will explore the various intersections between the academic and the obscene – in research, teaching, and in pornographic production – to trace the various uses each has made of their unlikely partner.

OBSCENE ACADEMY

The proliferation of academic work on pornography in the 1960s – largely questioning the operation and foundations of obscenity laws, and functioning to historicise old pornography and contextualise the new – worked chiefly to depathologise it. A causal connection cannot be proved between the surge in academic discourse on the topic and the concurrent contraction of the category 'obscene' to eventually exclude almost all printed works (for which some claim to literariness could almost always be made); it can, though, be postulated, and was at the time. In 1971 Irving Kristol claimed:

> For almost a century now, a great many intelligent, well-meaning and articulate people – of a kind generally called liberal or intellectual, or both – have argued eloquently against any kind of censorship of art and/or entertainment. And within the past ten years, the courts and the legislatures of most Western nations have found these arguments persuasive – so persuasive that hardly a man is now alive who clearly remembers what the answers to these arguments were. Today, in the United States and other democracies, censorship has to all intents and purposes ceased to exist. (1997: 174)

Walter Berns, himself a Professor of Political Science at the University of

Toronto, claimed that 'the work has not been written, staged, or filmed that cannot find its champions among the professors' (1972: 276). This conservative strategy of alleging an alignment of the interests of professors and pornographers was explicitly parodied in *The Obscenity Report*, a hoax publication whose success in fooling all commentators shows how accurately it mirrored the moralistic tone of the Nixon administration:[2]

> Supporters of the legitimacy of obscenity center on a respectable, if small, intellectual community. For the most part, they include college professors, their students, and other academics, many based in New York City and Washington, D. C. [...] They are joined, of course, by the actual purveyors of obscenity. (1970: 38)

While only the most conservative commentators accused intellectuals of intrinsic corruption or duplicity in regard to their attitudes to or relationship with pornographers, the engagement by academics with both the issues surrounding pornography and, implicitly, with the object itself led to an institutionalised doubt over their capacity to provide a useful contribution to debates around the issues of obscenity and censorship. It is significant that the test for obscenity determined by *Miller v. California* in 1973, replacing *Roth v. United States* which had pertained from 1957, marginalised expert witnesses on social effects and literary quality, and shifted 'the tastes of the average person ... from the position of object of the obscenity test to that of its legal reagent' (Hunter *et al.* 1993: 213). Judge Gewin expressed the populist contempt for allowing informed intellectuals to determine obscenity:

> To hold, in effect, that we must turn the application of obscenity statutes over 'to a collection of randomly chosen Ph.D.'s' as expert witnesses in such matters, is to require abdication of the judicial function of the judge or jury as triers of fact. (Nowlin 2003: 77)

Despite removing academics from the process of prosecuting pornography, and supposedly trespassing on First Amendment-enshrined rights, the new obscenity tests proved singularly incapable of 'stemming the tides of filth'. A series of problems in defining the tests' key terms (obscenity, prurience, community standards) were first addressed without recourse to the advice of experts, and then bypassed completely. Pornography became self-defining, and in the process automatically condemned itself – 'the films, obviously, are the best evidence of what they represent' (*Paris Adult Theatre 1 v. Slaton*, 413, US 49, 56).

A major problem arose, however, in satisfying the 'community standards' test in a society which was becoming increasingly fragmented and conflicted.

Impossible to define, and therefore categorically useless, obscenity, while still remaining legally proscribed as unprotected speech, became increasingly detached from the representational mode (genre) of pornography. The Supreme Court's assertion that (hard-core visual) pornography had a specific and identifiable form, together with its continued failure to securely attach the legal label of 'obscene material' to it, meant that for the first time pornography could be isolated from other, less explicit, forms of sexual representation and could be addressed in the public space without continual recourse to matters of constitutional law. Building on the sex research pioneered by Kinsey, Masters and Johnson, and others, and more particularly on the numerous studies of pornography and its effects commissioned by the Presidential Commission on Obscenity and Pornography, the 1970s and early 1980s saw a huge increase in research on pornography – its effects, how it is used, and attitudes towards it. As many of these studies took the form of psychological experiments in which groups of male students were shown pornographic films, and then subjected to questioning, surveys or role-plays to determine the effects of the viewing, university researchers were effectively becoming disseminators of pornography – not exactly producers, but almost certainly falling within the popular and political definitions of pornographers. Highly abstracted, artificial, and criticised for their methodology more often than their morality, these experimental studies were largely confined to university classrooms, and involved male psychology students who were typically debriefed following the viewing to remove any potential contamination (see Gunter 2002).

DESPISED DISPLAYS

Around the same time, though, less institutionalised and more activist intellectuals were bringing pornographic representations more nakedly into public spaces. Mirroring the peripatetic exhibition practices of soft-core porn distributors (see Schaefer 1999: 99–103), anti-pornography feminists created and toured 'roadshows' consisting of visiting speakers, panel discussions, displays and slideshows of pornographic images (see Webster 1981; Johnson 1997). Feminist pornographic displays were framed by politically activist discourses, and their chief purpose was exposure, to dispel '[w]omen's ignorance about the true nature of pornography' (Russell 1998: 37). Again, the attempt to have pornography define itself *as such* is the main principle of the processes inhering in both selection and display. While some of these interventions involve substantial sections of detailed textual analysis (see Dworkin 1981; Griffin 1981; Dines *et al.* 1998), the objective is always to make apparently diverse pornographic texts conform to a singular definition of it 'as what it is, that is to say as a violation of the Civil Rights of Women' (Mackinnon, cited in Everywoman 1988: 8). It is this clarity – almost as effortless in its perception as Justice Potter Stewart's re-cognisance, and a great deal more legalistically productive – which attracted conservative moralists to Andrea Dworkin and Catherine Mackinnon's anti-pornography ordinances. Avoiding the problematic and ultimately pointless notion of obscenity, Dworkin and MacKinnon's attempted ordinance materialised from academic engagement with pornography as both representational texts and social problem. Thoroughly informed by prior work on the topic, Dworkin's analysis of pornography emerged from the academy, and had its first effects there, both to inspire and to inhibit (see Downs 1989). Although textual analysis is not the main objective of this project, other than where it is required to more fully demonstrate the nature of the offence proposed, Dworkin was one of the first to treat hard-core pictorial pornography as representation, even if it would all eventually prove to be symbolically representative of violent oppression. The anti-porn publications and exhibitions are insistently repetitive about identifying pornography's own formulaic repetitions, across different media, national origins, and historical contexts; but their direct confrontation with hard-core pornography for educational purposes might be seen to have legitimised and, perhaps, prompted its usage in more nuanced pedagogical engagements.

The engagement with pornography in university-based research – other than in psychological and sociological effects studies, and legal discourse on obscenity – is largely subsequent to the feminist anti-pornographers' explicit activities. Rather than making pornography unacceptable or extinct, it seems as though the informed engagement with pornography by campaigners for censorship succeeded only in stimulating other forms of intellectual enquiry into the object. Many prominent writers on pornography cite the reductionist analyses associated with Dworkin and MacKinnon as a prime reason for their engagement with the subject (see Soble 1986: 1; Williams 1993: 57; Thompson 1994: ix–xi; Kipnis 1996: x; Winkler 1989). Pornography, whatever the individual academic's perspective or intention, became a very visible signifier of cultural radicalism. Entering academic and institutional practices retaining its problematic aura, pornography remains *sexy*, as Jennifer Wicke noted as far back as 1991:

> Courses are being offered, seminars suggested, books emerging apace, and even the instinctive feel one acquires for what will radiate as hot and imperative in a book or essay title is shifting to 'pornography', having supplanted the early 1980s thrill of 'power' and the delights later in the decade of 'sexuality', perhaps because pornography so neatly conflates the two. (1991: 68)

Wicke acknowledges that the conjunction of academia and pornography is not without problems, particularly in the area of display. The reproduced pornographic photographs in *Caught Looking* (Ellis *et al.* 1986), are, she believes, leached of their masturbatory or fantasy functionality, at least while securely contained within the academic context. As perhaps the two most clearly distanced species of communicative practice, pornography and academia cannot co-exist and, at least as the object of research, pornography succumbs under the transforming power of 'critical consciousness' (1991: 81).

SHOW AND TELL

Despite the confidence of many academics and censorians of various perspectives that explicit sexual materials can be looked at without being consumed, and so can be safely both researched and resisted, the ability of pornography to provide a cultural touchstone has re-emerged in responses to its pedagogical uses. The numerous moral panics which intermittently erupt over the classroom display of pornography demonstrates that it marks one of the few areas of academic enquiry in which clear distinctions can be drawn between attitudes to practices in research and teaching. Despite the wariness with which many responsible educators approach the issue, though, pornography has gradually secured a place in the curricula of higher education. The first display of pornography in a classroom for purposes other than sexual education, moral censure or political agitation, is now probably as lost as the earliest pornographic film itself – or, at least, none of the many academics who have related the story of their first exhibition of pornography to students has felt able to claim priority. But sometime in the early 1990s in America it seems that several scholars decided that their teaching of pornography would be better informed by the presence of the thing itself within the classroom. The typical justification for this (and many academics who teach pornography seem to have found themselves having to provide a rationalisation in public at some point) is ultimately to do with definitions; or, more accurately, the definite. Linda Williams, for example, ascribes her decision to teach, rather than merely research and write on, pornography to a need to counteract MacKinnnon's 'facile fantasy about the root evil of pornography' (2004: 12). While feminist anti-porn academics and activists occupied themselves attempting to distil a definition of pornography from various materials (not all of which were necessarily sexually explicit, but which were all supposedly degrading to women), 'anti-anti-porn' academics were selecting and exhibiting similar – often identical – texts as the very things which would define the area of study.

Although most critics writing on the genre acknowledge the slipperiness of the term, it is remarkable how few outside of the pro-censorship lobby even attempt to arrive at a generic description of pornography, either through making use of their identified 'typical' texts to delineate its boundaries, or by drawing on the typologies of genre models as they have been established in numerous studies of popular culture. Various avoidance strategies are frequently utilised. One is to invoke a series of contradictory definitions, typically drawn from the dictionary, feminist jurisprudence, and the law on obscenity, and to then ignore all of them while still allowing them some kind of spectral authority; this has been used by Gayle Rubin (1993) and, more extensively, by Laurence O'Toole (1998). A variation of this appears in Walter Kendrick's refusal to propose any definition at all, replacing it with a discussion of 'everything that has ever been called "pornography"' (1996: xii). But the commonest method is to use as criteria for inclusion some variation of visible sex with intent to arouse, and to justify it by appeal to other sources' similar criteria (Soble 1986: 8–9; McNair 1996: 44–5; Williams 1990: 29–30, 284). Though pornography can now be summoned into being in both academic discourse and the classroom environment, its effective detachment from the legal category of the obscene has not aided in its conceptual identification. It is still known only when it is seen, being the best evidence of what it represents, while hard-core is 'the genre's only apparent obviousness' (Williams 1990: 6). Ironically for this most apparently transparent of visual modes, the imperative to show it in class comes from a failure of representation, an inability to harness its meaning, define it or refer to it in its absence.

This, though, has not prevented the classroom display of pornography from becoming its own symbolic object. Since pornography has largely been denuded of scandal in the public sphere and the commercial environment, particularly as much of the browsing and acquisition has moved online and into the domestic space, its 'glamour', its 'peculiar power and significance' (Segal 1992: 67) has shifted elsewhere. Where has it gone? We think, just about everywhere. The 'pornographisation' of the mainstream, already a cliché, is a complex interplay of 'striptease culture' (McNair 2002) and a 'metapornographic' discourse of shock and scandal, familiar from earlier mediatised moral panics. (See Attwood 2007 for an analysis of this as it relates to academia.) While hip hop videos, lad mags, and 'pornumentaries' can provide a certain frisson of either excitement or vexation, metapornography of the outraged variety is more productively created if the colliding discourses are more traditionally distinct. Leaving aside the lucky accident of Janet Jackson's 'nipple slip' at the Super Bowl, and the regular appearance of home-made celebrity sex tapes on the internet, the most reliable source for newsvendors wishing to quote porn in public has become the American academy. The number of salacious stories on the topic is huge, and continually rising. Most of the articles which berate the phenomenon of 'porn studies', name and shame the persistent perpetrators, and bemoan the status of contemporary higher education are, like pornography itself, typically repetitive, breathless, and ejaculatory (see Jablonski 2001; Carlson 2003; Young 2003). And despite the valiant efforts of both the occasional dispassionate observer and the 'conservative commentators who can work themselves into a righteous lather about the decline of higher education' (Schaefer 2005: 105) to inform the public about 'porn studies', almost every encounter between pornography and academia is narrated as a first-time experience. 'Local prof teaching porn', always 'scandalous', always an 'expose', is firmly established as a reliable page-filler for regional newspapers.

So well established is the mode that it has engendered its less popular sub-genres, including the story of the academic who is also a part-time sex-worker. This narrative cannot make effective use of the functions typical to the main genre of corrupting young minds and wasting tax dollars, and it might be thought that what people do outside of their publicly-funded work is their own affair; but the fact that these stories are generated whenever circumstances allow illustrates the fundamental nature of the whole genre – it is the merest connection between the body of the academy or the academic and the idea of sex that provides the required disjunction. Intellectualising sexual practice, performance or presentation, and sexualising academic enquiry, threatens to rupture both. Academia and its critical authority is not perceived as immune to pornography's contaminating discursive power.

STUDENT BODIES

The figure at the centre of this discourse of pollution is the student – multitudinous, amorphous, pregnable, and subject to pornographic propaganda from radically disreputable professors. Given this trope, pornography becomes just another in a long list of thought-crimes verbalised by academics within the auditory and conceptual range of their students. Assaulted by communist agents in the 1950s, peaceniks in the 1960s, the political correctness police in the 1980s, American students have been continuously degraded by unscrupulous academics and infantilised by scare-mongering commentators. But an alternative narrative has also been suggested – one in which the students provide the motive force for the attitudinal adjustments which lead to institutional transformation (see Jacobs and Landau 1966; Bloom 1987). Critics whom align professors and pornographers ignore the active role which students have played in the insemination of pornography into the academy, and the constructions of themselves as pornographic subjects.

Pornography consumed on campus outside of the classroom has been a key indicator of various aspects within the evolving attitudes towards and campaigns against explicit sexual display. At the close of the 1960s, protests over *Playboy* in the university were among the earliest direct action campaigns against pornography (see Boler *et al.* 1982: 263). Students' attempts to screen *Deep Throat* (1972) caused it to be subject to more censorship attempts on university campuses than any other text in the 1970s, from both moralists and feminists (see Woods 1979). The relationship between pornographers and students has been reciprocal, with producers of pornography increasingly centring their product on students as consumers, and involving them in production. *Playboy*'s first 'college issue' was published in October 1955; their first 'college playmate' in September 1958; 'campus sex' specials appeared in September 1968 and 1969; 'campus nudity' in September 1972. September 1977 saw the first appearance of 'Girls of the Big Ten', student pictorials which continue to this day. Whereas the first of these specials generated at least some student protest at *Playboy*'s intrusion onto campus (see Lederer 1982: 183), recently they have only provided fodder for student newspapers and a healthy increase in *Playboy*'s circulation (see Dunphy 2003). The constant legitimisation of 'student porn' inevitably resulted in the entry of undergraduates into the arena of production, with a raft of sex magazines produced under the auspices of many of America's most prestigious universities (see Rudoren 2006). Students are also surreptitiously participating in and producing pornographic videos (see Moody 2007; Kruer and Stampfl 2005). The impression left by an endless series of shocked exposés, salacious feature stories, and apoplectic editorials is that the experience of American higher education consists of an incessant torrent of desire and its effortless discharge. Consumption, production and investigation of pornography by students on campus removes the pornographic professor from the picture, but retains many of the other pertinent aspects of pornography in an academic context. The issues raised by outraged commentators are still those around sexual harassment, educational degradation, and institutional support for obscenity (see Secor 2005). But in replacing analysis with entertainment, critics must engage with sexualised consumption, and therefore with the erotically charged 'student body'.

Students, usually in their late teens or early twenties, relatively unencumbered by fiscal, familial or social responsibilities, living away from home for perhaps the first time, encountering a large and disparate variety of new people, will inevitably be one of the most sexually active demographic groups. Given this predictable relative promiscuity, it might therefore be thought unusual that the involvement of students with pornography should generate the required conceptual disjunction to make it the subject of scandal stories. Two factors are, we believe, operating here. One is the metapornographic quoting of the eroticised young person, of either sex – this is primary in stories featuring students posing for pornographic magazines, or participating in filmed fraternity orgies. The script here is a straight-forward one of pornographic details (naming acts and titling publications), and the news-value is supplied

Fig. 6 Co-ed as sexual icon in *Cocksure Graduate*.

by peers' responses to a publicly active pornographer in their midst (see Kaye 1992). The other narrative is more complex, and occurs when students are the agents of their own eroticisation, when they control at least some of the means of production. These stories, despite the involvement of a greater number of students, are more nuanced than those involving one or a few models shedding their inhibitions. Again, we think the reasons are various. Exploitation is more difficult to establish, given the similar ages and statuses of all involved; but more particularly, the disjunctive move of these stories comes from the very fact of students appropriating their own eroticised image from the society responsible for its manufacture. It is the partial, confused and confusing, representational revenge of the co-ed.

Supposedly slang for 'co-educational' but only ever applied to female students, 'co-ed' has since its formulation carried connotations of sexual availability.[4] Rudy Vallee's hit song 'Betty Co-ed' (1931), purportedly a love song, characterised her thus:

> Flirtation is an art with Betty Co-ed
> Her station quite depends upon her charms
> She gets the men in rushes
> By well cultivated blushes
> And she's happy with a fellow on each arm.

Of the several dozen American feature films and shorts made between 1911 and 1946 which make reference to co-eds in their titles, most are romantic comedies or social problem films (*Confessions of a Co-ed* (1931), for example, includes illegitimacy and a love triangle). After a twenty-year on-screen hiatus the return of the co-ed in the 1970s was in sordid crime features and hard-core sex films. Since 1980, almost all titles including the word co-ed are hard-core and often fetish pornography, including *Coed Devirginizations* (2001). In erotic literature and pulp fiction, too, the co-ed has long been a 'sexual icon' (Scheiner 1996: 108); examples include *Memoirs of a Girl Student* (1934), *Coed for Hire* (1966), *Cocksure Graduate* (1975).

The protagonist of *Campus Call Girl* (1964) becomes a prostitute to support her illegitimate daughter, and is expelled from college when her spurned lesbian roommate informs the dean: '[We] did not build this seminary, not its enviable reputation, by allowing either *tarts* or *perverted* women among its students!' (O'Neill 1964: 34). The female student is figured as potentially and unnaturally lustful – not just the object and innocent derivation of desire, but embodying sex itself, and preternaturally enthusiastic in its initiation. The co-ed as signifier of sexual responsiveness is so well established that it aided resolution of one of the few mistakes made by the American stag film industry, usually so perceptive in determining its constituency's wants. When audiences were disturbed by the portrayal of *The Nun* (1949) as a sexual predator, the 'distributors trimmed both the beginning and end ... and reissued it under the innocuous (if misleading) title *College Co-Eds*' (Thompson 2007: 211).

Whereas other iconic female pornographised roles (nurses, stewardesses, housewives) can be depicted as either active or passive, the female student is usually represented as an enthusiastic sexual participant. Characterised by youth and attractiveness, of course, but also typically wealthy, privileged, intelligent and ambitious, the female student is narratively problematic in a genre which typically (not solely, of course) depends on the 'male dominat[ing] the sex behavior' (Smith 1976: 22). Aside from the usual method of enforced humiliation – frequent in pornographic paperbacks of the 1960s and 1970s and in many 'roughie' sex films of the time – which largely renders pointless having a sexually liberated and energetic female protagonist, there are two other methods whereby the female student's sexual agency can be safely contained. One is through intercourse with her co-ed peers, in lesbian encounters frequently involving sadomasochistic sorority rituals; the other is by engaging her in some kind of relationship with one or more of the teaching staff. While this is not an essential element of the campus-based pornographic narrative, having the female student involved in sexual encounters with faculty provides a distinctive sexual charge. Whereas the co-ed's relationships with male students are either mutually consensual or extremely brutal, introducing a male (occasionally female) professor evokes hierarchical structures which can be eroticised through power rather than violence. In addition to the adoption of the classic pornographic relationship where the male is of superior status, age and sexual experience, the professor/student pairing introduces a range of other possible relations of dominance, obligation, indebtedness, subservience, admiration, and transgression all of which can contribute towards an erotics of instruction.

Most modern pornography foregrounding the involvement of students ignores the potential for fiction, and tends towards a certain kind of 'reality porn' (as Ruth Barcan describes it, 'commercially made, for sale on the open market' (2002: 98)). The dominant and most apparently lucrative aspect of this category is the 'amateur' tag, clearly a partial misnomer but generally accepted to mean 'pro/am', where the male participant is a full-time pornographer, and the females are casual labourers (see Lehman 1999: 363). The long lists of 'coed', 'sorority', and 'college girl' websites which are brought up by a click on either 'amateur' or 'teen' in a porn web directory (we used sirrrodney.com) demonstrates the multiple functionality of the student for internet pornography. Female university students, always over eighteen, usually under twenty-one, in an unremunerated occupation, forming a large and already culturally eroticised demographic, have become the camera fodder of the 'amateur' genre. And by metonymic connection everyday student life becomes thoroughly pornographised on the web: dorms (*Dorm Amateurs*), sororities (*Lightspeed Sorority*), campus parties (*College Party Time*), spring break (*Operation Spring Break*). Minimal narratives, invoking authentic college scenarios such as frat parties, hazing, and study breaks, are utilised to provide justification for casual sexual encounters. The actual motivation for this activity is more honestly promoted in such sites as *Co-eds Need Cash* and *College Teens Book Bang*. The latter is predicated specifically on the student's need for the apparatus of learning, and sexualises their supposed diligence and academic ambition. One participant's profile runs:

> We ran into first year student Angelina at the local campus. She was upset that she had all these classes but no books and no cash to get them. That is when we told her about our scholarship program and she sucked & fucked for the cash!

It is at points such as this that the promiscuous co-ed begins to be reconfigured as the *student*, acknowledging her educational context and primary occupation. While the co-ed narrative is uncomplicatedly orgiastic, the student must be allocated more complex motivations, and can be potentially and variously susceptible, seductive, and calculating, particularly in relations with her educators.

PROFESSING PORN

Pornographic narratives of professor/student sexual interaction clearly partake of prior assumptions which can be traced elsewhere in cultural representations; '[t]he campuses in academic novels are places rife with sexual liaisons between professors and their students', though in most the students are passive, but not unwilling, recipients and 'the professors come across as sexual Lotharios who are driven by their libidos' (Tierney 2004: 172–3). Like all stereotypes, this is a reductive characterisation; it can, though, be differentiated. Five typologies of 'Lothario' are suggested in an analysis of campus-based sexual harassment: 'The Counselor/Helper', 'The Confidante', 'The Intellectual Seducer', 'The Opportunist', 'The Power Broker' (see Dziech and Weiner 1990: 122–4). Whilst all of these could operate in sexual discourses involving professors and students, they achieve even wider application when they encounter their corequisite notion of 'female students [who] have fantasised or even initiated sexual relationships with male teachers' (Pichaske 1995: B1). A similar typology of seductive students has not been performed, with even subtle analyses such as Jane Gallop's concentrating only on variations of 'smart, ambitious young women, many of them ... feminist academics today, [feeling] powerful because they seduced their teachers' (1997: 43). There is, though, discrimination between scenarios, from the potentially consensual to the blatantly exploitative, all of which are again narratorially applicable: 'seductive behavior', that is 'inappropriate sexual advances'; 'sexual bribery ... from grades, to fellowships, to recommendations'; 'sexual coercion ... [threatening] bad grades, poor references, poor evaluations, academic discipline' (Francis 2001: 7–9). Within the dualistic relationship of a professor and a student there are, therefore, a sizeable range of narrative opportunities; the only distinction between mainstream fiction and pornography is that in the former, there is a remote possibility that sex will not occur. Even here, though, the dynamics of the genre seem to lead inexorably towards a sexual encounter between professor/student. The assumption that this will occupy the central narrative of a campus novel is so well developed that if this is not the intention then strategies need to be developed to marginalise it. Howard Jacobson's *Coming From Behind* (1983) can only embark on its satirical route after the obligatory sexual encounter with a student is disposed of as a narrative issue at the outset; the novel begins with the protagonist in his office having sex with a student who is clearly a minor character, and who never appears again. Omitting any establishing scene prior to intercourse, and thus evading all the possible narrational scenarios, this attempts to figure the erotic fantasies regarding professors and students as pornography, stripped of character or motivation.

An entirely oppositional move is found in much of the hard-core pornography which deals with academic staff and students. These are frequently narratorially dense, and make fulsome use of the subtly distinct scenarios established by sexual fantasy and erotic literature; they might even be said to incorporate accounts of sexual harassment, appropriating them as pornographic discourses. In *Every Night Lover* (1969) by Les Tucker, the professor of American Literature is aggressively seduced by two successful and ambitious students. The first sex scene in *A Sea of Thighs* (1971) finds Professor Standish Bummpo arousing Haya Wantta, '[o]ne of his better students' (Kainen 1971: 10) by a display of brilliant poetic analysis. *The Oxford Girl* (1988) exploits the power of the professor to its fullest in a typical sadomasochistic fiction. Contemporary online pornography utilising this situation is similarly well informed on the eroticised potentiality of the pedagogical relationship.

Several websites specialise in this area, and they are typically listed in porn directories along with co-ed sites. Adopting this typology, in the absence of any better, they can be classed as a sub-genre of the college girl type. A content analysis, though, reveals distinct, even extreme, differences between sexual materials featuring students, and those also involving professors. Whereas co-ed sites focus almost entirely on the pornotopic possibilities of university

– with its concentration of sexually active young people, lack of familial or communal restraints, and semi-ritualised erotic display and behaviour – faculty/student pornography more frequently figures sex as a mode of exchange. Although intercourse is inevitable (this is pornography, after all), it occurs as a result of negotiations, and serves a purpose outside of itself. While the introduction of the professor means that the pornographic scenario can follow a culturally established path, each individual encounter needs to delineate a specific situational form and set of relations. Given the added complexity that this adds to the production process, what must be determined is the added pornographic value it provides which makes the narration and location worthwhile investments.

The most obvious answers to this question are that it is a fetishised sexual preference, or that it conforms to a common fantasy. These are, we believe, almost certainly incorrect. The typically fetishised elements of these sites ('the naughty schoolgirl look: the plaid skirt, the knee socks, nerdy glasse [sic]' (*Naughty Bookworms*)) are often actually not present, more easily accessed on other sites, or independent of the student in a classroom situation. Similarly, it is difficult to believe that it is a common fantasy to be a university professor, whatever the stereotypical opportunities for sexual dalliance. Unless the principle markets for these sites are male faculty staff expressing their own repressed or regulated desires, then it is unlikely that an empathic relationship with the male protagonist is the central attraction.

Some answers to this question might be forthcoming from a more detailed analysis of content. We examined four websites which adopted the theme of professor/student sex – three cursorily, and one in more depth. Of the four, *Old Man School* is the nearest to identification as essentially a fetish site, foregrounding as its attraction the disparities in age between male and female performers. It is also the one which most clearly conforms to the relationship between professor and student characterised as 'intellectual seducer', though its own performance of this is somewhat disappointing:

Fig. 7 *Old Man School.*
Courtesy of www.oldmanschool.com.

> So what if her lector [sic] is not so young and handsome? She knows young guys and they all sooo stupid! And here is DA MAN she even has to ask for his permission in French. When she wants to play with his penis. So charming!

All of the other sites feature males of varying ages – all older than the females, of course, but not consistently portrayed as noticeably elderly. *Dirty Teacher's Pet* and *Teen Teacher* have many features in common, including much of the actual content. Despite the overlap, they establish different approaches to the material. *Dirty Teacher's Pet* comes the closest to figuring the female student in a similar manner to the co-ed sites, questioning a female addressee 'Why work your way through college when you can fuck your way through?' The nature of this exchange is more clearly spelt out by the profile attached to Chloey, who 'couldn't pass her first year of University based on her brains, but she's managing to pull straight A's by spreading her legs for her hunky professors!' (*Dirty Teachers Pet Chloey*) The scenarios in *Teen Teacher*, though frequently featuring the same videos, are given a more apparently coercive framing, headlined by 'Poor Little Schoolgirls Exploited by Their Dirty Teacher'.

Naughty Bookworms (formerly *Bookworm Bitches*) seems to be the largest and best-established professor/student site. The scenarios on this site are also the most varied, making extensive use of the dynamic interplays suggested by placing the characters in their environment. They range from Bree Olsen, who wants to make Professor Savage happy as a birthday present to herself, through to Keiko, who is spanked for cheating and then submits to sex to obtain a passing grade. Between sexual exuberance and punishment come varied degrees of seduction, compromise and coercion. Sasha Grey begins her scene by writing 'I can and will fuck for my A' on Professor Vega's chalkboard; when he refuses her, she goes to see her counsellor, Professor Savage, and demands assistance. Refused again, due to her being 'the worst student he's ever had', she retorts: 'Now that Professor Vega's married, he's a pussy, and he doesn't want this pussy, so maybe you do.' She begins to masturbate, and Professor Savage resists for a few minutes, before she deep throats him while he pants, 'This is so wrong'. Charlotte Stokely has similarly worked her way through several members of the faculty. Ashley Jensen goes straight to the top and approaches the Dean with a sexual offer, even though it is established that the previous incumbent was dismissed following a sexual scandal involving a student. Jodi and Gretchen are called in together to see Professor Lobo because their essays are very similar; both deny cheating, continually abuse each other, but agree to have sex with each other and with their professor for passing grades. While these scenarios are clearly fulfilling a heterosexual male fantasy about sexually available young women, each one fabricates some obstruction, however minor and easily overcome, between desire and satisfaction. It is the nature of the hindrance which varies across the samples, and provides some element of difference.

A much more nuanced scenario is supplied for Christina. She has made some errors in her paper on physical therapist Joseph Pilates, and Professor

Johnson is unhappy with her references. Exasperated, she tells her professor 'you're bitter that you're just a schoolteacher that makes a little over minimum wage.' It emerges that her wealthy father has attempted to bribe the staff to improve his daughter's grades. She denies the accusation, offers to rewrite the paper, then tries to bribe the professor. He claims the moral high ground – although many institutions are corrupt, he is not for sale. He compliments her dress; she retorts that he could never afford her. Despite this clear opportunity for him to make a sexual advance, several more minutes of negotiation over her grade ensues, as he offers her a C- to take her top off. Even while undressing and displaying herself she maintains her self-confidence and sarcastic demeanour. The majority of the ensuing sex scene follows the usual pattern for heterosexual pornography, though it is occasionally punctuated by Christina's pointed comments, including an accusation that he gives poor grades in order to manipulate students into situations such as this. The scene ends with Christina receiving the customary facial cumshot, and immediately insisting that the grade on her paper is changed.

Some of the other *Naughty Bookworms* videos exhibit comparable oscillations in verbal ascendancy, though all follow basically similar sexual activities. As with all pornography it is, of course, the penetrative genital sex which is the defining factor of the videos. This is framed, though, by a narrative which is particular to each individual text, and typically interspersed with dialogue which rearticulates the characterisations and reactivates the story. Although each narrative can occupy a subtly distinct location on the spectrum of professor/student relations, all, even the promiscuous student scenarios, are effectively enactments of institutional dominance, in which either the male participant's sexual demands are enabled by a culture in which harassment seems to be accepted, or the female's sexual agency is figured as commodity. Therefore they apparently replicate the accepted pornographic narrative in which male power is enacted and eroticised. However, the continual presence of obstruction and patterns of bartering in professor/student pornography modify porn's simplistic hierarchies; exchange is clearly not submission, and in this mode of pornography negotiation is eroticised as an alternative form of power. Although the genre demands that the outcome of these negotiations must always be the usual ejaculatory conclusion, the narratives which lead to this are actually pornographic enhancements of appropriated academic relations. They work because they are culturally recognised. Porn plagiarises academia's institutionalised roles and exchanges, and in return reveals the complex erotics of pedagogy.

Perhaps, then, the problem of pornography in the classroom is that it reveals too much, and not only about the sexual dynamics within pornography. These concerns could be linked to John Glavin's claim that '[a]ll teaching, all successful teaching, falls into one of two kinds: abusive or seductive' (1997:

13). While this might seem to adequately describe the identification between pornography and academia that we have explored, it does not fully recognise the complex dynamics that are revealed even in the porn, let alone the intricate patterns of exchange which make up classroom interaction. Glavin may be correct, however, in suggesting that all professor/student relations are potentially sexualised, and, like the pornography, operate through dialectics of domination and resistance, obstruction and instruction. The ease with which these sexually charged relations can become actually sexual is recognised in wider society by the cultural stereotype of the promiscuous academy, and within the institution by university regulations against even consensual staff/student relationships. To show pornography in the classroom, to display explicit representations of sex to students, is to reify and perhaps reinforce this sublimated sexual apparatus of pedagogy. The object of analysis begins to open up the frame which has attempted to contain it. While the cool strategies of textual analysis, the gravitas of informed contexts, and the rhetoric of academic freedom and responsibility seem to provide an educational prophylactic, porn remains pornographic. It is not exhausted by critical analysis; incorporating pornography into the pedagogical performance makes that pedagogy pornography, whatever else it may also be. This is not to say, however, that we should avoid engaging with, or exhibiting, pornography in the university classroom. In a society saturated with sexual imagery the academy would be irresponsible were it not to critically reflect on such representative forms. The responsible educator will be aware that reflection works both ways, however, and that the university itself remains part of the same network of political, social and sexual relations in which the pornography it examines is produced and consumed.

NOTES

1. This is the US professional organisation for English teachers; the UK equivalent, the National Association for the Teaching of English has not, to the best of our knowledge, sponsored any publications dealing with pornography as an educational issue. Most of the experiments, innovations and controversies in the teaching of pornography have occurred in the United States; hence, our chapter deals almost exclusively with the US experience (and, incidentally, tends to use the appropriate terminology). The UK, as always, trails only a few years behind.
2. This is not the *Report of the Commission on Obscenity and Pornography*, commissioned by President Johnson, but eventually reporting to President Nixon, with which is sometimes confused. *The Obscenity Report* continued to fool commentators for many years

(for examples see Rist 1973 and Greek and Thompson 1992). The actual authors were Jethro K. Lieberman and Sandor Frankel (personal email, 27 February 2008).
3   The earliest example we have traced of filmed pornography screened in class was in a 'coeducational sociology class of 250 persons' at California State College in January 1970, and was designed to ridicule 'America's prudishness about sex as contrasted with its toleration of … such "glaring obscenities" as the Vietnam war, violence on television and pollution of air and water' (cited in Krattenmaker & Powe 1978: 1197). Both of the teachers responsible were suspended without pay.
4   A citation from 1895 in the *OED* bemoans that 'There is even danger that soon "co-ed" institutions will degenerate into mere matrimonial agencies'.

WORKS CITED

Abbott, P. (1988) *The Oxford Girl*. New York: Blue Moon.
Attwood, F. (2007) '"Other" or "One of Us"?: The Porn User in Public & Academic Discourse', *Particip@tions*, 4, 1, May. On-line. Available: http://www.participations.org/Volume%204/Issue%201/4_01_attwood.htm (accessed 1 April 2009).
Barcan, R. (2002) 'In the Raw: "Home-made" Porn and Reality Genres', *Journal of Mundane Behavior*, 3, 1, February, 87–108.
Berns, W. (1972) 'Beyond the Garbage Pale, or Democracy, Censorship and the Arts', in D. Holbrook (ed.) *The Case Against Pornography*. London: Tom Stacey, 273–94.
Bloom, A. (1987) *The Closing of the American Mind: How Higher Education has Failed Democracy and Impoverished the Souls of Today's Students*. New York: Simon & Schuster.
Boler, M., R. Lake and B. Wynne (1982) 'We Sisters Join Together…', in L. Lederer (ed.) (1982) *Take Back the Night: Women on Pornography*. New York: Bantam Books, 261–6.
Carlson, T. (2003) 'That's Outrageous: Porn 101: Yep that's *Penthouse* on the Syllabus', *Reader's Digest*, March, 31–3.
Dines, G., R. Jensen and A. Russo (1998) *Pornography: The Production and Consumption of Inequality*. London: Routledge.
Downs, D. A. (1989) *The New Politics of Pornography*. Chicago: University of Chicago Press.
Dunphy, M. (2003) 'Model Students Show Their Stuff in *Playboy*', *The Daily Illini*, 24 September. On-line. Available: http://www.illinimedia.com/di/sep03/sep24/news/stories/news_story08.shtml (accessed 29 September 2008).
Dworkin, A. (1981) *Pornography: Men Possessing Women*. London: The Women's Press.
Dziech, B. W. and L. Weiner (1990) *The Lecherous Professor: Sexual Harassment on Campus*. Second edition. Urbana and Chicago: University of Illinois Press.
Ellis, K., N. D. Hunter, B. Jaker, B. O'Dair, and A. Tallmer (1986) *Caught Looking: Feminism, Pornography and Censorship*. New York: Caught Looking.
Everywoman (1988) *Pornography and Sexual Violence: Evidence of the Links*. London: Everywoman.
Francis, L. P. (2001) *Sexual Harassment as an Ethical Issue in Academic Life*. Lantham, MD: Rowman & Littlefield.
Frank, J. P. (1966) 'Obscenity: Some Problems of Values and the Use of Experts', in J. P. Frank and R. F. Hogan, *Obscenity, the Law, and the English Teacher: Two Papers*. Champaign, IL:

National Council of Teachers of English, 1–47.
Frank, J. P. and R. F. Hogan (1966) *Obscenity, the Law, and the English Teacher: Two Papers*. Champaign, IL: National Council of Teachers of English.
Gallop, J. (1997) *Feminist Accused of Sexual Harassment*. Durham, NC: Duke University Press.
Glavin, J. (1997) 'The Intimacies of Instruction', in R. Barreca and D. D. Morse (eds) *The Erotics of Instruction*. Hanover, NH & London: University Press of New England, 12–27.
Greek, C. E. and W. Thompson (1992) 'Antipornography Campaigns: Saving the Family in America and England', *International Journal of Politics, Culture and Society*, 5, 4, 601–16.
Griffin, S. (1981) *Pornography and Silence: Culture's Revenge Against Nature*. London: The Women's Press.
Gunter, B. (2002) *Media Sex: What are the Issues?* New Jersey and London: Lawrence Erlbaum Associates.
Hogan, R. F. (1966) 'Obscenity and the Teacher: Another View', in J. P. Frank and R. F. Hogan, *Obscenity, the Law, and the English Teacher: Two Papers*. Champaign, IL: National Council of Teachers of English 1966, 49–61.
Hunter, I., D. Saunders and D. Williamson (1993) *On Pornography: Literature, Sexuality and Obscenity Law*. Basingstoke: Macmillan.
Jablonski, J. (2001) 'Porn Studies Latest Academic Fad', *Accuracy in Academia*, October. On-line. Available: http://www.academia.org/campusreport_2001.html (accessed 1 April 2009).
Jacobs, P. and S. Landau (1966) *The New Radicals: A Report With Documents*. New York: Random House.
Jacobson, H. (1983) *Coming From Behind*. London: Chatto and Windus.
Johnson, E. (1997) 'Appearing Live on Your Campus!: Porn-education Roadshows', *Jump Cut*, 41, May, 27–35.
Kainen, R. (1971) *A Sea of Thighs*. London: Olympia Press.
Kaye, A. (1992) 'Student Poses in "Hustler"', *The Daily Pennsylvanian*, 23 September. On-line. Available: http://media.www.dailypennsylvanian.com/media/storage/paper882/news/1992/09/23/Archive/Student.Poses.In.hustler-2186323.shtml (accessed 28 September 2008).
Kendrick, W. (1996) *The Secret Museum: Pornography in Modern Culture*. Expanded edition. Berkeley and Los Angeles: University of California Press.
Kipnis, L. (1996) *Bound and Gagged: Pornography and the Politics of Fantasy in America*. New York: Grove Press.
Krattenmaker, T. G. and L. A. Powe, Jr. (1978) 'Televised Violence: First Amendment Principles and Social Science Theory', *Virginia Law Review*, 64, 8, December, 1123–297.
Kristol, I. (1997) 'Pornography, Obscenity, and the Case for Censorship', in L. Gruen and G. E. Panichas (eds) *Sex, Morality, and the Law*. New York: Routledge, 174–82.
Kruer, R. and K. Stampfl (2005) 'Porn Producer Recruits 'U' Students', *The Michigan Daily*, 20 April. On-line. Available: http://www.michigandaily.com/content/porn-producer-recruits-u-students (accessed 29 September 2008).
Lederer, L. (ed.) (1982) *Take Back the Night: Women on Pornography*. New York: Bantam Books.
Lehman, P. (1999) 'Ed Powers and the Fantasy of Documenting Sex', in J. Elias, V. D. Elias, V. L.

Bullough, G. Brewer, J. J. Douglas and W. Jarvis (eds) *Porn 101: Eroticism, Pornography, and the First Amendment*. Amherst: Prometheus, 359–66.
McNair, B. (1996) *Mediated Sex: Pornography and Postmodern Culture*, London: Arnold.
____ (2002) *Striptease Culture: Sex, Media and the Democratization of Desire*. London and New York: Routledge.
Moody, E. (2007) 'Instructor Might Have Acted in Pornography', *Ball State Daily News*, 12 February. On-line. Available: http://media.www.bsudailynews.com/media/storage/paper849/news/2007/02/12/News/Instructor.Might.Have.Acted.In.Pornography-2712427.shtml (accessed 29 September 2008).
Nowlin, C. (2003) *Judging Obscenity: A Critical History of Expert Evidence*. Montreal: McGill-Queen's University Press.
The Obscenity Report: The Report to the Task Force on Pornography and Obscenity (1970) New York: Stein & Day.
O'Neill, S. (1964) *Campus Call Girl*. Derby, CT: Gold Star.
O'Toole, L. (1998) *Pornocopia: Porn, Sex, Technology and Desire*. London: Serpent's Tail.
Pichaske, D. R. (1995) 'When Students Make Sexual Advances', *The Chronicle of Higher Education*, 41, 24, 24 February, B1–B2.
Rist, R. C. (1973) 'Polity, Politics, and Social Research: A Study in the Relationship of Federal Commissions and Social Science', *Social Problems*, 21, 1, 113–28.
Rubin, G. (1993) 'Misguided, Dangerous and Wrong: An Analysis of Anti-Pornography Politics', in A. Assiter and A. Carol (eds) *Bad Girls and Dirty Pictures: The Challenge to Reclaim Feminism*, London: Pluto Press, 18–40.
Rudoren, J. (2006) 'The Student Body', *The New York Times*, 23 April. On-line. Available: http://www.nytimes.com/2006/04/23/education/edlife/MAGAZINES.html (accessed 29 September 2008).
Russell, D. E. H. (1998) *Dangerous Relationships: Pornography, Misogyny, and Rape*. Thousand Oaks, CA: Sage.
Schaefer, E. (1999) *'Bold! Daring! Shocking! True!' A History of Exploitation Films*. Durham, NC: Duke University Press.
____ (2005) 'Dirty Little Secrets: Scholars, Archivists, and Dirty Movies', *The Moving Image*, 5, 2, Fall, 79–105.
Scheiner, C. J. (ed.) (1996) *The Essential Guide to Erotic Literature Part Two: After 1920*. London: Wordsworth Classics.
Secor, S. (2005) 'New Lows of Higher Education', On-line. Available: http://www.obscenity-crimes.org/espforparents/efp0505.cfm (accessed 29 September 2008).
Segal, L. (1992) 'Sweet Sorrows, Painful Pleasures: Pornography and the Perils of Heterosexual Desire', in L. Segal and M. McIntosh (eds) *Sex Exposed: Sexuality and the Pornography Debate*. London: Virago, 65–91.
Smith, D. D. (1976) 'The Social Content of Pornography', *Journal of Communication*, 26, 1, 16–24.
Soble, A. (1986) *Pornography: Marxism, Feminism, and the Future of Sexuality*. New Haven: Yale University Press.
Thompson, B. (1994) *Soft Core: Moral Crusades Against Pornography in Britain and America*. London: Cassell.
Thompson, D. (2007) *Black and White and Blue: Adult Cinema from the Victorian Age to the*

VCR. Toronto: ECW.
Tierney, W. G. (2004) 'Academic Freedom and Tenure: Between Fiction and Reality', *The Journal of Higher Education*, 75, 2, March/April, 161–77.
Tucker, L. (1969) *Every Night, Lover*. New York: Bee-Line Books.
Webster, P. (1981) 'Pornography and Pleasure', *Heresies*, 12, 48–51.
Wicke, J. (1991) 'Through a Gaze Darkly: Pornography's Academic Market', *Transition*, 54, 68–89.
Williams, L. (1990) *Hard Core: Power, Pleasure and 'The Frenzy of the Visible'*. London: Pandora.
───── (1993) 'Second Thoughts on *Hard Core*: American Obscenity Law and the Scapegoating of Deviance', in P. Church Gibson and R. Gibson (eds) *Dirty Looks: Women, Pornography, Power*. London: BFI, 46–61.
───── (2004) 'Porn Studies: Proliferating Pornographies On/Scene: An Introduction', in L. Williams (ed.) *Porn Studies*. Durham: Duke University Press, 1–23.
Winkler, K. J. (1989) 'Research on Pornography Gains Respectability, Increased Importance Among Scholars', *The Chronicle of Higher Education*, 14 June, A4–A5, A8.
Woods, L. B. (1979) *A Decade of Censorship in America: The Threat to Classrooms and Libraries. 1966–1975*. Metuchen, NJ: Scarecrow Press.
Young, C. (2003) 'Skin Flicks 101: What Porn Studies Profs Don't Get About Sex', *Reason*, 1 May, 20–1.

COME AGAIN?
Hard-core in History

CHAPTER FIVE

'WHITE SLAVERY', OR THE ETHNOGRAPHY OF 'SEXWORKERS': WOMEN IN STAG FILMS AT THE KINSEY ARCHIVE[1]

Linda Williams

In February of 2003 I was invited to give a talk on women in stag films at the Kinsey Institute for Research in Sex, Gender, and Reproduction at Indiana University. The organisers invited a number of lectures on topics of female sexual behaviour and representation. My talk was appended to a screening of four stag films from the Kinsey Institute Film Archive. This 'historical stag collection', which now includes 1,697 8mm and 16mm black and white titles, is the heart of the Kinsey film archive. To my knowledge this was the first time the Kinsey Institute had engaged in a public screening of any part of its stag collection.

Stag films are anonymously made, short, undated silent films displaying one or more hard-core sex acts.[2] These uncredited, or bogusly credited, films flourished in an underground circuit in the US and internationally during that extended period between the 1910s and the early 1970s before moving-image pornography became quasi-licit. From the 1910s through the early 1950s, they were shot and distributed on 16mm and presented by travelling road show men to lodges, fraternities and smokers. The showmen set up the projector and brought the films. However, Eric Schaefer (2007) has recently argued that in the post-World War II period smaller 8mm gauge films and projectors came into use; the travelling road show slowly died. It became possible for individuals to purchase 8mm films for home or party viewing through bars, gas stations, photography shops, barber shops and even through the mail.

It may seem a little odd for the Kinsey Institute to have celebrated 'Women and their Sexualities', as this lecture series was called, through a lecture-screening of hard-core stag films made by and for men. However, Kinsey film archivist Rachael Stoeltje chose four films from the collection which were unusually marked by what she called 'women-in-charge' themes and which thus seemed appropriate to the celebration of Kinsey's famous book on women's sexual behaviour. I was eager to see how the Kinsey Institute would handle this public campus screening. For while the Institute has been instrumental in preserving this excoriated and neglected heritage of cinematic and sexual history, they had never, to my knowledge, organised a public exhibition of these once entirely clandestine materials.

The Kinsey Institute Archive is unique in the world. Kinsey collected anything pertaining to sex: books (scholarly and popular), photos (art, ethnography, dirty pictures), art (drawings, paintings and the proverbial etchings), films (hard-core stag films, art films and the films of sexual acts that Kinsey himself had made in his famous attic), and ephemera (phalluses,[3] decorative condoms, sadomasochistic paraphernalia, and so forth).[4] One of the great delights of doing research in the Kinsey Archive is its spirit of inclusion. No item is too obscene, too ridiculous, too rare to be excluded.

Rachael Stoeltje kindly sent me video copies of the four films she had chosen for screening. They are: *Modern Pirates* (c.1930s), about the captain of a yacht and the five female pirates he services sexually until he becomes exhausted and jumps ship; *A Free Ride* (c.1923) about a man who picks up two women in his Model T and then has a sexual party with them in the woods; *Getting His Goat* (a.k.a. *On the Beach*, c.1925), about a man who steals the clothes of three women skinny dipping at the beach and bargains for sex through a knot in a fence in return for their clothes. The tables are turned, however, when a goat is substituted for a woman. Finally, *Bring 'em Back Nude*, is a 1930s-era film depicting the erotic jungle-inspired daydreams of a woman who dreams about a gorilla who guards two naked white females. Just as the action heats up and the natives get restless, the woman is awakened from her dream (there is no hard-core action in this film).

The following is a revised version of my talk. I use the occasion of this publication to reflect upon the question of which stag films should be shown to represent 'the stag archive', the problem of the representation of women in it, and the larger question of this ambivalent and fascinating film heritage.

WOMEN IN STAG FILMS

Heterosexual pornography is conventionally considered to be the place for the display of the female body. Much writing by feminists about this pornography (both from pro- and anti-censorship perspectives) has been about the uses and abuses of the female body in serving the power and pleasure of men. Recently, however, gay critic and historian Thomas Waugh (1996) has pointed out that heterosexual pornography, including that of stag films, is also about the display of male bodies to men. Straight pornography, then, has a homosocial, and even homoerotic, component. These films rather insistently seek to explore what the title of a stag film from the 1920s calls the 'Wonders of the Unseen World' – the hidden secrets of female anatomy that proper heterosexual males were at least supposed to be obsessed with in a pre-pornographic era. However, what these films actually end up featuring, either to their viewers' great interest or to their embarrassment, is the penis.[5] Waugh cites, for example, the 'traumatized silence' he experienced on seeing the famous 1950s era stag *Smart Aleck* with his 'dormitory peers in 1968 and the queer difference I and others must have felt' (2001: 281).

It makes good sense, then, to discuss, as Waugh does, the homosocial element of these films, made by men for men, that enact ritual exchanges of, and pleasures taken in, women. But homoerotic and homosocial pleasures are not the whole story of stag films and if we focus only on them, we may too wilfully ignore the female body that functions as the ostensible attraction of such films. So with the caveat that women were never the intended audience for these films, but with the urge nevertheless to think about their subjectivity and performativity as circumscribed within a larger system of male power, let us consider the possibilities, and limits, of female agency in stag films from the Kinsey archive.

From the perspective of female agency, it is important to realise that the four films chosen to be screened by the Kinsey Institute to reveal strong, 'women-in-charge' themes are about as good as it gets in stag films. The narratives of these films pointedly do not depict the relatively common scenario in this era of hard-core films in which women are coerced to please men (see Williams 1999: 164–5). Rather, they depict the camaraderie of women having a good time with one another, sometimes along with a man, or as in *Getting His Goat* and *Modern Pirates*, at the expense of a man. In other words, these are stag films even a feminist might be able to enjoy and it is not accidental that, in this instance, they were chosen to please a contemporary mixed-gender audience.

Indeed, two of the stag films in this programme – *A Free Ride* and *Getting His Goat* – have earned a sort of place of pride in the poorly reproduced stag film anthologies that circulate on video today. The popularity of these two films may have a lot to do with the fact that they place their displays of female nudity and sex acts in 'nature' as opposed to the often depressing and stifling furnished rooms and motel rooms so common in many stag films. The third film, *Modern Pirates*, is notable for some nice outdoor photography when its five women who have pirated the captain's yacht romp on the beach of an island. (This film's hard-core footage is cinematically distinct from the rest and has most likely been inserted from an entirely different film). *Bring 'em Back Nude* also stresses the great outdoors of the African jungle and is an exceptionally well-shot and well-produced film that, despite its interest as a female racial-sexual fantasy, does not seem to belong to the stag genre at all since it has no hard-core footage.[6] The 'wild' outdoor settings of all these films simply look better than those set in ill-lit and depressingly similar motel rooms. The bodies of the women romping on the beach in both beach films, or prancing about the depleted man in *A Free Ride*, are enhanced by a play of light and shadow that seems a gratuitous boon, not necessary to the genre's mission of bodily and genital display, but all the more wonderful for that very reason.

These open-air settings, these 'wide open spaces where men are men', as an intertitle from *A Free Ride* puts it, posit the existence of places of momentary sexual 'freedom' where it is 'natural' to strip. This is precisely what each of the five female sailors who board the captain's yacht in *Modern Pirates* do once they are beyond the 'three mile limit'. And it is what the three women who go skinny dipping at Idyllwilde beach also do in *Getting His Goat* before the man spying on them takes their clothes and insists on sex. In a much more circumscribed way, it is also what the man in *A Free Ride* does after picking the women up in his Model T. Spying on the man peeing in the bushes, the two women are interested and, as another intertitle puts it, 'the party is on'. In short, these films, among the most idyllic in the entire Kinsey stag collection, all depict places in nature where sex might take place with abandon.

Of course when the women strip in these films they are stripping for the view of men. The simple fact that absolutely none of the male bodies strip as completely or frolic in nature with the same abandon as the female bodies suggests the erotic limits of such films: if the penis is crucial and must be shown to confirm that actual penetration in the 'meat shot' does takes place, the rest of the male body is under no such similar compulsion to be put on display. Indeed, not only do the men not strip, but, common to all stag films, many wear false moustaches, masks, and false noses to disguise their identities. While a few women wear disguises too, the more naked the women are, the more the men seem to cover up.

The scrawny, short man with a patently fake moustache who picks up the two women in *A Free Ride* and has sex with each of them, the overweight captain who pursues the naked female sailors in *Modern Pirates* and brings them back, and the day dreamer with glasses on the beach in *Getting His Goat*, all suggest that the pleasures of stag films may have been originally founded on a different sort of spectacle than that of the unrealistically endowed male bodies of contemporary porn performers. In these earlier pornographic films the pleasure of watching seems to lie, at least partly, in the revelation of randiness in the balding, fat, scrawny, short men with (often) very ordinary penises. Though the men in these films reveal unexpected appetites, they remain quite human, not the perfect sex machines found in contemporary incarnations, and they almost never display their bodies the way the women do. A typical plot terminates sex by showing a man who simply wears out. For example, the plump captain in charge of the bevy of beauties on the boat in *Modern Pirates*, who certainly does not look like a stud, leaves the boat because he is expected to be a stud for the pleasure of the women (his exit line is 'I'm a captain and not a stud horse').

Waugh's (1996) argument would interpret the frequent unloveliness of these 'stag' men as a defence against homoerotic pleasure. I wonder, however, if this unloveliness does not also represent a kind of punishment on the women for having sex in the first place? Some stag films seem to insist on rubbing the woman's face in the presumed dirt of sex as if it were funny. Consider another film in the Kinsey stag collection, *The Passionate Farmhand* (c.1920s) not shown in this public screening, but also in the Kinsey archive. In it, a woman named Lena visits her farmhand boyfriend, Rufus, who invites her to a 'Speak Easy'. While there, he slips her a mickey, inserts a candle in her vagina and another in her anus and lights both. Later she wipes his anus before rimming him, remarking in another title card: 'You must have had spinach for dinner'. The film ends with Rufus peeing on Lena in the bathtub. Such a film offers the reverse of the idyllic, women-in-charge frolics screened by the Kinsey Institute at my lecture. Or consider any number of films which delight in deploying the derogatory slang that goes along with sex; *Loaded Dice* is full of it: a fully-clothed man strokes a woman's naked behind. When he enters her, a title informs us that he is 'drilling for oil', then that he has 'struck a gusher'. Vaseline is used after he hits a 'dry hole'.

I mention these examples because if we want to understand the humour of stags it is not always the case that it is subversive of male power. A number of recent scholars have suggested that the study of pornography in general, and stag films in particular, would benefit from a greater appreciation of their humour. Film critic Peter Lehman, for example, has argued that my own discussion of pornography overlooks the 'fleeting moments of humour in porn', which is entirely true (1995: 9). Feminist critic Constance Penley notes the 'ubiquitous use of humour', in stags, 'and not just any kind of humor, but bawdiness, humorously lewd and obscene language and situation' (1997: 94). Penley adds that stag films especially 'are often structured like a joke. And here we are talking about really bad jokes, ranging from terrible puns to every form of dirty joke – farmer's daughter, traveling salesman, and aggie jokes' (1997: 95). Penley excludes the short peep show loops which consisted of earnestly direct views of sexual action with little set-up and no story, but she insists that 'the majority of the few hundred American stag films made for collective male viewing depended on this popular brand of humour' – especially, she notes, in the pre-World War II era.

Both Penley and Lehman are right, I think, to point to the uses of humour in pornography. However, I'm not sure that we do a service to the modest field of porn studies by characterising the whole of pornography or even the 'pre-World War II films that were made on the edges of the entertainment world and thus shared the qualities of both burlesque and silent film comedy' (Penley 1997: 95) as humorous, even bad-joke humour, especially if we assume, along with this assessment, that the joke is often on the man. Penley's re-evaluation is based on highly selective examples at which women viewers today can comfortably laugh and ignores the less comfortable examples in which the joke is on the woman.

For example, Penley argues that part of the humour in stag films comes from the fact that it is the women who both initiate and, as she says, 'set the terms' for sex. Thus *Getting His Goat* illustrates 'both the kind of humor and the level of commentary on masculinity found in the typical stag film of the era' (ibid.). The women, she maintains, offer a 'charming mischievousness' while the man deserves what he gets because 'of his sexual and social ignorance' and the final moral, 'There's one born every minute', is a 'cautionary address to the male audience not to be fools to their own desires' (1997: 96).

Penley invites us to connect the tradition of humorous stag films to an older tradition of dirty songs and limericks and to a low-class tradition of mocking the mores of professional and bourgeois classes in which female agency is often strong. I think it is important to open up this discussion of the class dimensions of pornography (and Penley does so, appropriately in the context of a volume entitled *White Trash: Race and Class in America* (1997)). However, if the very fact that women perform sex, or cleverly negotiate the ways in which they give it, is itself the source of the humour, then we must remember that it is only so in a world that normally thinks women's pleasure in sex, or savvyness about it, is either strange or wrong.

If we want to cast stag films as part of the lost history of American folk humour, we do well to realise that technically all stag films qualify as humorous to the degree that they put in play a Rabelaisian reversal of the usual norms of decorum. It is considered funny that women want and initiate sex in a world where, as the men in the era of illicit stag screenings probably believed, sex is scarce and the women who initiate it often do so for money. But on whom is the joke in this case? Penley wants us to see that it is on the man, which is literally true in *Getting His Goat*, her primary example. In this film not only does the man have sex with a goat through the knot hole of a fence thinking he has coerced a woman to have sex in exchange for the return of her stolen clothes, but later, when he encounters the group of women on the beach again, the women 'get his goat' again by faking pregnancy and extorting money.

However, it would be a mistake to take the joke of this particular film as typical of all stag films or even of those low forms of bawdiness typical of folk humour. At least as typical, I would argue, is the joke about Lena and the farmhand, or the joke I will describe below about the Klansman and the black woman. Jokes, especially tendentious ones, often have very precise gender, class and race-based targets. To the extent that sexual urges in pornography tend to overcome the usual divisions that separate classes, races, and even species, they may seem subversive. As in musicals, primitive urges and rhythms override the taboos of civilisation. But this does not mean that the barriers that separate genders, classes and races are not also reasserted, often in insidious ways.

If *Getting His Goat* offers a Rabelaisian bawdy humour in which women literally and figuratively get the man's goat, extorting money from him to boot, we should not then re-assess the whole of stag cinema as subversive folk humour on the basis of this one film which deftly manages to make bestiality funny even to a female audience. The recent popularity of this film in college classrooms and at public screenings – it also figured prominently in Al Di Lauro and Gerald Rabkin's (1976) illustrated history – attests to the fact that it is perhaps the only one of quite a few films with bestial themes that is palatable to today's audiences.[7] One is also quite relieved to discover, for example, despite the implication in the plot that the man on the beach has sex with a goat as a kind of punishment for his extortion, that we never actually see the sort of insertion shots or sexual acts in the same frame that are the *sine qua non* of hard-core, at least not with the goat.

Penley argues that stag films and, by extension, similarly low-class forms of pornography in the later era of video porn in the 1980s, after the heyday of 'porno chic' in the early and mid-1970s, have an element of subversion because they depict female agency (1997: 19). Yet the agency she points to is always part of the joke: 'Proper' women do not seek or lustfully engage in sex with strangers; the women who do so are always compromised. The very fact that women, presumed to be more chaste than men, are lustfully having sex with these strangers – the plumber who comes to fix the pipes, the dentist who pulls the tooth, the perennial doctor who must look at private parts, or, as in our examples, the idle man on the beach, the random man with the car, or the captain of the ship – does, indeed, seem to be half the joke.

We should consider that the women depicted in this particular film exhibit something more than what Penley calls 'charming mischievousness' – they exhibit, rather, a kind of calculation and blasé manipulation. For example, the woman who orchestrates the goat substitution, first collects the man's money and then efficiently warms up his penis manually through the knot hole in the fence while her friends bring the goat. In other words, as Waugh

Fig. 8 *Getting His Goat*. Courtesy of the Kinsey Institute.

(2001) has astutely noted, the women who so brazenly jiggle their breasts, wiggle their hips and manipulate penises are often, in real life as well as on the screen, professionals, while the men who are so awkwardly hidden under those moustaches, masks, and so many more clothes are often, in real life as well as on the screen, amateurs. Waugh writes: 'The 'hooker' presides over the entire corpus of stags ... inflected by the familiar hypocritical class-centric contempt for the working girl' (2001: 285).[8]

So there certainly is Rabelaisian humour in stag cinema. However, if it is raunchy and bawdy, if it has aspects of the systematically pointed class antagonism and resentment that Laura Kipnis (1996), for example, attributes to the more recent phenomenon of *Hustler* magazine, it does not then automatically place itself on the side of the women, the lower classes, and the racially marked. Rather, as Waugh suggests, following Kinsey and Gagnon and Simon's earlier work, audiences (at the Elks Club or the American Legion) tended to be class homogenous themselves and to consist of 'upper-lower and lower-middle' classes who take out their class antagonism on women lower down on the social scale than themselves, especially prostitutes (2001: 286).

THE ETHNOGRAPHY OF 'SEXWORKERS'

The women in stag films know how to perform for, and on, men as for the camera. The men, comparatively, do not. This does not mean, however, that the women therefore have more power. As Waugh notes, 'the female performers were undoubtedly assumed by the audience to be sexworkers – and most clearly often were as much, just as their inept male partners were assumed to be and were visibly amateurs' (2001: 285). This is why, I believe, the men are more often seen hiding themselves. In the context of the stag film, then, the woman is in control but only in the way the prostitute is in control in order to better serve the john who hires her. The 'charming mischievousness' we observe in *Getting His Goat* may thus well come from the fact that these particular women did not have to 'work' in the usual way. The goat does it for them.

Though in most films the prostitute/john relation is implicit, a few films depict, and even name, this interaction between whore and client for what it is. In *A Country Stud Horse* (c.1920s), another Kinsey film which I have discussed at length elsewhere, an early title states, 'Mary picks up some business'; we then see Mary pick up a john (see Williams 1995). In *Easy Money* a punning title informs us that a girl having sex in a college dorm room is 'working her way through college'. In a more contemporary porno we might think that the girl is the college student and the men with whom she has sex help fund her education. In this case, however, the then all-male Ivy League institution whose sign (Yale) is on the wall, could only mean that the intertitle is a pun.

Another Kinsey Archive film, *The Pay Off* (c.1950s) is dramatically structured around the tension over money between a man who may be a pimp and a woman who may be a whore. In an opening scene a well-dressed man asks a woman, 'Did you bring the money?' and grows angry when it appears not to be enough. The man then grabs the woman's purse and an intertitle says, 'I ought to take it out on you'. 'You're afraid to!' she retorts. In a sex scene that is extraordinarily arty in its play of shadows, at least for a stag film, we then see how this situation is resolved, with sex of course, but with sex acts that are aggressively negotiated over money. This film would thus indeed seem to be an example of Penley's female agency. The woman not only prevails in the argument, she quite boldly takes a break between sex acts to take money from the man's coat and put it in her pocketbook before returning to the bed. Once again, however, this agency is that of the professional who knows what she is worth on the market and insists on her price, just as the women in *Getting His Goat* do.

Whatever female agency we witness in stag films is very often circumscribed by the fact that in them the woman is selling herself in a way that the men are not and that, as Waugh points out, there is always a greater contempt for the seller than there is for the buyer (2001: 286). This is true even in films that do not directly – as in *Getting His Goat*, *Easy Money* or *The Pay Off* – show an exchange of money. Thus, in *The Casting Couch* (c.1920s), the actress who wants a role but refuses the advances of the casting director reads in a book, *How to Become a Star*, that she should comply with the casting director. She does and the film's final title puns 'the only way to become a star is to get under a good director and work your way up'. Sex, like money, is clearly a medium of exchange. Penley argues that this film mocks the professional classes, and while this is certainly the case, Waugh's argument that the woman is portrayed as a professional herself but one who is despised by a 'gynephobic and erotophobic culture' is also relevant (2001: 286). The logic of the dirty joke is thus often quite punitive to the woman.

Penley also argues that one of the best known stag films of all time, *Smart Aleck* (c.1952), demonstrates female agency when its then 16-year-old star, Candy Barr, refuses to perform fellatio on a man who had picked her up at the motel pool. Penley writes: 'she gets up in disgust and calls a female friend who does want to have oral sex with the man. While that's going on, Candy gets back into the scene to get the man to go down on her' (1997: 97). Because it is 'the woman who orchestrates the sexual activity', because she induces the man to 'go down on her', she argues, the film illustrates 'female agency' (ibid.). While I suppose I could be pleased that *Smart Aleck* stopped short of showing Barr being forced to perform fellatio, I would emphasise that what we actually see is a prolonged tussle in which the man repeatedly tries to hold her mouth over his penis and she wriggles out. It is the man who then gets up in disgust and then Barr phones her friend. Once again the agency demonstrated is circumscribed by the situation of prostitution. Indeed, the negotiation over fellatio shown in this motel room seems very much to be over what Barr will and will not do for money, and the 'friend' she calls in to perform fellatio would certainly seem to be yet another working girl.

I cannot say the extent to which the narrative of this film depicts what actually happened to Barr in the motel room – that is, whether as a sexual performer in a stag film she was asked to perform an act she found distasteful and resisted, or whether the tension over fellatio was part of the script.[9] It is interesting, however, to listen to Barr's own description of this period of her life in a brief interview in the recent *Playboy*-produced documentary, *The Story of X* (1998). As the first 'porn star' whose *nom de porn*,[10] was known to her public, Barr's description of her situation at the time she made the film is of interest for its revelation of the grey area between working girl and prostitute:

> I ended up, eventually, from being a working girl in a restaurant as a waitress into a white slavery involvement that involved itself over a period of time into motel people and this is how it all started. If I had not been under duress I certainly would not have gone and willingly done it. I had other things to do in my life than go run out in a motel room and let people take pictures of me.

I am not absolutely certain to what the 'it' in 'this is how it all started' refers – her unprecedented fame as a porn star or her involvement in prostitution – but I think we can see in the tortured syntax of this statement that Barr is grappling with the fact that to be a low-class working girl in a restaurant slides rather easily into the other kind of working girl in a motel room. Barr is of course also claiming that she performed these acts 'under duress' and the phrase 'white slavery involvement' raises all sorts of flags, managing to be both sensational and vague.

The term 'white slavery' first became current in the US in the Progressive Era to describe the buying and selling of young girls into prostitution. As is well known today, the burgeoning social scientific and reformist discourses defining it were deeply racist. They were racist both in the sense of worrying only about the sexual slavery of white women, never that of women of colour, and in the frequent allegations that the sexual traffic of white women was an organised conspiracy run by Jews and foreigners. They were also dubious as examples of overt coercion. It is likely that social factors such as poverty, low wages and other deprivations were more responsible than evil foreigners coercing young girls to sell themselves (see Staiger 1995; Schaefer 1999: 18). 'White slavery', used to describe evil exploiters of the virginal sexuality of young white women, was certainly an anachronistic term by the time Barr used it in this documentary (even allowing for the possibility that the interview may have been shot sometime before it was used in this 1998 film). Yet Barr does not go on to claim, as her more famous early 1970s successor Linda Lovelace would do, that she was corrupted or damaged by her involvement in pornography itself. Indeed, she is quick to clarify that what bothers her today is not the outrage to her innocence, or the trauma of the event, but something else entirely: 'I know one thing: that was a tacky guy they got for me and that's an insult.' The interview then concludes with Barr's remarkably benign observation about pornography: 'Let's face it: it's here it's slapping us in the face. Let's make it ... respectable.'

It would seem – despite the inflammatory reference to 'white slavery', invoked as a way to suggest that forces beyond her control led her, at the age of 16, to a career in stag films – that Barr's fundamental identification is as a working girl who seeks respect as such. She does not go on to blame pornography or the traffic in women as the source of her 'ruin' – that would be to play into the logic of the police and the johns who condemn the sellers, not the buyers of female 'goods'. Rather, she goes on to wish for better, more 'respectable', working conditions and status. The fact that the narrative of the film then shows her negotiating for one aspect of these conditions in her refusal to perform fellatio is thus quite apt. In this interview Barr's intonation as she gropes for the word 'respectable' is both tentative and poignant. In an earlier era, when the kind of illicit, underground stag films in which she performed were made, when pornography was precisely not 'slapping' anyone but the men at the stag parties 'in the face', a plea for respect would have been out of the question. Women in porn were whores whether they played them as characters or not.

Waugh's insight that 'the stag corpus may well be the best visual ethnography of sexworkers in America during this period' is worth taking seriously as a consequence of his reading of the 'chance flickers' of documentary truth occasionally found in these films (2001: 285; 278). The value of a term like 'sexworker' is its emphasis on the field of sexuality as a place where women, and of course some men, do, indeed, work. I would not want to assume that every film depicts the relations between a prostitute and a john – the men in the films were doubtless paid for their work as well, though the consequences of their actions were never as stigmatising to them as the actions of women performers, their performances did not make them 'sluts', but 'studs'. Nor is the work performed in stag films by men or women 'simply' the work of prostitution, since the requirement of this work is not only to please the customer, but to please the viewer.

'Sexworker' can be a useful term that allows us to focus on the work of giving pleasure in sex. Invented by San Francisco-based prostitute and activist Carol Leigh (a.k.a. Scarlot Harlot) in the late 1970s, it offers an umbrella term to apply to all persons who sell sex – whether strippers, lap dancers, male, female, or transgendered prostitutes, phone sex providers, or porn performers – without distinctions of class. It connotes a freely chosen profession. It was precisely the sort of term Barr might have been looking for in the interview cited above as she sought to redefine her earlier stigmatised work in an increasingly on/scene sexuality – a term that would help accomplish the greater 'respectability' she seeks. The exact opposite of 'white slavery' – with its lurid connotations of racialised exploitation and spoiled innocence – sexworker has served as an effective counter to the notion that women who perform sex for money are enslaved and then hopelessly fallen.

Nevertheless, the word 'sexworker' is also anachronistic for the period in which stag films were the dominant form of explicit sex films. It has a euphemistic tinge of political correctness that does not quite fit the historical attitudes towards the women who performed sex for hire from the 1910s through the late 1960s and towards the women who can be seen to repeat those sex acts in the stag film archives. Though the racial baggage of a term like 'white slavery' rings equally anachronistic (and worse) from the other direction to our ears today, it has the advantage of expressing what seems to have been Barr's own ambivalence about the sequence of events that got her to that motel room where she performed in *Smart Aleck* Cleary she did not feel she had freely chosen her line of work, though the coercion she experienced may have been more economic than physical. If we gravitate to this film today for its glimpse of a moment's struggle around the performance of fellatio, it may also be because this act has become so generically commonplace – almost *de rigueur* – in today's pornography. Indeed, for a variety of reasons, most prostitutes and most female porn performers would rather perform fellatio than intercourse.

Contemporary feminists rightly resist the notion that women in pornography are sex slaves of any sort. Penley's efforts to see the humour and female agency in stag films is, I think, part of this resistance. But we need a more historically nuanced way of reading female agency in stag films, something that can be located *between* white slavery and the ethnography of sexworkers, something that can also include the different situation of American women of colour in stag films, and something that can avoid melodramatic scenarios of extreme victimisation while acknowledging the grey areas between coercion and work. In order to qualify just what sort of agency we can imagine for the various women of stag films, let us consider one more such film – one that I was only able to see during my most recent visit to the Kinsey Institute, and which was therefore not included in my talk.

Entitled *KKK Night Riders*, it looks to be from the 1930s, though it is hard to tell given the poor quality of the print and the fact that the only clothes worn are a Klansman's robe and hood. It portrays a corpulent white Klansman in full regalia, including hood, who invades the cabin of a black woman and forces her to have sex at knife point. As in all stag films depicting rape, the woman is portrayed as succumbing to the pleasures of coerced sex. Also as in all such films, one can never be sure if the woman's pleasure is faked or real. After the crudely hand-written title we see a hand knock on a door. A man in full Klan regalia enters a knotty pine cabin. A hand holds aloft a short sword. A black woman reading a newspaper in bed slowly recognises the Klansman's presence. The man's hand pulls down the sheet covering her to reveal her naked (and also plump) body. A title card reads: 'Oh Lordy don't hurt me I'll give you my all' after which the knife is held to her belly, 'Here I am Mr. Klansman I'm all yours'. When they begin to have sex another card, speaks the misogynist and racist ethic of the film: 'All night riders must have their fun.'

The 'fun' portrayed is about ten minutes of sex in a wide variety of positions (coitus, fellatio, cunnilingus, anal) in which the Klansman removes his robes but keeps on his hood. Eventually, however, he removes his hood ('your [sic] sure hot, I'll remove my white mask') though his face still remains obscured in what appears to be a dark stocking. At one point the woman asks in another intertitle, 'Does you all feel good now Mr. Klansman [sic]?' At another point, during an interlude, their portly black and white bodies form a surprising picture of intimacy – as if the Klansman's assault had actually formed the kind of intimate interracial couple that the Klan itself abhorred – as they stroke one another. The film concludes with more sex, an odd moment in which the man

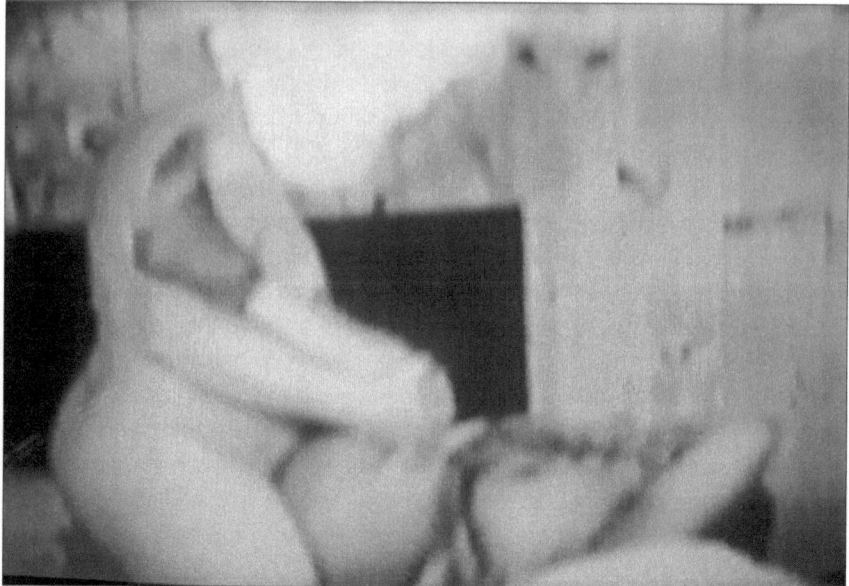

Fig. 9 KKK Night Riders. Courtesy of the Kinsey Institute.

holds the newspaper to his face as if to cover it, and a final exterior ejaculation that shows the woman tasting the ejaculate.

What interests me in *KKK Night Riders* are its similarities and differences to the coercive scenarios of stag films that involve class, not racial, differences. The working girls in *Getting His Goat* are coerced by a dreamer in glasses who looks to be a college kid. The class differences between them are part of the reason for our contemporary feminist satisfaction at the revenge of the girls. The Klansman who so carefully guards his face from view is also of a different class from the woman whose cabin he invades, as indicated by the rough cabin as well as the grammatical lapses in the representation of her dialogue, not present in his.[11] But this man is of a different race as well, and he is cloaked in the very costume of white supremacy. His coercion of the black woman evokes a long history of racial and sexual servitude in which the ethic of 'honest' work for pay does not exist.

One reason I think this film is an important historical document of the limits of female agency in stag films is that it reminds us of a history of actual sexual slavery that the term 'sexworker' cannot encompass. Here, indeed, is a situation that grows so directly out of slavery – though not the 'white slavery' of Barr's formulation – that it might be wishful thinking to consider the woman who performs in this film as a sexworker. The term is too progressive; it says too little about the historically determined, coercive context of black female and white male sexual interactions depicted here under the very sign of a white supremacy designed to reassert the race- and gender-based prerogatives of white men. This woman has historically less agency than her white sister performers and less chance of asserting herself as a worker; the man with whom she performs, hides himself even more than his white brothers in stag films; and the film itself, if it can be seen as an ethnography, speaks its particular 'chance flickers of documentary 'truth" about a tradition of black servitude to white desires (Waugh 2001: 278).

Only if one buys into white supremacist beliefs can we think that the joke in this film is on the man. It could only be on him if we believe that he degrades himself by having sex with the black woman, just as the dreamer in *Getting His Goat* degrades himself, albeit without knowing it, when he has sex with a goat. Although it would be comforting, from where we sit today, to read this Klansman without a horse, whose only ride is on the black woman he rapes, as giving the lie to the myth of the Klan as the rescuers of white womanhood, I fear that for most of the white men who saw it in its circulation at stag parties and fraternal organisations during the depression that the only possible way to see the film as a joke on its night rider would have been to buy into the white supremacism that views sex with a black woman as degrading.

EPILOGUE

My talk at the Kinsey Institute, and its subsequent rewriting for this article, has left me with some lingering questions that might best be posed to the readers of this piece. Obviously, an archive of stag films is not like any film archive. It was not acquired to preserve film history but as a record of sexual practices; all of its films were illicitly made and distributed and no one properly 'owns' their copyright. It is something of a miracle – and a tribute to Alfred Kinsey's voracious, non-judgemental interest in everything having to do with sex – that this archive exists at all. I do not claim to know how an archive of hard-core films should present its contents to scholars and to the public, but I do believe that any archive, even a sex film archive, exists in order to be preserved and for its contents to be made available to those interested in its materials. Today, we are interested in the details of sexual history that were once hidden away in 'secret museums' (see Kendrick 1987). In my work on pornography, it has become increasingly clear to me that sexual representations that were once considered obscene, in the quite literal sense of being hidden away from public view, have increasingly come on/scene in all sorts of ways.[12] Stag films are no exception.

The lecture-screening in which I participated was a new public display of a kind of film that had once only been for private consumption by prurient men. The purpose of my scholarly and feminist talk – rather like the man in the white coat who legitimised the taboo and prurient contents of the old exploitation films – was at least partly to inoculate against the prurient interest of the films. There is no law, however, saying that prurient interest cannot coexist with scholarly interest. Kinsey himself is the most striking example of this fact. The student who was quoted in the Institute's house organ, *Kinsey Today*, was, I think, expressing that possibility when he/she stated: 'Historic silent stag films, in a room packed with hundreds, with Linda Williams' thought-provoking analysis. What an experience!' The quote was followed by a photo of an expectant, and fairly young, crowd of spectators. The experience, I would venture, is never only 'thought provoking', but neither is the excitement only sexual.

The Kinsey Institute's choice to screen outdoor, 'humorous' films with 'women-in-charge' themes is quite understandable, especially in the context of the Kinsey celebration of *Sexual Behaviour in the Human Female* (1953). My choice to bring in other examples of less humorous films in which women are not in charge is also understandable lest the Institute encourage a perhaps unwarranted nostalgia for an earlier era of hard-core cinema. The real issue is how to best present the heritage of stag films. Stag film compilations that offer tinkling piano accompaniment, as if the films were the equivalent of Harold Lloyd or Charlie Chaplin comedies, run the risk of a bogus nostalgia associated with mainstream silent films. Nor did American stag films, as far as I have been able to tell, even have musical accompaniment. Much more likely all male audiences sat in an embarrassment of silence punctuated by laughter and crude jokes. We should not seek to reproduce the atmosphere of a smoker for screenings of stag films but neither should we seek to produce a bogus nostalgia for the 'good old days'.

A 2002 French compilation of stag films has recently attempted to generate such nostalgia. Entitled *Polissons et Galipettes* (2002) it was shown at Cannes and released in French theatres in 2002. In 2003 the English version of this film was released on DVD under the terminally cute title, *The Good Old Naughty Days*. The audiences for this film were seemingly invited to witness the charming frolics of their grand and great grand parents' generations to the anachronistic accompaniment of a tinkling piano. Most critics reviewing this film celebrated the dirty movies of yesteryear in contrast to presumably more 'brutish' contemporary hard-core practices as if the plumper, more varied bodies of the stag film era also represented a happier, more polymorphous era of sexual play.[13] Part of the fun of such compilations is the mere spectacle of people from the 1920s and 1930s, photographed in black and white – and in increasingly anachronistic silence after the late 1920s – having sex at all.

Neither the Kinsey programme, chosen for its humour and relative female control, nor the Reilhac collection, chosen, as French cultural historian Jann Matlock suggests, to portray 'a delightful romp of prelapsarian sex that you can practically take home to Mom' (2004: 30), may fairly represent the archives from which they are chosen. I thus share Matlock's scepticism about the historical claims offered up in the brief intertitled commentary of *The Good Old Naughty Days*. Though it might comfort us to think that family togetherness was fostered when 'teenage boys were brought to the screenings by their uncles' (as one intertitle informs us) and that these state-operated interwar brothels afforded a relatively healthy form of state sanctioned prostitution, sex-education and bourgeois sociability, Matlock argues that the compilation may pass on a number of dubious myths about the 'jovial homosociality of the brothel salon' (2004: 30), the most fundamental of which is the assumption that brothels in Europe actually were the primary venue for screening these films (see Koch 1993; Williams 1999: 58–92; 295). Matlock also suggests that that even French stag films, with their distinctive French characteristics – including abundant culinary metaphors and an actual preference for what English speakers like to call 'French kissing', not to mention the relative nonchalance exhibited towards male/male sex acts presented within a larger heterosexual context – must have offered a wider range of hard-core action than the rather cute, pretty and extremely well-made examples served up in this particular compilation.[14]

What we really need are better ways to examine the entire history of the stag era of illicit films most of which has remained *terra incognita* compared to what we know about other silent cinema.[15] As the history of stag films effectively comes on/scene, we need restorations, public screenings of representative samples of actual films – not just video copies such as were screened at Indiana University. We also need DVD compilations that make available the best available prints. We need, for example, an American version of *The Good Old Naughty Days* – only one that is more historically probing and actually representative of the archive from which it is taken – not only the cute examples and without that tinkling piano. Such a selection, placed on DVD would be a real improvement over the bad duplications of duplications currently in circulation.

During the course of my stay at the Kinsey Institute, Rachael Stoeltje brought up the idea of producing just such a compilation – a two-disc DVD compilation of about thirty stag films to be restored and produced by Kino. The compilation would be accompanied by interviews with scholars, introductory text and historical notes modelled on the excellent Treasures of the American Film Archives DVD set, produced by the National Film Preservation Foundation in 2000 – in other words, a sort of hard-core 'Treasures of the Kinsey Archive'. I wrote an enthusiastic letter of support for the plan to the Kinsey Board of Trustees arguing that a collection of stag films from the Kinsey would be an invaluable resource to many scholars and teachers who believe that the heritage of hard-core cinema is crucial to understanding the impact of moving images on American life and culture and that such a collection would easily replace the existing cheaply produced anthologies of stag films with poor prints and random music which either strive to make the films seem cute or which offer heavy-handed, defensive commentaries.

Unfortunately, Indiana University lawyers threw up obstacles. They wanted Kino to accept all liability for the project and were fearful that if they did not, the University and the Institute could be sued by the grandchild of one of the film's performers. To date, no progress has been made on the Kinsey DVD and the Institute itself no longer even has an archivist for the stag collection. Nor, I have been told by a potential donor of films, do they take good enough care of the films they do have to be a place where one would feel good about donating more films. I may be dreaming to hope that the great American archive with the most stag films will rehire its archivist and produce a representative, restored, scholarly edition that will include the lyrical and the humorous alongside the misogynist, the racist and the ugly, but I firmly believe that scholars and students should be able to screen and study the ethnography of sexworkers in addition to the myriad other possible approaches to the history of stag films through the greater access to the Kinsey collection. It is no longer enough to be able to view stag films on Kinsey Institute premises at Indiana University in private screenings. The stag film heritage needs the collaboration of scholars and archivists to preserve and study a body of work that has been far too long neglected.

NOTES

1. A longer version of this paper has previously been published in *The Moving Image*, 5, 2 (Fall 2005), 106–35.
2. The American term 'stag' is derived from the all-male parties, or smokers, where such films were shown, often by itinerant projectionists, to an exclusively male audience.
3. At my first visit to the Kinsey Institute before I had been introduced to the collection, I met one of the librarians carrying a statue of a monkey. In his shirt pocket was a large detachable phallus belonging to the monkey.
4. For descriptions of the Institute's library and the growth of the collections see the three major biographies of Alfred Kinsey by Wardell Pomeroy (1972), James Jones (1997) and Jonathan Gathorne-Hardy (1998).
5. Scott McDonald (1983) notes the awkwardness of this view of the penis from an ostensibly heterosexual viewpoint as well. Waugh thus describes a viewing situation that comprises 'men getting hard pretending not to watch men getting hard watching images of men getting hard watching or fucking women' (2001: 280).
6. Because this film, interesting as it was, did not seem to belong to the true stag film genre I did not address it then and do not now.

7   See, for example, *Mexican Dog* (c.1930s) and *Beauty and the Boxer*, which is about a woman and a prize fighter.
8   Waugh adds that few 'literally drawn prostitute characters appear in the stag stories as such, but the recurring exchange of money and services implies that most female characters are candidates' (2001: 285).
9   Even improvised stag films acted out someone's idea of a sexual 'script'.
10 I borrow this term from the masterful director of hard and soft-core films of the 1970s and 1980s, Radley Metzger.
11 There are, however, spelling lapses throughout the intertitles.
12 If *obscenity* is the term used to mark the unspeakability of explicit sex acts, the truly underground, illicit status of stag films, for example, during their hey-day, *on/scenity* is the term I have coined to mark the greater speakability and visibility of explicit sex acts in our own day. (see Williams 1999: 280–314; Williams 2004: 1–21).
13 For example, Maitland McDonagh (n.d.) refers to its 'agreeably prelapsarian landscape of desire', and contrasts the 'absence of the narrow focus and distasteful sheen of meanness that oozes off much 21st-century pornography'; Linda Ruth Williams describes the 'charmingly anachronistic' qualities of the film and the way 'Everyone seems to be having a jolly good time' (2004: 50–1).
14 Matlock (2004) suggests, for example, that the anthology includes examples that tend to range from the flirtations to bawdy, but to exclude the kind of 'woman threatened by rape' scenarios, or examples of bestiality (here, I would not really count the fluffy white dog who cutely licks both women and men as bestiality).
15 We certainly need the kind of detailed historical inquiry that Thomas Waugh (1996) has been carrying out with respect to homoerotic films and photos in the article cited above and in his beautiful and richly researched book, *Hard to Imagine: Gay Male Eroticism in Photography and Film from Their Beginnings to Stonewall*.

WORKS CITED

Di Lauro, A. and G. Rabkin (1976) *Dirty Movies: An Illustrated History of the Stag Film, 1915–1970*. New York: Chelsea House.
Gathorne-Hardy, J. (1998) *Alfred C. Kinsey: Sex the Measure of All Things*. London: Chatto and Windus.
Jones, J. (1997) *Alfred C. Kinsey: A Public/Private Life*. New York: W. W. Norton.
Kendrick, W. (1987) *The Secret Museum*. Berkeley: University of California Press.
Kipnis, L. (1996) *Bound and Gagged: Pornography and the Politics of Fantasy in America*. New York: Grove Press.
Koch, G. (1993) 'The Body's Shadow Realm', in P. Church Gibson and R. Gibson (eds) *Dirty Looks: Women, Pornography, Power*. London: BFI, 22–45.
Lehman, P. (1995) 'Revelations about Pornography', *Film Criticism*, Fall/Winter, 3–16.
Matlock, J. (2004) 'Keeping Up Appearances', *Sight & Sound*, 14, 4, 28–30.
McDonagh, M. (n.d.) 'Review of *The Good Old Naughty Days*'. On-line. Available: www.tvguide.com/movies/database/ShowMovie.asp?MI=44539 (accessed 2 April 2009).
McDonald, S. (1983) 'Confessions of a Feminist Porn Watcher', *Film Quarterly*, 36, 3,

10–17.

Penley, C. (1997) 'Crackers and Whackers: The White Trashing of Porn', in M. Wray and A. Newitz (eds) *White Trash: Race and Class in America*. New York: Routledge, 89–112.

Pomeroy, W. (1972) *Dr. Kinsey and the Institute for Sex Research*. London: Nelson.

Schaefer, E. (1999) *Bold! Daring! Shocking! True!: A History of Exploitation Films, 1919–1959*. Durham and London: Duke University Press.

____ (2007) 'Plain Brown Wrapper: Adult Films for the Home Market, 1930–1969', in J. Lewis and E. Smoodin (eds) *Looking Past the Screen: Case Studies in American Film History and Method*. Durham: Duke University Press, 201–26.

Staiger, J. (1995) *Bad Women: Regulating Sexuality in Early American Cinema*. Minneapolis: University of Minnesota Press.

Waugh, T. (1996) *Hard to Imagine: Gay Male Eroticism in Photography and Film from their Beginnings to Stonewall*. New York: Columbia University Press.

____ (2001) 'Homosociality in the Classical American Stag Film: Off-Screen, On-Screen', *Sexualities*, 4, 3, August, 275–91.

Williams, L. (1999 [1989]) *Hard Core: Power, Pleasure, and the 'Frenzy of the Visible'*. Berkeley: University of California Press.

____ (1995) 'Corporealized Observers: Visual Pornographies and the "Carnal Density of Vision"', in P. Petro (ed.) *Fugitive Images: From Photography to Video*. Bloomington: Indiana University Press, 3–41.

____ (ed.) (2004) *Porn Studies*. Durham: Duke University Press.

Williams, L. R. (2004) *'The Good Old Naughty Days'*, *Sight & Sound*, 14, 4, 50–1.

CHAPTER SIX

LOST IN DAMNATION: THE PROGRESSIVE POTENTIAL OF *BEHIND THE GREEN DOOR*

Darren Kerr

Described as a 'misogynist classic' by Linda Williams in her influential study, *Hard Core: Porn, Pleasure and the 'Frenzy of the Visible'* (1999), the Mitchell Brothers' *Behind the Green Door* (1972) is a feature-length hard-core porn film that is renowned for its series of spectacular psychedelic slow-motion 'money shots' (male ejaculation) that are the climax of both its ritualistic sexual centrepiece and its experimental visual style. The film stars Marilyn Chambers whose resulting stardom, like many porn performers, eclipses the idea that she may indeed be playing a character. In *Behind the Green Door* Chambers plays Gloria Saunders but, it can be argued, is more accurately thought of as representing an anonymous young woman who is abducted and then taken to a sex club, where she performs various sex acts in front of a mixed audience. Whilst acknowledging *Behind the Green Door*'s uncomfortable narrative of sexual coercion, it is worth noting in detail that the film's self-reflexive address calls attention to the *performance* of sex and sexuality that explores the role of porn as a *fantasy* space. This chapter then is an attempt to revisit a key moment in the history of pornography on screen that has, for too long, been contained within problematic debates concerning media effects, the often superficial styling of porno-chic and anti-porn sentiment which, whilst not entirely without merit, tries to sweep aside any potential notion of a relationship between pornography and how issues of sexuality might be rearticulated. The central objective here is to reappraise *Behind the*

Green Door's significance and status as an often-overlooked milestone in the 'Golden Age' of porn that should be lost in damnation no more.

BEFORE THE *GREEN DOOR*...

In 1970, two years before the release of *Behind the Green Door*, the US Commission on Obscenity and Pornography published its initial findings, which concluded that there was no link between the increased availability of pornography and sexual crime. However, by 1986, the Attorney General's Meese Report had declared a causal relationship between pornography and sexual aggression. It was a claim problematised by the researchers whose work it was based on. Edward Donnerstein and Daniel Linz complained that their findings were misused in the report (see Williams 1999: 319). Of course what occurred during the intervening years, between the Commission on Obscenity and Pornography and the Meese Report, were 'the porn wars' debates.

These debates on porn emerged from, firstly, the explosion of pornography on the big screen and porno-chic, secondly, porn's subsequent move into the domestic sphere with the advent of home video in the 1980s, and thirdly, came as a response to a time by which the industry and story forms had evolved into foregrounding male fantasy and female subjugation in mainstream screen porn. Such debates are indeed important if we are to reclaim the progressive potential for a film too often damned simply as enacting a fantasy of ravishment. The strength of feeling around the ill effects of porn are expressed in the vitriolic rhetoric found within the writings of Catherine MacKinnon (1993) and Andrea Dworkin (1979) and the debate-within-the-debate from the many feminist writers who objected to this anti-porn feminism (see O'Toole 1999).

Whilst this chapter will not reproduce or outline these debates it is important to note how vernacular theories attached themselves to screen porn, which determine the popular discourses around it. These emerged through the 1970s and 1980s where the context of a growing awareness of sexual harassment, the explication of feminist issues and broader political agendas seeking to tackle domestic violence and rape, circulated. Furthermore, concerns of what left-leaning sexual politics meant for the embittered right existed and spread in response to such liberalisation. Realistically it is little wonder that such rancour dominated debates about porn during the widespread (and relatively immediate) advent of its increased availability. This was, after all, a time when porn *form* on the screen was transitional and developing in a financially aggressive industry that demanded a cheap, easy and generically repetitious product. Furthermore pornography carried with it the weight of a somewhat unfortunate history in the production and distribution of sexually explicit still-image photography, magazines and early stag reels.

Even before moving-image pornography emerged, stills photography of both the erotic and pornographic began to establish what appear to be the parameters in which early erotic and stag films were seen. As Williams (1999) notes it was these technologies of the visible and the protocinematic, which came together with explorations of sexuality, that allowed the body to reveal itself. Such still images not only draw attention to a shift in representing the female form, from the idea of the nude in art to naked in photography, but also reveal the female body as imagined, encased in superfluous detail and, perhaps most importantly, fetishised. This means of visibly mastering sexual difference is carried through into early stag films. One such anthology, both nostalgically and temptingly titled *Taboo: The Beginning of Erotic Cinema* (2004), offers a collection of short films that provide a significant snap-shot of the different ways in which women were imagined.

Taboo contains six undated shorts from the 1930s and 1940s that reveal the ways in which early erotic and pornographic films contained the 'confession' of women's sexuality from a male point of view. *Roman Holiday* presents women in a performance of a play in which they adopt various roles and emotional expressions but mostly offer the body and movement as the film's focus. *Caught in the Barbed Wire* offers an 'accidental' striptease as the sole female's clothes are caught and untangled for the voyeuristic pleasure of the viewer. *Nude Diversion* and *Uncle Si and the Sirens* are early films that acknowledge the links between technology, sexual spectacle and pleasure. The former offers us a naked woman being filmed as she is looking and moving around a camera of her own. She clearly exists to simply 'appear' (rather than to be in any way active or with purpose) and acknowledges her presence with repeated, knowing gazes to the viewer that rupture the diegesis. Such gazes are also evident in the latter film, *Uncle Si and the Sirens*, which foretells the coming of television and its surreptitious use for personal pleasure. The 'sirens' of the title are the mostly topless women Uncle Si comes across as he tunes and re-tunes his television receiver. In both of these films the relationships between technology, audience and the sexual subject are made clear, with the camera existing to reveal the women through a male mode of address.

The final two films, *Anonymous French Shorts* and *Dressage au Fouet*, introduce the crude aesthetics of early hard-core – caught between amateurism, sexual spectacle without context and, quite simply, sexual play. The former presents two women groping, grabbing and mutually masturbating on a bed whilst the latter introduces two other women engaging in a performance of S/M. Together the films in this collection frame women's pleasure as connected to display, technology and, as suggested by the collection's title, taboo. Interestingly though the anthology, when viewed collectively, draws attention especially to sex on screen as sexual fantasy.

The problem of course lies in the author of such fantasies being a male who is constructing/imagining the sexual female. This should lead us into a debate about the problems and intricacies of sexual *fantasy*, but the socio-political history of pornography has been more concerned with the damning of porn's connection to 'reality'. And that reality is inevitability marked by porn's critical history which is itself inextricably linked to violence. This comes from a prevailing perception that porn produced by men reveals how pervasive misogyny is in Western patriarchal culture. Thus porn is perceived to construct female sexuality through women's submission to male domination, objectification and dispossession, hence rendering pornography as a *form* of violence against women. To repeat some of these ideas may seem somewhat outdated, but it is the continuing influence of these formative ways of how porn is thought about that the problem of porn still persists to this day. As Cynthia Carter and C. Kay Weaver note of the contemporary 'there is ... general agreement that mainstream, heterosexual (patriarchal) pornographic representations should be a cause for concern' (2003: 107). This concern is dominated by how women are imagined on screen and yet a conflicting position is demonstrated through a growing body of work on women and porn. These include the growing number of women as producers of pornography, ideas around how women in S/M occupy positions that challenge mainstream gender roles (see Rubin 1993) and how women actively watch hard-core (see Smith 2007) and challenge the idea that porn is degrading (see Juffer 1998).

BESIDE THE *GREEN DOOR*...

It is, however, undoubtedly the relationship between porn and coercion that influences how the Mitchell Brothers' *Behind the Green Door* may be read, since it is a film which is ostensibly about the abduction of a woman for the gratification of male fantasy. To follow Diana Russell's (2000) model of the proposed relationship between porn and sexual violence, *Behind the Green Door* appears complicit with such a thesis. The film would, on the surface, appear to present men as predisposed to desire such coercion and undermine any inhibitions they may have against acting it out. Additionally, it not only presents its victim as unwilling to express or enact any resistance, but it also shows this coercion as narratively progressing towards female pleasure, which arguably functions to vindicate any sense of violation *and* sustain the position of male dominance. The difficulty though is in reconciling the idea that the *representation* in such a fantasy (and its polysemic nature) becomes displaced in favour of *real* acts of sexual coercion. The result is that representation is denounced by the same measure as a real act of sexual coercion would be. The (already condemned) representation then gets caught up in pre-existing notions of sexual politics and power relations which, I would argue, can inadvertently limit the reading and understanding of female sexuality and agency in pornographic film. As Williams states, this critical position concerning porn's patriarchal phallocentrism and its inherent violence unintentionally implies 'that if female sexuality were ever to get free of its patriarchal contaminations' it would offer no expressions of violent fantasy, transgressive use of power or indeed engage in fantasies of coercion (1999: 20).

While this relationship between porn and violence is undoubtedly problematic and in need of further exploration, *Behind the Green Door* nevertheless offers us a potentially progressive moment in porn history that has previously been lost amidst the public health discourses that the very concept of pornography attracts. Part of this loss can further be attributed to Gerard Damiano's infamous *Deep Throat* (1972), released the same year as *Behind the Green Door*. The controversy that *Deep Throat* attracted stole attention away from *Behind the Green Door*, which is still most often grouped together with other films of the period such as *The Devil in Miss Jones* (1973) and *The Opening of Misty Beethoven* (1975). In *Deep Throat*, Linda Boreman (Linda Lovelace) expresses her dissatisfaction at failing to achieve sexual pleasure until Dr Young (Harry Reems) examines her to find her clitoris in her throat. What follows is the infamous deep throat sequence that renders Boreman only capable of achieving orgasm by performing oral sex. Aside from its explicitly comedic male fantasy pretensions *Deep Throat* is often noted for its attention to female pleasure – a point addressed in Fenton Bailey and Randy Barbato's documentary *Inside Deep Throat* (2005) (also see Flint 1999; Turan and Zito 1974). The potential to see *Deep Throat* as a politically liberating account of female sexuality however is not matched by its narrative coherency which descends into negating Boreman's satisfaction, in favour of a series of sexual numbers that denies female pleasure and seems to forego its oral promise and premise.

Similarly *The Opening of Misty Beethoven* and *The Devil in Miss Jones* are less obviously constructed as a fantasy within the diegesis compared to *Behind the Green Door*. Misty (Constance Money) and Justine Jones (Georgina Spelvin) each engage in a sexual odyssey which, like *Deep Throat*, places them in a narrative of supposed sexual freedom that is most obviously undermined and contradicted by their being either disengaged in the sexual acts or damned for partaking in them. Regardless, these films made stars of the female leads and none more so than Lovelace whose presence and celebrity was to dominate the 1970s porn scene and influence many of the subsequent debates about porn and exploitation.

The celebrity of *Behind the Green Door*'s Marilyn Chambers, by comparison, remained within a character constructed somewhere between the purity of her role as the Ivory Soap 'Snow Girl' and her accomplished sexual performances on the hard-core screen. On reflection, I argue that *Behind the Green Door* merits attention in its own right for the way in which it prompts a reading, not just of the film's problematic fantasy, but of sex on screen itself, that is concerned with the complexities of porn production, exhibition and consumption. What this reading demands though is not only closer attention to what appears *between* the sequences of sex (which is normally elided in favour of the spectacle of the act) but also a need to attribute narrative agency to the trajectory of each subsequent sex scene in the film (much like traditional narrative analysis in any other genre). Indeed, a consideration of narrative and textual analysis prompts a re-reading of the film that marks it out as something quite different from its contemporaries.

BEHIND THE *GREEN DOOR*...

The film begins in the traditionally male space of the truck-stop diner and the Waitress (Adrienne Mitchell) greeting two truck drivers before significantly absenting herself from this space after hailing the Cook (Dana Fuller) over with the line 'Your buddies are here'. It is from this point that the Cook solicits the story of the Green Door from the truck drivers (credited as Barry and Truck Driver). In a bid to stimulate anticipation both men express hesitation at sharing such a tale. The idea of men telling tales is to be noted in how the story appears somewhat guarded by the men who open the narrative – it is clearly not the first time that the topic has come up and its framed as if it belongs to the realm of modern folklore. The Cook clearly wants access to (and desires) a Foucauldian will-to-knowledge about the modern and hidden sexual activities and performances that go on through the green door. The brief debate over who should tell the tale concludes with Barry's comment, 'No-one tells it like you' which indicates that this contemporary tale has indeed been recited before and, like modern folklore or an urban myth, is still circulating. A glimpse of hesitation marks the Truck Driver's face as he yet again adopts the mantle of storyteller and thus the implicit narrator of the film's action.

Fig. 10 Men telling tales...

The story that the film is based upon (like the unreliable authorship of its telling within the film) is one of uncertain origin, being a tale that its co-director Artie Mitchell encountered during military service. *Behind the Green Door*'s opening, in spite of its poor production qualities, sets the scene effectively for the flashback that dominates the majority of the film's narrative and importantly the construction of its diegesis. This places it firmly within the realm of male fantasy, which can lead to an assumption that such a fallible construction of women's sexual agency is inherently wrong. My contention though is that in spite of the diegesis being informed by a tale told by men, it is nevertheless a tale that *explores* and *elevates* the sexual agency and independence of women.

As the main flashback begins we are introduced to Gloria Saunders through the first signs of her independence and freedom as she careers down an open road in a sports car, alone. A cut to a hotel terrace re-introduces (in flashback) Barry, listening once more to the storytelling Truck Driver who is recounting anecdotal tales of his job, working and dating. Gloria enters, sits at an adjacent table and is framed between the two men before the scene alternates its focus between her face and the Truck Driver's dialogue who is now recounting the pressures experienced on a previous date.

What follows this is the abduction of Gloria, orchestrated at the hotel by men who have been expecting her. It is a key moment, but it is shrouded in mystery as we are left with no knowledge about the abductors, whether there was any degree of complicity on Gloria's behalf or whether the Truck Driver and Barry had any part to play in her abduction. Perhaps what is more productive in this pivotal and contentious moment is to consider how the film presents the abduction in a way, we may assume, that mirrors how this sequence is being described in the Truck Driver's tale – a way that sustains the anticipation that is central to the telling of this narrative. What is more evident is that the Truck Driver and Barry were at the hotel in preparation for the evening's events due to take place on stage in an underground club for a variety of invited (and masked) guests only. It soon becomes apparent that these guests differ greatly from the exclusively, and traditionally, male-oriented spectators of hard-core performance: these adult spectators are diverse in their gender, sexuality, ethnicity and age.

From this point onwards, sexual activities dominate the rest of the film. So it seems an apt moment to investigate the narrative agency that is attributed to each of these subsequent performances. Prior this though, it is important to note that Gloria's arrival on stage is pre-empted by a routine from a mime artist (Angela Castle). The make-up of the mime artist indicates that she is wearing a neutral mask and, in expressive mime, an oversized lipstick is applied followed by blusher to her cheeks. Once this 'new face' is on, an exaggerated smile emerges. This face is then 'removed' through hand gestures, signalling a return to the neutrality of the mask before being put back on, then off and again on in an overly emphasised series of signs and movements which imply the *putting on* of a face, a mask and a *performance*. The mime draws attention to the construct of stage performance and does so especially in relation to enacting gender. The skit concludes with the face removed and an imaginary oversized jacket and trousers put on. This would seem to indicate that whilst being dressed and prepared, the masks are soon to come off. In the context of hard-core porn, the mime's act also seems irritatingly extended and, for the cinema audience that it was originally exhibited to, intentionally inescapable. As viewers then, we are made to share in the audience's anticipation of the main event but encouraged to acknowledge its performative qualities as drama and enactment.

This exaggerated performance of preparation serves as an introduction to the main show and occurs whilst Gloria receives a massage backstage from a solitary female. Taking the massage into account there is a clear narrative of sexual performance that moves from ritualistic preparation to a multi-coloured, psychedelic climax. It is also a narrative that is informed by the fluidity of both sexual boundaries and sexual dominance that goes through a number of different (theatrical and sexual) 'acts'. Being brought onto the stage Gloria is attended by a group of women who follow an expressive theatrical style in their caresses of her that graduate towards oral and penetrative sex. This orgiastic routine dissipates as the African Stud (Johnny Keyes) appears. Again his performance and dress is overtly stylized which is carried over into his sexual performance as he and Gloria have sex. At first glance this may appear to confirm the discourses around the 'film as rape fantasy' as the Female Attendants (as they are credited) appear to prepare Gloria for this all powerful and potent symbol of masculinity and sexual performance – the well-endowed black male. However, close reading of the sex on screen illustrates how Keyes' character actually follows the lead established by the group of women in an oral sex segue performed on Gloria. The women then are not the handmaidens that the idea of a coercive fantasy requires, but rather the initiators.

The way in which the sex is shot reveals how elevating male pleasure (which male-produced porn tends to heavily to rely on) is deferred in the film. Also, instead of the usual close-ups on genitalia that fragment the hard-core body, which had long been established in early stag loops and was revisited again in video-produced porn of the 1980s, we tend to see more of Gloria's face and her *entire* body in movement in an attempt to capture visceral pleasure and experience. This counters the idea of the woman's body in pleasure on screen as being cut-up in a bid to both fetishise her and reduce her to a fragmented collection of sexual parts. Moreover it is her frenzy that is prevalent, not his, as we cut to shots of an aroused audience. Keyes' character completes his part of the performance without focus on his gratification – indeed his costume renders *him* as just primitive cock – as he simply exits the stage with no money shot delivered.

Just as the narrative of this staged sexual performance moves from a single female to several women, so too does Gloria's experience with men on the stage. As Gloria is carefully directed into position by stage-hands, trapeze swings are lowered to almost surround her. Four men take to the stage: three take to the swings whilst the remaining man lies beneath her. She then proceeds to masturbate two of the men, perform oral sex on the third whilst having penetrative sex with the fourth. The significance of this act lies in the fact that it is she who is presented as being in control. To encase the film within the idea of it being a rape fantasy is to deny female sexual agency, activity and pleasure as it is expressed in the performance *and* in the context of men imagining that sexual agency. Additionally this deferential treatment of men is arguably apparent in the trapeze scene in which the men solicit a voyeuristic gaze in their passive posturing, once again having to follow a female lead.

It is worth recounting here that this is indeed presented as a flashback of men telling tales because this male fantasy is one that denies male agency over sex acts and sexual pleasure. This is not to say that the film is fixated solely on exploring female pleasure but rather that pleasure in *Behind the Green Door* as it filters outwards, across performers in the theatre, is arguably deferential.

The climax of the sex on stage is one of prolonged and repeated male ejaculation. It is a scene that lasts for almost six minutes and it shifts from freeze-frame stop-motion to slow-motion. It incorporates graphic overlays, multiple colours and split-screen imaging. It is a moment that appears to typify the truly primitive moments of spectacle on screen in the film's demonstration of its (then) sophisticated use of technology to emulate the psychedelic and hallucinogenic qualities associated with the period *and* the visual evidence of male sexual pleasure. Traditional readings of the money shot in porn focus on its currency as evidencing satisfaction just for men. This is supported through ejaculation often being the narrative climax to the sex act and presented as the resolution to the sexual pleasure – both of which inherently centre on male-only gratification. In spite of its heightened spectacle though, *Behind the Green Door* decides not to conclude its narrative of sexual performance at this point. Like all modern folkloric tales this one is about to further evolve in its retelling in the diner.

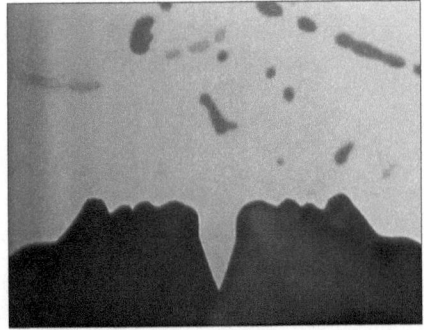

Fig. 11 *Green Door's* premature narrative climax.

After the climactic scene on stage Gloria is carried off by an unidentified male. Outwardly it appears to be Barry but the overhead shot makes identification difficult to ascertain. It is at this point that we return to the truck-stop diner wherein our storyteller concludes with, 'When they went through the green door it was the last I saw of them'. This implies that it was not Barry who took Gloria from the stage but, significantly, it *is* he that tells the Cook the story will continue 'some other time'. This 'other time' emerges as Barry returns to his truck and hits the road. A dissolve signals a continuation of this fantastic tale as Barry and Gloria engage in the sex that concludes the film. Again, whilst demonstrating mutual fulfilment it is Gloria's agency that is fore-grounded in Barry's imagination as she emerges as the focus, in control, active and in charge of her pleasure. In contrast to the performance of sex on stage this sequence is shot in soft focus, employing slow dissolves and is gently lit. It ends face-to-face with a simple kiss which neatly denies the genre the hard-core currency attributed to the male climax that dominates the form.

Fig. 12 Gloria's sexual agency denies hard-core currency.

As evidenced in the audience's participation the pleasure in *Behind the Green Door*, normally a male preserve, is seen to be disseminated mutually, not just restricted to serve men *and*, importantly, this position comes from the auspices of male fantasy. This is men (average men, working men, men telling tales) denying men privilege in hard-core sexual performance for public consumption.

BEYOND THE *GREEN DOOR*...

The conclusion takes this close reading of sexual spectacle into the audience within the film whose activity during the stage performance not only supports the idea that hard-core pleasure *isn't* an inherently male domain, but also appears self-reflexive in its honesty about what it is to consume porn. Unsurprisingly for a porn film the relationship between the hard-core performance and its audience takes place within the realms of the underground (the exclusive sex club), the forbidden (in its sexual displays) and the experimental (in its theatrical style).

Despite being masked, unknown and anonymous, the audience come to be known to us as consumers of porn through their own reactive play, performance and recital of what they are watching and experiencing. The move from observers to participants occurs as the stage-sex passes its halfway point during the African Stud sequence. Significantly this moment in the narrative of sex has begun to establish the diverse performance of pleasure which is taken up and expanded by the audience. As previously noted, the audience is diverse in age, gender, ethnicity, even size and shape, but it is in bringing together the eclecticism of differing sexualities that the shared performance becomes most notable. Gay, straight and transgendered players move from being individually framed to collectively displayed. As the stage show builds to its literal climax the audience become more significant players to the point that the stage performers are displaced in favour of the camera's gaze cutting between the now active audience members. Masks are slowly lost as the lines along which the audience can be differentiated erode as a result of the pleasure accrued from consuming hard-core performance. What we are presented with negates the sight of the idealised bodies of the stage performers to impress upon us the assorted range of bodies and sexualities in these 'consumers'. It is worth noting that the anonymity of the audience returns once the sexual energy on stage is expelled in all its technicoloured glory.

Traditionally, establishing a diegesis in film demands the segregation of the audience from the actors – the viewers from the action. The porn film, of course, does not function in this way. Cinema's 'fourth wall' in the porn film repeatedly collapses as it invites the viewer's pleasure to meet that of the performers. This is nothing new when considering how image technologies (photography, film, video and more recently the internet) and pornography relate to their audiences. The same notion is enacted in *Behind the Green Door* as the stage-performance calls into being the sexual proclivities of the audience. It is worth briefly mentioning the importance of the theatrical setting in the film here. As well as aligning itself to porn's heritage of inviting the spectator in, *Behind the Green Door* seems to draw its influence from the notion of theatre as a conceptually 'open' or 'empty' space. This experimental approach, advocated by directors such as Peter Brook (1968), expresses the notion that there is no line between the stage and the audience: a performance is made possible because of the space occupied both on- and off-stage. Meaning is generated as a result of the presence of performers *and* audience in that 'open' space. Intentionally or otherwise, presenting this theatrical notion, the Mitchell Brothers seem to acknowledge the call-to-response that the porn film could be said to request of its audience. In *Behind the Green Door*, the very experience of viewing porn is recognised as the co-ordination of cognitive engagement followed by physical response, as evidenced in the sexual activities that the diegetic audience engage in.

With its predilection for the avant-garde – in its use of the stage, the Mime, the 'open' space – *Behind the Green Door* offers a significantly self-reflexive moment in porn film history that is not attempting to distance itself from cinematic hard-core or escape a faux construction of male fantasy (it is after all part of the narrative) but rather accept its own construction and its consumption *as* pornography. To these ends *Behind the Green Door* not only credits the performance of sex with narrative significance but also demonstrates how the film demands a progressive reading that is aware of the complexities of producing fantasy, exhibiting sexual performance and consuming hard-core pornography.[1]

NOTE

1 Thanks to both Donna Peberdy and Claire Hines for their support and comments on earlier versions of this chapter.

WORKS CITED

Brook, P. (1968) *The Empty Space*. London: Penguin.
Carter, C. and C. K. Weaver (2003) *Violence and the Media*. Buckingham: Open University Press.
Dworkin, A. (1979) *Pornography: Men Possessing Women*. New York: Putnam.
Flint, D. (1999) *Babylon Blue: An Illustrated History of Adult Cinema*. London: Creation Books.
Juffer, J. (1998) *At Home With Pornography: Women, Sex and Everyday Life*. New York: New York University Press.
MacKinnon, C. (1993) 'Turning Rape into Pornography', *Ms.*, July–August, 24–30.
O'Toole, L (1999) *Pornocopia: Porn Sex Technology and Desire*. London: Serpent's Tail.
Russell, D. E. H. (2000) 'Pornography and rape: a causal model', in D. Cornell (ed.) *Feminism and Pornography*. Oxford: Oxford University Press, 48–93.
Rubin, G. (1993) 'Misguided, dangerous and wrong: an analysis of anti-pornography politics', in A. Assister and C. Avendon (eds) *Bad Girls and Dirty Pictures: The Challenge to Reclaim Feminism*. London: Pluto, 18–40.
Smith (2007) *One for the Girls! The pleasures and Practices of Reading Women's Porn*. Bristol: Intellect.
Turan, K. and S. F. Zito (1974) *Sinema: American Pornographic Films and the People Who Make Them*. New York: Preager.
Williams, L. (1999) *Hard Core: Porn, Pleasure and the 'Frenzy of the Visible'*. London: University of California Press.

CHAPTER SEVEN

THE LIMITS OF PLEASURE? MAX HARDCORE AND EXTREME PORN

Stephen Maddison

Enrico Biasin and Federico Zecca (2009) have noted what they describe as a 'new' hyperbolic proliferation of Linda Williams' famous characterisation of hard-core porn as a 'frenzy of the visible' (1990). This 'new' frenzy of the visible, Biasin and Zecca suggest, has led to the proliferation and institutionalisation of fetishistic sex practices (such as reverse double penetration, ass-to-mouth, cum swapping, anal gaping and so on) that characterise the gonzo style, in which the relationship between realism and amateur filmmaking is emphasised. In effect, this analysis alludes to the process of contemporary porn genres (and not just gonzo) becoming more extreme, with popular styles becoming widely influential. The rise of gonzo in the current era of digital porn is easy to understand. Gonzo can be cheaply produced, with a seamless digital workflow from filming to publication and retail. And the camera-as-spectator in the scene reflects the increasingly intimate relationship porn spectators have with smaller screens and browsing-as-viewing modes of consumption. But a key implication of Biasin and Zecca's suggestion of a 'new' frenzy concerns the status of pleasure in pornography, as a materiality on which its commodity value rests. That is, consumption of porn (and we seem to be consuming ever more of it all the time, in different formats) is driven by the promise of pleasures as yet to be experienced. In practice, this means that there is high demand in the industry for sexual innovation and novelty value. Thus, gonzo's popularisation of what Biasin and

Zecca describe as fetishistic practices (2009: 144) can be seen as a kind of commodity innovation that high levels of competition in the industry mean will be copied widely.

But the question of pleasure in pornography is problematic and rarely located in the context of subjectivity and capital (as opposed to being located in the context of say, gender inequality or psychoanalysis). This chapter aims to begin to question what it might mean to think about the mainstream hardcore porn industry as an engine of pleasure. In Williams' (1990) now iconic formulation, the pursuit of pleasure in porn is literally that – a diegetic frenzy to seek out the mechanisms of pleasure in bodies and represent them. This remains a compelling way of understanding the history of pornography. But it is becoming increasingly difficult not to relate pornography's search for pleasure to wider patterns of governmentality in neoliberalism, where pleasure lies at the axis of consumer culture, ideologies of freedom and choice, and the mechanisms for proliferating capital, as a kind of injunction by which the individual secures their selfhood. In this context, what does it mean to suggest that the pursuit of pleasure in porn rests upon it becoming increasingly extreme? And what are the limits of pleasure?

'A BOIL ON THE ASS OF PORNOGRAPHY': IS MAX HARDCORE TOO EXTREME?

In 2007 Paul Little (aka Max Hardcore) was indicted on ten counts of federal obscenity charges in the USA relating to five movies – *Pure Max 16: Euro Version* (2004), *Max Hardcore Fists of Fury 3* (2004), *Max Hardcore Extreme Schoolgirls 6: Euro Version* (2004), *Max Hardcore Golden Guzzlers 5* (2003), and *Max Hardcore Golden Guzzlers 6* (2003) – showing fisting, urination and vomiting. He was found guilty on all charges and sentenced to 46 months in prison. Little began serving his sentence, following an unsuccessful appeal, in January 2009 and was released in July 2011. Prior to re-election in 2005, the Bush administration had promised 'to make the investigation and prosecution of obscenity one of [our] highest criminal enforcement priorities' (Tapper 2005). Following the unsuccessful attempt to prosecute porn producers Extreme Associates in 2003, the imprisonment of Little is the only significant high-profile porn conviction in the US since the Reagan administration (see Maddison 2009a). Max Hardcore makes 'extreme' porn, and he is widely disliked in the industry. But what does this notion of 'extreme' mean in this context? For many in the porn industry itself, Max Hardcore is *too* extreme. Patrick Collins (of porn company Elegant Angel) has called Max Hardcore 'a boil on the ass of pornography' (in Hoffman 2003), whilst a representative review of *Max Extreme 4* (1998) says:

> Way too much choke fucking and slobber on her face for my taste... I gave up on this piece of shit pedophile scene so I didn't have to rag on the use of the fucking speculm [sic]. What a fucking waste of thrity [sic] minutes of tape. Max, even you should be ashamed of this fucking garbage... This scene has zero sex appeal, it sucks and it's not worth the tape it was copied on. (Pipe 1999)

The understanding of Max Hardcore's 'extremity' enabled the Bush administration to appease anti-porn constituencies by tackling the apparent worst excesses of porn in prosecuting him, whilst notably leaving the rest of the industry untroubled. At the same time, Max Hardcore, as many commentators have noted (for example Rotten.com), sets a standard for the rest of the industry. What today may appear 'extreme' in his films will soon become part of hard-core's generic standards. For example, commentators have argued that Max Hardcore invented 'extreme anal', a style of heterosexual eroticism that arguably now dominates much mainstream porn (see Scholtes 1998). And thus Max Hardcore's 'extremity' serves dual purposes. Firstly, it provides mythic inoculation of the industry against the threat of extremity (he is extreme and misogynistic, so they cannot be). As Barthes suggests, the myth 'immunizes ... by means of a small inoculation of acknowledged evil; [and] thus protects it against the risk of a generalized subversion' (1993: 164). Secondly, Max Hardcore's output serves as a site of innovation that drives porn production across the industry.

There is no question that hard-core is becoming more extreme. I have written about this critically in the collection *Mainstreaming Sex* (Maddison 2009a). In this context we need to be cautious about simplistically scapegoating Max Hardcore. There are a number of important shifts that distinguish the increasing extremity of hard-core porn (for example the relationship between porn and biotechnology, micro-publishing, production technologies, use of migrant and disadvantaged workers also exploited by biotech). Primary amongst these features of 'extreme' porn is the intensification of a dehumanised female body that, as Paul Willeman has noted, is the 'meat' repository for the demonstration of performances by 'plant' machinery (2004: 21). I do not want to underestimate the gendered effects of extreme porn, but having written about them elsewhere, I want to pursue other, related, issues here.

The idea I want to isolate in these discourses of 'extremity' is an often-repeated one about Max Hardcore's films being too extreme to be pleasurable as viewing experiences. For example:

> He reduces the likes of vapid, vacuous *Vivid Video* girls to the functional equivalent of discardable Chinese take-out menus dangling from your front doorknob [...] In Mr. Hardcore's arena, anal sex became less of a plot point

and more of a full-throttle narrative engine designed to humiliate and degrade multiple female performers at once, and as much as humanly possible [...] *Sorry if you can't jerk off to that*, but more often than not Max's films are less about masturbation and more about showing the audience something they don't exactly see every day. (Rotten.com n.d.; emphasis added)

This proposition that Max Hardcore's films are too extreme to be pleasurable raises interesting questions about the role of pleasure in pornography, and in capital more widely. The idea of a pornography that is not pleasurable to watch, or which cannot be successfully masturbated to, runs counter to our understanding of the form. Hard-core porn is, after all, a representation of affective responses in bodies on screen designed to solicit affective responses in viewers. Is it not? In order to answer this question I want to widen my focus for a moment and consider the role of pleasure more generally in neoliberal capital.

THE INCITEMENT TO PLEASURE AND NEOLIBERAL SUBJECTIVITY

We could say that in the neoliberal society of control, pleasure is not a frill or a bonus but an injunction, a requirement of our subjecthood. Critics of post-feminist ideologies have well-documented the extent to which this structure is gendered: post-feminist ideology is distinguished by its claim for women's 'right' to sexual pleasure. This 'right' works to naturalise heterosexuality: however economically and professionally emancipated (or not) the post-feminist woman is, this will be culturally less significant than the continuing plausibility of her sexual desirability within heterosexuality, as a legion of iconic post-feminist texts, from the novel *Bridget Jones's Diary* (1996) to the *Sex and the City* (1996) anthology, attest. This 'right' to sexual pleasure is intricately bound up with the extension of pornography into popular culture, and owes as much to commodification as to feminist sexual politics. Esther Sonnet (1999) has written about post-feminism in relation to the Black Lace series of erotic novels for women. She suggests that post-feminist values foreground individual, rather than collective, empowerment, and an entitlement to pleasure, where that pleasure is not a function of political struggle, but is instead a function of consumer choice. Post-feminism describes an ideological formation in which the rhetoric of female empowerment has been assimilated by capital, where it represents a hegemonic concession to the political success of feminism, but where female empowerment becomes a function of consumer culture, rather than a function of a structural redistribution of gender power.

Angela McRobbie offers a subtle analysis of this process, identifying two key emblems of what she describes as the 'aftermath' of feminism. Firstly, the post-feminist masquerade is a new form of feminine deference literally clothed in the privileges of consumer culture, arising self-consciously from women's capacity to earn, and seeking approval not directly from men but from the 'fashion and beauty system' (2007: 723–4). Secondly, the figure of the 'phallic girl' who superficially refuses deference and assumes a licensed form of phallicism, enjoying culture, but renouncing feminism in order to preserve masculine approval (2009: 83). McRobbie suggests that 'the regulatory dynamics of this sexualized field of leisure and entertainment [defined by a tabloid language of masculinist pleasures] are disguised by the prevalence of the language of personal choice' (2007: 733).

These feminist analyses of pleasure and depoliticisation relate to a wider account of neoliberalism that locates the incitement to pleasure as one of the ways in which we either become subjects of neoliberal governmentality (in Foucauldian paradigms), or the society of control (in Deleuzian paradigms). Mark Fisher, drawing on both approaches, identifies interpassive 'depressive hedonia' as a characteristic mode of engagement with an endless flow of content: texting, YouTube, Facebook, iTunes, fast food: always on, instant gratification, seemingly endless choices, endless pleasure (2009: 21). This is an appropriate and important model for understanding porn consumption in the current conjuncture. There has never been more porn, nor has it been more easily available. Most online porn sites offer weekly updates of short individual scenes rather than more infrequent (and expensive) feature-length films. The very saturation of porn, not only in terms of its abundance and accessibility, but its integration into so much of our cultural life, seems to exemplify the idea that we consume porn interpassively, whilst it performs our sexuality for us. Rather than inciting our desire to go out and find some 'real' sex, porn generates desire for porn itself: an endlessly updating parade of posthuman bodies, freakishly endowed and reassuringly standardised. 'Real' sex recedes as porn becomes the dominant mode through which sex is experienced. Fisher, following Deleuze, suggests that we experience authority as an 'indefinite postponement', an unresolved state of perpetual deferral in which 'external surveillance is succeeded by internal policing' (2009: 22) and which makes us subject to what Nikolas Rose has called 'government at a distance' (1996: 44, 54–9). Rose suggests that the individual's desire 'to govern their own conduct freely' and pursue 'a version of their happiness and fulfillment that they take to be their own' actually 'entails a relation to authority' even 'as it pronounces itself the outcome of free choice' (1996: 59). Whilst neoliberalism strives to operate government at a distance, apparently dissociating formal political institutions from an enfranchised set of communities of interest, in fact it 'specifies the subjects of rule in a new way: as active individuals seeking to "enterprise themselves", to maximize their quality of life through acts of choice' (1996: 57). However freely individuals may pursue choices in the name of personal fulfillment, and however much these choices may feel owned, and freely made, they in fact bind the subject to authority (1996: 59). For Fisher, the consequence of all these choices and of being hooked into 'the entertainment matrix' is 'twitchy, agitated interpassivity, and an inability to concentrate or focus' (2009: 24). Consequently we are unable 'to do anything else *except* pursue pleasure' (2009: 22; emphasis in original).

Fisher's formulation is reminiscent of the Frankfurt School's analysis of the culture industry and Adorno's (1991) concept of distraction in particular. But in the new analysis pleasure is no longer either a distraction or an amelioration of oppression (as in Foucault's (1978; 2003) society of sovereignty or society of discipline) but is agency itself, offering choices that feel like empowerment but which actually require our alienation as competitive individuals. Pursuing pleasure is one of the key ways in which we work, as Rose puts it, to constitute ourselves in approved forms. It is a form of government at a distance, producing individuals looking to 'maximize their quality of life through acts of choice' (1996: 57). And so the role of pleasure in neoliberal capital is not merely to distract us from the apparent privations of our economic and social disenfranchisement, but is rather the mechanism by which desire and creativity become channeled into commodity culture and its modes of subjectification (see Gilbert 2008: 181).

HARD-CORE AND PLEASURE

The history of porn is a history of increasing explicitness, a frenzy to capture sexual pleasures in representational form that are inherently physiological, buried in the mysterious mechanisms of the body. Williams has famously argued that porn may be driven by the fantasy of capturing the 'truth' of female sexual pleasure ('indiscreet jewels'), but that its frenzied gaze upon the female body is in fact a 'narcissistic evasion of the feminine "other" deflected back to the masculine self' (1990: 267). Williams' analysis suggested that historically the hard-core feature becomes characterised by a linear progression of genital acts, from arousal and foreplay, through to penetration and orgasm, that offers a logic of human sexual physiology derived from Kinsey. As I have argued elsewhere, this progression of genital events has become increasingly reconfigured in the context of the impact of gonzo styles, web-based forms of distribution, and the relationship between sexual cultures and biotechnology (see Maddison 2009a; 2009b). Where once hard-core strove to offer physiological verisimilitude, it now foregrounds posthuman displays of organs and acts only plausible as functions of porn's production technologies and sexuo-pharmacology.

Despite these changes in the style of sex and the proportions and capacities of bodies on display, pornographic realism continues to seek the truth of affective pleasures. And as ever this truth is representationally elusive, in both technical and philosophical terms. Performers may or may not be convincing; the camera has to be in the right place at the right time; bodies and acts need to be lit so that we can see enough, but maybe not too much; performers need to manifest a degree of mutual responsiveness; relays of identification and desire are unstable and complex (as a generation of psychoanalytic film theory has demonstrated).

Porn genres have historically worked to mitigate these instabilities, though not always successfully. Thomas Waugh suggests that in stag films, 'masculinity [is] on display in spite of itself' and that 'this paradoxical, primitive, and innocent art form ... seeks cunt and ... discovers prick' (2004: 129–30). Nina Power suggests that the money shot has long been a key device in hard-core, designed to ensure that 'the audience get their money's worth' by proving that what they've seen 'has finally, irrevocably been proved to be "real"' (2009: 54). But Anne McClintock argues that the male cum shot is an 'overdetermined contradiction' in heterosexual porn which represents the failure of phallic logic and signifies the 'asymmetry of female and male sexual pleasure' (1992: 123). She goes on to suggest that

> to portray a 'vaginal orgasm' means rendering the penis invisible inside the woman, while at the same time obscuring the vagina ... to portray a clitoral orgasm, excited by hands or mouth, is to refuse the primacy of the penis. (1992: 127)

And thus, in the context of a pornography driven by a phallic logic, female pleasure becomes unrepresentable; hard-core is, in one sense, fundamentally homoerotic in its invitation to men to 'identify vicariously with the spectacle of another man's pleasure' in the absence of its ability to account adequately for female pleasure in the context of heterosexuality (1992: 123). The identification of this contradiction is the basis of Williams' iconic analysis, and for hard-core producers, it is a locus of obsessive attention that drives an internal incitement to sensation.

In the films of Max Hardcore, we find an intensification of these effects. In order to demonstrate this, and to critically evaluate the way in which his films attempt to represent affect in the bodies of performers, and stimulate response in the bodies of spectators, I want to consider a scene from a typical Max Hardcore film. In the second scene of the compilation *Extreme Schoolgirls 1* (2003), Max performs with Drew, a young woman who is dressed in a tight pink baby-doll top and tight miniskirt and high platform shoes with frilly white ankle socks. Her hair is in pigtails, tied with purple and pink plastic baubles, and her face is made up in lurid pinks and purples. The scene takes place outside, with Drew lying on her back on a table for most of it. Max stands naked, either between her legs or he stands over her head tipped back over the edge of the table. The scene is shot gonzo-style, with one camera that follows the action jerkily in medium shot, with occasional close-ups of Drew's face or genitals. The scene begins with Max noting how Drew has put weight on. He pulls up her top and caresses the curve of her belly. She agrees and asks him to help her lose weight. She kneels and performs oral sex on him, before Max leads her to the table and performs an enema on her. Drew lies on her back, top pushed up over her breasts, and miniskirt round her waist. After withdrawing the enema hose, Max steps to one side, masturbating as Drew squirts the water out of her rectum. The camera pans from between her legs to a mid-shot of Max masturbating beside her. Drew tells him, 'Oh Max, please help me lose some weight'. Drew giggles and laughs as he performs the enema. Max penetrates Drew anally and she tells him to 'Plunge-fuck me, Mister'. Max withdraws and walks around to her head. He tells her 'let's make you skinny' as her pushes down on her breasts and then throat until her neck is bent back over the edge of the table. Max stands over her head and throat-fucks her. In close-up we see Drew vomit copious clear liquid over his penis which runs over her nose and eyes as Max asks her 'isn't that sexy?' The vomit smears her purple and pink makeup. As she wipes the vomit from her face Max returns between her legs and in medium shot we see him penetrate her anally. He performs another enema, telling her to gag herself with her own fist. We see a close-up of the hose entering Drew's anus and then a medium shot of her lying on the table pushing her fist in her mouth as Max masturbates and performs the enema. He tells her to 'make yourself gag you little cunt'. He penetrates her again, and in close-up we see water pouring out of her anus as he removes his penis. Max returns to Drew's head, tipping it back over the edge of the table. He stands over her and throat-fucks her again. We can hear choking and gagging sounds. At the edge of the shot we can see her hand pushing at Max's thigh. He withdraws his penis and in close-up we see him masturbating into her mouth. He ejaculates, telling her to swallow it. He throat-fucks her again and she vomits over his penis and her face. We hear Max saying, 'and now you're really fucking skinny baby'. The scene cuts to a shot of the two performers standing side by side as they admire Drew's less rotund belly.

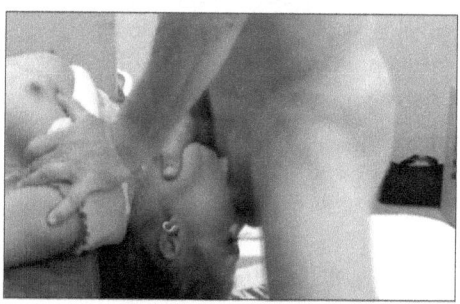

Fig. 13 Max Hardcore and Drew in *Extreme Schoolgirls 1*.

This scene typifies the work of Max Hardcore in a number of ways. Max himself is significantly older and less well-endowed than is the norm for male performers in hard-core. The scene is characterised by a constant stream of instructions given by Max to Drew, and by her total passivity. The lack of vaginal or clitoral stimulation certainly signifies what McClintock calls the 'asymmetry of female and male sexual pleasure' (1992: 123), and the use of medical instruments is very common in Max Hardcore films. In this scene he uses an enema hose and bag; often he uses steel forceps to hold open the mouths, anuses or vaginas of female performers. And aesthetically, Drew is a characteristic Max Hardcore performer with her mix of sleazy and childish attire.

Max Hardcore's films usually include a characteristic variation on the staple cum shot, in the guise of what he calls 'facials'. In Max Hardcore's films, makeup is used not to naturalise the standards of glamour set by the 'fashion and beauty system' (as McRobbie suggests is the case for the post-feminist masquerade; 2007: 723–4), but to parody these forms and make female performers look younger than they are. Interviewed by Rotten.com (n.d.), Hardcore talks about his use of cheap makeup brands marketed at teens:

Fig. 14 The climactic shot of Drew's face in *Extreme Schoolgirls 1*.

> Repeated reamings, piss and puke, and it's still there. Really amazing stuff. I had tried the brush-on high price crap and that's just useless. The eye shadow and cheek makeup I use is the low-cost stuff used by teens. Those are the only ones who have the bright pinks and blues that really pop on camera.

The culmination of most scenes in Max Hardcore's films are close-up shots of the faces of female performers, smeared with urine, semen, makeup and their own saliva from being throat-fucked. In the scene from *Extreme Schoolgirls 1*, the climatic shot of the scene shows Drew's face, with her makeup smeared with semen, vomit and saliva. Here the search for pleasure, Williams' frenzied gaze, tips over into an incitement to sensation, where the involuntary convulsions of Drew's anus ejecting water, or her gag reflex causing her to vomit, displace the more conventional fetish (semen as pleasure). If female pleasure in this scene is potentially unrepresentable, Max Hardcore, as performer, director and producer, is not going to try. Instead, Drew's body is the opportunity to display affective responses to his domination of it by a combination of penis, camera, medical implements, and parodies of feminine masquerade (both in the use of makeup, jewellery, shoes and clothing, and in the exercise of the disciplinary injunction to be thinner). That this is '*hard work*' (Power 2009: 51; emphasis in original) for Drew as a performer, as it is for Max, seems unquestionable, but importantly the object of this work is less his cum shot (as would normally be the case, and where this cum shot would stand in for both his pleasure and hers) but her involuntary vomiting in response to his choke-fucking of her. The potential pleasures of being anally penetrated or given an enema by Max may be representationally obscure, but we are in no doubt that her body is responding strongly to stimulation when Drew vomits over her own face. These are, by any standards, spectacular ejaculations from her bodily cavities, directly related to Max Hardcore's stimulation. To what extent are such ejaculations meaningful as pleasure? We have already noted that some porn industry commentators suggest that the point of Max Hardcore's work is not to solicit masturbation; that is, it is not designed to establish a set of correlative set of affective pleasures between performers and spectators. So what is the meaning of films like *Extreme Schoolgirls 1*?

One answer is that the meaning of Max Hardcore's work lies in the pleasures of subjugating women. His website Maxhardcore.com has been sequestered as a consequence of his trial, but before it was taken offline it boasted that he will 'Savagely Sodomize Stupid Sluts!' who will 'get Throat-Reamed, Ass-Drilled and Fucked-Up Beyond Recognition!' because 'THEY deserve it – Because YOU demand it – Because I Alone Must Do It!' Hardcore's work perhaps best exemplifies the trend identified by Lauren Langman as the 'grotesque degradation' of women 'in retaliation for their assertiveness' (2004: 201). Watching Max Hardcore's work makes it difficult to disagree with Langman's assessment. But this broadly anti-porn position fails to adequately account for what I would argue to be the crucial aspect of this conjuncture, and that is the prevailing neoliberal injunction to pleasure. Anyone who makes porn, or watches porn, knows that despite its rigidly generic forms that make many mainstream films look the same, finding 'good' porn, porn that successfully manages to stimulate affective responses in your body, is surprisingly hard, and itself necessitates the consumption of a lot of porn in order to find work that is satisfyingly stimulating. Indeed, given the prevalence of downloaded, serialised, one-scene films, hard-core consumption now often takes the form of restive file browsing, one hand frequently occupied not in stroking the body, but the mouse or trackpad, opening and scrubbing through files to patch together a bricolage of quality pornographic moments. This is perhaps one reason why Power has recently likened porn to work: 'the sheer *hard work* of contemporary porn informs you that … sex is just like everything else – grinding, relentless, boring' (2009: 51; emphasis in original). We might say then that porn is the pre-eminent neoliberal cultural form. It promises an almost endless supply of products, is easily accessible and cheaply produced, with practically weightless forms of distribution, that deliver expected, anticipated stimulations across an apparently diverse range of tastes and kinks (teen whore, painful anal, amateur, high budget, and so on), but where this choice offers not freedom but Fisher's 'twitchy, agitated interpassivity' (2009: 24). Porn cannot deliver on its promises. We know this. This is the 'real' that pornographic realism seeks to suppress. There is no satisfaction, only the affirmation of interpassivity, and 'reflexive impotence' (Fisher 2009: 21) as a form of neoliberal subjectification. So-called 'extreme' porn should be shocking not for the extremity of the sex acts (which by porn standards are neither extreme nor shocking) but for its limited construction of human sexual possibility, as Power suggests: 'the excessive taxonomical drive of contemporary pornography is merely one element of its quest to bore us all to death and remind us that everything is merely a form of work, including, or even most especially, pleasure' (2009: 55).

What I would like to suggest is that the extremity of Max Hardcore may have worked for the Bush administration, and for porn industry commentators, as a form of inoculation, but that his films may offer a fault line in which we can see the limits of the neoliberal incitement to pleasure. Desire for mainstream hard-core is driven by a desire for authentic affect, for 'real' stimulation that is elusive, despite the seemingly endless stream of content. Max Hardcore offers a glimpse of the limits of this desire, where frenzy to find signs of pleasure tips over into incitement to sensation (you may not be able to tell whether she has cum, but you can tell that she has been choking when she vomits). Max Hardcore may be an engine of innovation in an industry dependent on slowly evolving and conservative generic conventions, but his films do not breach the standard conventions of porn, or refute the idea that by offering a range of niche tastes, the industry is offering 'choice' and freedom. In one sense, he simply offers, in Adorno's (1991) words, novelty and 'pseudo individualization', and a vision of porn, like any other, full of disciplined bodies working to stimulate standardised, contained pleasures in spectators. Max Hardcore exemplifies the 'new' frenzy of the visible, the next stage of porn's continuing history of the search for the 'truth' of pleasure. But for all the vomiting and the spectacular ejaculations of fluids from body cavities, for all the subjugation of women with implements and new sexual positions, Max Hardcore's work is typified by a kind of performative blankness.[1] Despite their relative extremity, and their drive for increasingly intense bodily responses, Max Hardcore's films suggest a limit to pleasure, not only because they may fail to get you off (as the Rotten.com reviewer above suggests) but because they perfectly characterise Fisher's 'depressive hedonia' (2009: 21), with (literally) no pay off, predicated on our investment in the idea that the existence of 'extreme' porn is a marker of our access to differentiation, choice and selfhood.

NOTE

1. Rocco Siffredi, another iconic porn performer and auteur, whose output is even more prolific than Max Hardcore's, and whose films contain comparable levels of choke-fucking and extreme anal, nevertheless achieves a strikingly different effect through the intensity of his sexual performances.

WORKS CITED

Adorno, T. (1991) *The Culture Industry*. London & New York: Routledge.
Barthes, R. (1993 [1959]), *Mythologies*. London: Paladin.
Biasin, E. and F. Zecca (2009) 'Contemporary Audiovisual Pornography: Branding Strategy and Gonzo Film Style', *Cinema & Cie: International Film Studies Journal*, 9, 12, 133–50.
Fisher, M. (2009) *Capitalist Realism: Is There No Alternative*. Ropley: O Books.
Foucault, M. (1978) *The History of Sexuality: An Introduction*. London & New York: Penguin.
____ (2003) *Society Must Be Defended: Lectures at the College de France, 1975–76*. London & New York: Picador.
Gilbert, J. (2008) *Anticapitalism and Culture: Radical Theory and Popular Politics*. Oxford & New York: Berg.
Hoffman, H. (2003) 'Hoffman Hardballs Hardcore', *Luke is Back*, February. On-line. Available: http://www.lukeisback.com/stars/stars/max_hardcore.htm (accessed 29 April 2010).
Langman, L. (2004) 'Grotesque Degradation: Globalization, Carnivalization and Cyber-porn' in D. Waskul (ed.) *Net.SeXXX: Readings on Sex, Pornography and the Internet*. New York: Peter Lang, 193–216.
Maddison, S. (2009a) 'Choke on it, Bitch!': Porn Studies, Extreme Gonzo and the Mainstreaming of Hardcore', in F. Attwood (ed.) *Mainstreaming Sex: The Sexualisation of Western Culture*. London: I. B. Tauris, 37–54.
____ (2009b) '"The Second Sexual Revolution': Big Pharma, Porn and the Biopolitical Penis', *Topia: Canadian Journal of Cultural Studies*, 22, Fall, 35-54.
McClintock A. (1992) 'Gonad the Barbarian and the Venus Flytrap: Portraying the Female and Male Orgasm' in L. Segal and M. McIntosh (eds) *Sex Exposed: Sexuality and the Pornography Debate*. London: Virago, 111–31.
McRobbie, A. (2007) 'Top Girls?', *Cultural Studies*, Vol. 21, Nos. 4-5, 718-737.
____ (2009) *The Aftermath of Feminism: Gender, Culture and Social Change*. London: Sage.
Pipe, R. (1999) 'Max Extreme 4', *RogReviews*. On-line. Available: http://www.rogreviews.com/reviews/read_review.asp?sku=512 (accessed 26 April 2010).
Power, N. (2009) *One Dimensional Woman*. Ropley: O Books.
Rose, N. (1996) 'Governing "Advanced" Liberal Democracies', in A. Barry, T. Osborne and N. S. Rose (eds) *Foucault and Political Reason: Liberalism, Neo-liberalism and Rationalities of Government*. London: UCL Press, 37–64.
Rotten.com (n.d.), 'Max Hardcore'. On-line. Available: http://www.rotten.com/library/bio/pornographers/max-hardcore/ (accessed 29 April 2010).
Scholtes, P. S. (1998) 'Devil in the Flesh', *City Pages*, 14 January. On-line. Available: http://www.citypages.com/1998-01-14/arts/devil-in-the-flesh (accessed 29 April 2010).

Sonnet, E. (1999) '"Erotic Fiction by Women for Women": The Pleasures of Post-Feminist Heterosexuality', *Sexualities*, 2, 2, 167–87.

Tapper, J. (2005) 'Court Deals Blow to US Anti-Porn Campaign', *ABC News*. On-line. Available: http://abcnews.go.co/Nightline/print?id=433956 (accessed 2 May 2010).

Waugh, T. (2004) 'Homosociality in the Classical American Stag Film: Off-Screen, On-Screen' in L. Williams (ed.) *Porn Studies*. Durham & London: Duke University Press, 127-141.

Willeman, P. (2004) 'For a Pornoscape', in Pamela Church Gibson (ed.) *More Dirty Looks: Gender, Pornography and Power*. London: BFI, 9–26.

Williams, L. (1990) *Hard Core: Power, Pleasure and the 'Frenzy of the Visible'*. London: Pandora.

CHAPTER EIGHT

PLAYMATES OF THE CARIBBEAN: TAKING HOLLYWOOD, MAKING HARD-CORE

Claire Hines

A month prior to the DVD release of *Pirates* (also known as *Pirates XXX*) in September 2005, the official trailer opened with the bold statement that this was to be 'THE BIGGEST ADULT FILM PRODUCTION IN HISTORY'. Watching the one-minute-forty-three-second-long teaser trailer, it is clear that, as promised, everything about *Pirates* is remarkably ambitious, expensive and, well, just plain big. The trailer demonstrates that, unusually for a hard-core porn film, *Pirates*' deliberate emphasis on size and scale will extend well beyond the anatomical. In addition to the generous proportions of surgically enhanced breasts, designer vaginas and epic penises so often associated with the genre's biggest stars, the film's Hollywood-style production values, including special effects and an original musical score, augment a feature-length plot and characters that borrow heavily from Gore Verbinski's blockbuster film *Pirates of the Caribbean: The Curse of the Black Pearl* (2003).

Pirates' teaser trailer is then exactly that, a big tease. It offers a potential audience the porn film's choicest (coming) attractions and a range of pleasures. These extend from the industrial – A-list porn stars, an award-winning director, and influential adult film studios – to the aesthetic – detailed costumes and sets, sea battles and special effects. In this way *Pirates* was immediately advertised as a hard-core porn film with mainstream aspirations. Following the film's successful release, media responses to what has become the *Pirates* phenomenon suggest that these aspirations have since been met, and possibly even exceeded. The aim of this chapter is to explore this particular porn phenomenon and to investigate *Pirates* as a contemporary feature-length hard-core film that has, to some extent, managed to achieve crossover status. I will consider how some filmmakers in today's porn industry might take from Hollywood in order to make hard-core.[1]

HOLLYWOOD-STYLE HARD-CORE:
THE ADULT FILM INDUSTRY AND THE STUDIO SYSTEM

At a general level, it has been argued that the structure and development of the adult film industry shares a number of similarities with Hollywood. For example, writing for the *New York Times* in May 2001, journalist Frank Rich recorded his expedition to 'the San Fernando Valley ... on the other side of the Hollywood Hills', where his mission was simply to learn more about the adult film business. Reflecting on his experience, Rich notes that 'Among other things, I learned that the adult industry is in many ways a mirror image of Hollywood'. Not only is the centre of adult film production geographically close to Hollywood, located just over the Hills in the San Fernando Valley area of Los Angeles, but like mainstream cinema the adult industry also controls what Rich calls 'its own starmaking machinery' and functions as a highly-lucrative and integrated system of production, distribution and marketing (2003: 49).

Nicola Simpson's critical work on the business of pornography (2004; 2005) takes this comparison one step further. She argues that the model of the studio system, dominant in Hollywood from the 1920s until the 1960s, has supplied the all-important blueprint for the organisational strategies adopted and adapted by the contemporary adult film industry. The parallels that Simpson draws between the two systems – in particular economic organisation and style of the studios, the significance of the star system and uses of new technology – are worth discussing in some detail here as they also shed light on the similarities between Hollywood and hard-core that I suggest is clear in the case of *Pirates*.

The first point to consider is the characteristics that the leading US adult film companies share in common with the major studios that dominated the Hollywood studio era. From the early 1930s to the late 1940s, the Hollywood film industry was almost entirely dominated by a small number of companies with controlling interests in the production, the distribution and the exhibition of films. The 'studio system', as it has become known, was made up of a hierarchy of eight major companies: Warner Bros., 20th Century Fox, RKO, MGM and Paramount, and Columbia, Universal and United Artists. Of these eight companies, the first five (or 'Big Five') were vertically integrated – as well as production studios they all also owned distribution companies and chains of film theatres to exhibit in – the other three (or 'Little Three') were structurally similar but were not fully integrated as they did not own large theatre circuits. During this period, the eight majors monopolised Hollywood and together they had 'effective control over the ... entire market' (Kuhn and Schatz 2007: 19).

The economic organisation of the studio system also had important implications for the development of Hollywood's production practices. Generic production, for example, is said to have grown out of the system, as each of the major studios attempted to build on and repeat their initial successes. Thomas Ryall has described how 'the standardisation of product obliged by the economic necessities of large scale industrial production led to particular studios concentrating on particular genres' (1978: 4). This in turn led to the development of recognisable studio or house styles. For instance, a major company such as Warner Bros. would be associated with certain genres (gangster, backstage musical) and a characteristic visual style (low-key lighting, minimal sets). In theory then, the Hollywood studio system offers the contemporary adult industry a historical model of fast and economically efficient film production.

Similar to the Hollywood studio system, most major adult film companies today also maintain tight control over all aspects of production, distribution and exhibition. Simpson cites the renowned adult film company Vivid as one of many contemporary porn studios located in Southern California to have adopted the integrated 'business practices characteristic of the Studio System' (2005: 25). Outlined by Simpson, Vivid's production process resembles an assembly line procedure in which studio style (or branding) and the contract system are both crucial to achieving a constant flow of 'quality' output (2005: 24–7). During the studio era, the contract system, like studio style, was a vital part of the industry's overall economic organisation as it became common for each of the majors to directly employ its own technical and creative personnel. So, for example, Warner Bros.' gangster film *The Roaring Twenties* (1939) was created by contract screenwriters Mark Hellinger, Robert Rossen, and Jerry Wald, made by contract director Raoul Walsh, and featured contract stars James Cagney and Humphrey Bogart.

As Richard Maltby states, like the rest of the cast and crew, 'Most stars were employed on long, fixed-term contracts with a single studio, and had relatively little control over the roles they were cast in or movies they made' (2003: 142). The star system was therefore central to the standardisation of the Hollywood film product from 1930 to 1950: stars were closely associated with the studio that they were contracted to and studios often produced 'star vehicles' in order to either build up or trade on a particular star's talents, audience appeal or persona. Since the decline of the studio system in the early 1950s, mainstream Hollywood is of course no longer able to exert such absolute control over its films, filmmakers and stars, but it appears that in the major adult production studios this old model is still dominant.

Digital Playground and Adam & Eve, the two adult film companies that co-produced *Pirates*, certainly seem to have made good use of many of the organisational strategies developed in studio era Hollywood. For example, founded in North Carolina in 1970, Adam & Eve currently consists of a production company, commercial website, retail stores, wholesale distribution department and range of branded products such as Adam & Eve lubricant, condoms, sex toys and even cologne. In this way, Adam & Eve's involvement in all three branches of its business – manufacture, wholesale and retail – mirrors the working model of vertical integration employed by the most successful film companies of the Hollywood studio system.

Stars are also as important to the organisation of the contemporary adult film industry as they were to the major studios in classical Hollywood; Adam & Eve and Digital Playground each have a list of contracted stars who regularly feature in their porn productions. *Pirates*' central female cast is made up of contract performers from both film companies: Adam & Eve's Carmen Luvana and Austyn Moore, and popular 'DP Girls' Jesse Jane, Janine, Tegan Presley and Devon. Casting these contract stars together gave *Pirates* a unique opportunity to appeal to the fan following of each actress and to maximise on the impact of them literally being together in the same film.

In *Pirates*, the scenes featuring Jane with Janine and Luvana provide useful examples of the enormous novelty value and spectacle that their combined billing afforded both the film's production companies and the actresses' many fans. *Pirates*' publicity traded heavily on the fact that this was the very first time that Jane had shared a girl/girl scene with either fellow DP Girl Janine, or Adam & Eve's contract star Luvana. During interviews all three performers were extremely enthusiastic about one another and the experience of finally getting to work together: Luvana couldn't enough of Jane, 'Jesse's insatiable sexuality was a fantasy I can dream about over and again'. Janine agreed, 'What a pleasure to experience Jesse Jane's authentic sexual energy, which I'm still reeling from. She is the future of porn. The scale of this production is nothing I've ever experienced [before].' Jane enjoyed them both, 'I have had sex with girls on and off camera for most of my adult life. No one has ever compared to Janine or Carmen Luvana' (Digital Playground 2005a). With these words, the film's contract stars promised its audience an event so exciting and so intense, they were still aroused by it.

This discourse of mutual appreciation, satisfaction and endorsement was part of the hype around *Pirates* controlled by its production companies. Simpson notes that, similar to actors in studio era Hollywood, the adult industry's use of the contract system means that 'Porn stars are bound to a particular producer or production company... This obligation includes willingness to participate on studio-arranged publicity and image "branding"' (2005: 34–5). Indeed, image branding was used extensively to promote *Pirates*' DVD release; Luvana and Jane were paired up by Adam & Eve and Digital Playground and sent out together on a two-month-long promotional tour across America. During the tour Jane and Luvana made appearances on local radio stations and in adult stores where they reportedly autographed full size film posters and DVDs 'to hundreds of fans for hours, well beyond their scheduled signing time'. Their pairing can be read as symbolic of mutual promotion: it supports the image of the performers as A-list porn 'super stars', the image of alliance between the two 'esteemed' contract companies they represent, and by association the image of *Pirates* as a high quality hard-core production (Digital Playground 2005c).

In addition to its contract stars, Digital Playground also supplied *Pirates* with its production crew. The film's director (and DP's co-founder) Joone, screenwriter Max Massimo, and editor Joey Pulgadas, are all regular members of the company's production team. In total, DP employs three contract directors: Robby D. makes the company's gonzo releases including the *Jack's Playground* series (2003–); female director Celeste (also known as Bunny Luv) produces erotic and artistic couples-orientated films such as *Intoxicated* (2005) and *Jesse Jane Sexy Hot* (2008), and Joone directs the annual big budget features like *Pirates* and the *Island Fever* series (2001–07). It seems reasonable to assume that, similar to the discussion of the studio system above, the presence of regular creative and technical personnel at DP might give them the opportunity to exert an influence over the studio's house style. Notably, the company's mission statement stresses that all of its releases, which ever one of its filmmakers is responsible, aim to emphasise

> quality first employing fastidiously high production values in erotic film for women, men and couples. Digital Playground's commitment to excellence, innovative technology, brilliant full-length productions and exclusive contract stars are the secret to its success. (2006a)

This rather grand mission statement highlights the importance of new technologies to the development of the adult industry as a whole, and to Digital Playground in particular. In this respect *Pirates* is also a film that showcases the studio's distinctive house style, using new technologies and formats to enhance its overall look and content.

TECHNOLOGICAL DEVELOPMENTS IN A DIGITAL PLAYGROUND

It is well documented that the rapid growth of the hard-core porn business, like all media industries, has been closely linked to ongoing developments in technology. In *Pornocopia*, Laurence O'Toole examines the ways in which new technologies such as video, cable and the internet have shaped and impacted on the contemporary porn industry. From its humble pre-cinematic origins in photographic stills and peep shows to the first vintage stag reels, porn, O'Toole says, 'has never been slow to embrace new technologies' (1999: 61). Before the introduction of the internet, he identifies the rise of video hard-core in the 1980s as 'a truly major event' in the evolution of the porn industry; one that 'changed everything, for better and for worse' (1999: 103). Video technology helped to democratise porn, making hard-core easy and affordable for people to watch, and even to make, in their own homes.

However, most significantly for this investigation into the relationship between Hollywood and hard-core, is that the boom in home video and amateur porn during the late 1980s was accompanied by what O'Toole describes as 'the decline of big-budget cinema hard-core productions. The last of the theatre, the costumes, the sets, the glamour' (1999: 104). It was during porn's so-called 'Golden Age' from the 1970s to the early 1980s that a number of hard-core features with plots, including *Deep Throat* (1972), *Behind the Green Door* (1972) and *The Devil in Miss Jones* (1973), had successfully managed to crossover into the mainstream where they were widely promoted and watched in cinemas as regular films.

The (lack of) importance of porn's narrative structure is discussed in more detail later in this chapter, when *Pirates* is considered as a hard-core version of the Hollywood blockbuster *Pirates of the Caribbean*. However, the point to stress here is that technology has influenced trends in porn production, as evidenced by the example of the introduction of domestic video. O'Toole goes on to connect the new computer technologies of the 1990s to a return – by some of the larger hard-core production companies wishing to stand out from the low-end suppliers – to relatively high-cost, high-quality 'porno de luxe' films that are capable of making a huge profit (1999: 181). Founded in 1993, Digital Playground can be understood as part of this trend of contemporary porn producers who continually invest in and sometimes even pioneer technological innovations in order to prosper in an ever more competitive marketplace.

Digital Playground's image as an upmarket porn studio is, therefore, based chiefly upon the company's contributions to and uses of the various new technologies available to the adult film industry. Beginning in 1994, for instance, DP created, produced and trademarked (in 2005) its 'Virtual Sex' line of interactive DVDs. Titles from the *Virtual Sex* series such as *Virtual Sex with Janine* (2002) and *Virtual Sex with Jesse Jane* (2003) allow viewers to experience interactive sex with the company's contract performers. Using DP's 'advanced cyber sex simulator', referred to as 'FantaVR', the viewer is able to control and direct the featured porn star, choosing the camera angle (multiple angles are available, including 'POV'), sexual position ('regular', 'titty' and 'anal') and mood ('innocent' or 'nasty') from a menu of basic options ('story', 'foreplay', 'strip' and 'sex') at the push of a button (see Digital Playground 2006a).

In this way, the *Virtual Sex* series uses technological advances in DVD to offer the viewer a first-person experience and tailor the hard-core action according to his/her own fantasies and desires. As a result, the series has been featured in a number of media articles that deal with recent technological developments made by the adult industry, including a report in the *New York Times*, 'The Fantasy of Interactive Porn Becomes a Reality' (Kennedy 2003). But while interactive DVDs have been criticised by some members of the porn industry, who argue that they are devoid of storyline and therefore of questionable value, other more mainstream, and less controversial, technological advances are also used by Digital Playground to develop its high-quality brand image.

Beyond the *Virtual Sex* series, then, Digital Playground has a long list of other technological firsts to its credit. In 2004, the company released *Island Fever 3*, the first adult title to be filmed, edited and delivered in High Definition (HD) format. In 2005 it released the first adult iPod trailers, and in 2007 it launched websites that made the first hard-core sex scenes available for purchase on the new iPhone. Most recently, having become the first adult studio to announce its future commitment to the Blu-ray format instead of rival HD-DVD in January 2006, the porn industry trade paper *Adult Video News* (*AVN*) reported that DP 'will release all new titles simultaneously on standard DVD and Blu-ray disc' (Sullivan 2008).

To add to these firsts, having been shot using high definition digital video cameras, *Pirates* was the company's first Blu-ray release at the end of 2007, ranking as online retailer *Adult DVD Empire*'s number one bestselling Blu-ray disc 'of all time' to date (September 2008). The Blu-ray version of *Pirates* was 'the first to offer the movie and all of its supplemental features in 1080p resolution, containing over six hours of footage on a single disc' (Warren 2007). Interviewed by Peter Warren for *AVN* about *Pirates*' high volume Blu-ray sales, DP's co-founder and CEO Samantha Lewis stated:

> I think especially in adult, there's nothing like [high definition] ... if you shoot with the good cameras, and you're lighting it correctly, and you're shooting it like a true filmmaker, there's nothing better. You are as close and as real as you can get. (Ibid.)

This comment calls attention to the major draws that new media formats like Blu-ray have for both porn producers and consumers. High-end producers, such as DP, continue to market hard-core films based on their superior production values, but can now offer versions in a new format that delivers exceptionally high-quality playback and more data storage than a standard

DVD. Porn consumers are given the opportunity to experience high-definition adult productions with advanced video and audio qualities that, it is argued, make the sex on screen appear crisper, clearer and closer to the Hollywood cinematic experience of 35mm film.

As stated above, historically, porn studios are well known for being 'ahead of the curve' when it comes to technology, and in media articles about the war between HD-DVD and Blu-ray it has widely been acknowledged the adult industry can greatly impact on and influence the future of the high-definition format (see Gardiner 2007). Significantly, Sony's initial refusal to allow companies to mass-produce hard-core porn on Blu-ray discs has not stopped the adult industry from embracing this new technology and responding with typical speed to consumer demand, in this case, for high-definition adult material (see Richtel 2007).

Returning once more to Simpson's work on the porn business, a final point of comparison can thus be made between studio system Hollywood and the contemporary adult industry. She notes that, 'The pornography business and Studio-era Hollywood have both adapted quickly to new technology that helps them reach audiences' (2005: 33). For, in the same way that major technological advances made during the studio era, such as sound, colour and widescreen, were all quickly appropriated in order to provide novelty value and attract audiences, companies like Digital Playground have also used new technical developments to reinvigorate the porn industry and enhance the viewing experience.

Although it must be acknowledged that there are, of course, several points of difference between the two systems (see Simpson 2005: 33–5), the many parallels that can usefully be drawn between them suggests that the contemporary porn industry has effectively 'skimmed' (Simpson 2005: 32), or perhaps more fittingly 'knocked off', the most successful features of the business model provided by studio-era Hollywood. The result is a hard-core version of a classic mainstream model and a point of crossover between sex and the Hollywood system that, I argue, the production of Adam & Eve and Digital Playground's pornographic feature film *Pirates* demonstrates at the levels of industry *and* content.

PIRATES DOES DISNEY: ADVENTURE, SPECIAL EFFECTS AND 'SWASHBUCKLING SEX'

In terms of subject matter and storyline *Pirates* is in fact just one of the many contemporary hard-core productions that have in some way parodied or played on the mainstream success of Disney's multi-billion dollar *Pirates of the Caribbean* franchise. Following the 2003 release of the first instalment in the original *Pirates of the Caribbean* trilogy, a flurry of porn films and series, such as *Girl Pirates* (2005–06), *Surrender the Booty* (2005–06), *Butthole Pirates* (2005–06) and *Seymore Butts' Butt Pirates of the Caribbean* (2006), has sought to appeal to audiences by punning on the title or theme of the popular Hollywood original. Dependent on genre, category and audience, each of these porn versions develops a unique (if sometimes dubious) relationship to the original film, defined by hard-core sex.

For example, similar to *Pirates*, Loaded Digital's *Surrender the Booty* combines pirate iconography and settings with sex, including anal and girl-on-girl, for a straight audience. As a result, *AVN*'s reviewer recommends this film as a kind of pornographic stop-gap for fans of the original: 'hot action, fun costumes and settings make this a winner for those who have already watched *Pirates of the Caribbean* 500 times and need something else to watch while they're waiting for the sequel' (LeRoy 2005).

In contrast, aside from the allusions made by its title and the pirate ship logo featured on the DVD box cover, Clydesdale Studio's *Butthole Pirates* (2005) makes no direct reference to either the Hollywood film, or piracy at sea. Consequently, *AVN* acknowledges that the title of *Butthole Pirates* is rather 'misleading' – for whilst scenes of hard-core gay sex are clearly a given, surprisingly there isn't a single jolly roger or a cutlass in sight, and none of the scenarios are based around what would commonly be understood as a pirate theme (see Patrick 2005).[2] Clydesdale Studio's disingenuous titling of *Butthole Pirates* is, then, a perfect illustration of the adult industry's opportunistic ability to exploit popular mainstream film titles, series and genres, however tenuous the connection between them might turn out to be.

In a collection of essays that charts the international impact of another mainstream film trilogy, *The Lord of the Rings* (2001–03), cult film critic I. Q. Hunter explores the intertextual relationship between contemporary cinema and its porn parodies by examining *Lord of the G-Strings: The Femaleship of the String* (2002), an erotic spoof of *The Fellowship of the Ring* (2001). Situating *Lord of the G-Strings* alongside such memorable titles as *Harry Potter Made the Philosopher Moan*, *Lawrence of Labia* and *The Sperminator*, Hunter states that, beyond the obvious joke made at the beginning, these porn versions 'rarely go much further than punning on the titles and lifting the basic situations of the original films' (2006: 318). He does however note that, for the critic at least, some porn parodies still prove engaging, especially when they 'reimagine' certain aspects of the original film. Thus he goes on to argue for the subversive potential of *Lord of the G-Strings*, which he says helps to unlock some of the 'repressions and erotic possibilities' of the original, including homoeroticism and the punishment of female sexuality (2006: 325). At the very least, Hunter suggests, pornographic versions – particularly hard-core pornographic versions – of mainstream films provide 'raunchy reproaches to Hollywood's squeamishness about sex' (2006: 318). For these reasons *Pirates* can also be thought of as a typical hard-core porn version. Arguably, it is this emphasis on hard-core sex that makes *Pirates*, like so many other contemporary porn versions, a film that is at once so much more and so much less than the mainstream original it takes from. It is therefore essential that the key differences and similarities between the Hollywood film *Pirates of the Caribbean* and the porn film *Pirates* are taken into account. This is a comparison that must, inevitably, centre on the representation of sex.

Like *The Lord of the Rings*, *Pirates of the Caribbean* is part of the wider fantasy film genre and combines action, adventure, humour and romance to appeal to both children and adults. The story of the first film follows blacksmith Will Turner (Orlando Bloom) and eccentric pirate Captain Jack Sparrow (Johnny Depp) as they join together in an attempt to rescue Turner's childhood love, Elizabeth Swann (Keira Knightly), and recapture Jack's ship, the Black Pearl, from the cursed Captain Barbossa (Geoffrey Rush) and his undead crew. Unusually for a Disney labelled release, *Pirates of the Caribbean* received a PG-13 certificate at cinemas in the US and a 12A in the UK. But this was because the film featured action/adventure violence and undead pirates rather than any nudity or sex and, aside from Captain Jack's innuendo-filled banter with just about every character he meets during the course of his adventures, the narrative contains very few direct sexual references. As a porn version aimed solely at an adult audience of men, women and couples, *Pirates* is, by comparison, made up of dialogue, performers and a plot that are motivated principally by sexual fantasy and hard-core sex. Nevertheless, the film does still manage to either imitate or adapt important elements of the mainstream original, including setting, special effects, storyline and character.

For example, in what remains a relatively rare departure from the porn industry's otherwise familiar tendency for sticking to low budgets and artificial studio settings, Digital Playground used location shooting, costumes, props and even a replica sailing ship to create *Pirates*' eighteenth-century backdrop and stage its main action. The filmmakers also construct a detailed setting that, although far from historically accurate, supports both the narrative and spectacle of sex. This selection and control over aspects of *mise-en-scène* begins with the film's very first sex scene between newlyweds Isabella (Carmen Luvana) and Manuel Valenzuela (Kris Slater).

Pirates opens with an establishing shot of a ship at sea, followed by a cut to a cabin on board in which the couple are about to consummate their marriage. The characters and set are given, as much as possible, a generic eighteenth-century feel. In contrast to noticeable twenty-first-century modifications such as shaved genitals, tattoos and false fingernails, Isabella and Manuel both wear period-themed costumes and their cabin is lavishly furnished with oil paintings, a lace dressing screen, draped curtains and a large comfortable-looking bed that is surrounded by candles. The lighting quality of this scene is relatively soft and emulates candlelight, alternatively masking and revealing parts of their bodies. The style of the actors' sexual performance is similarly romanticised and the couple's first encounter certainly appears tender, by porn standards at least, as they lovingly move from oral sex to penetration followed by the obligatory 'money' (ejaculation) shot, before finally ending the scene with a kiss. In the context of the overall film, these elements of *mise-en-scène* all add to the narrative function of this particular scene, establishing Isabella and Manuel as a romantic couple whose relationship will form one of *Pirates*' two major plotlines.

For a porn film, *Pirates* can also be thought to feature especially 'lavish' visual effects, including green screen and CGI animation (see McGinn 2005: 8). Much has been made of the numerous special effects (in total they allegedly number over three hundred) used in the making of *Pirates*, not least of all by the film's co-production company Digital Playground. Even prior to the film's release, DP's marketing emphasised *Pirates*' mix of special effects, sex and storyline, and it was widely publicised that 'skeleton warriors, awe-inspiring Incan magic, grandiose sea battles *and* ten of the most arousing sex scenes' combined to make this porn production 'an action packed, electrifying and swashbuckling sex-tale' (Digital Playground 2007). This publicity material calls attention to the fact that, in addition to the obvious primary spectacle of hard-core sex, *Pirates* also seeks to offer its audience a secondary, but no less stimulating, form of visual spectacle more closely associated with Hollywood cinema in general and *Pirates of the Caribbean* in particular.

In many ways, such pornographic feature films share with mainstream Hollywood the tension that exists between narrative and spectacle. Writing about the contemporary Hollywood blockbuster, Geoff King observes that, 'The narrative coherence of the blockbuster is often said to have been undermined by an emphasis on the provision of over-powering spectacle'; this is because 'spectacular imagery, of various kinds, sells' (2002: 179). This is of course a discussion that can just as easily be applied to porn production. Linda Williams has explored how for the first time, during the 1970s, certain pornographic feature-length films mentioned above successfully 'managed to integrate a variety of sexual numbers ... into a narrative' (1990: 99). Like these 'Golden Age' porn classics, *Pirates* integrates hard-core sex into a narrative, but unlike them, it also employs the visual effects typical of contemporary Hollywood blockbusters.

For *Pirates of the Caribbean*, the visual effects company Industrial Light & Magic (ILM; founded by George Lucas) used CGI to stage key action sequences such as the ships at sea and the skeletal pirates. Designed by Digital Playground's own in-house post-production effects team (another rarity among contemporary adult studios), *Pirates*' use of special effects

– admittedly unimpressive when compared to Hollywood, but rather impressive when compared to most porn – clearly takes its cue from the mainstream original. Similar to *Pirates of the Caribbean*, *Pirates* uses digital animation to enhance location shooting, simulate scenes of ships at sea, and create an army of skeletons.

Granted, these effects are far from sophisticated, and they might even be thought to threaten the porn film's generic foregrounding of sex and thus the viewer's all-important masturbatory pleasures. For instance, at sea, the ships glide serenely over the waves rather than rolling realistically through them, and the armed skeletons are more reminiscent of Ray Harryhausen's stop-motion animation in *Jason and the Argonauts* (1963) than ILM's digitally-layered designs that reveal Barbossa's undead crew, complete with decomposing flesh, under the moonlight in *Pirates of the Caribbean*. In an otherwise enthusiastic review of DP's film for *Adult DVD Reviews*, Dr Jay complains, 'I remember thinking to myself "gee, why isn't the ship rocking" as I watched couples fuck aboard the ship. That's not what my mind should have been on during sex scenes' (2005). Nevertheless, it is significant that *Pirates* uses special effects to imitate the visual style of the original film, and in both cases CGI is an important part of the overall fantasy, storyline and aesthetic.

Compared to *Pirates of the Caribbean*'s Hollywood budget, which is estimated on the Internet Movie Database at somewhere around US$140 million, *Pirates*' cost at just over one million dollars might sound rather cheap, but still reportedly made it the most expensive porn film in history. Even for Digital Playground – a contemporary adult company which has worked hard to foster its image as an upmarket studio – the film was recognised by the porn industry and its audiences as an extraordinary landmark achievement and 'a blue movie for the ages' (McGinn 2005: 8). Adult film critic and fan Roger Pipe's opinion that '*Pirates* is a perfect blend of technical brilliance, entertaining storytelling, gorgeous babes and hot sex' (2005) and *AVN* reviewer Jared Rutter's admiration for director Joone's 'sure hand with story material, pacing the action well' (2005) are indicative of this largely positive response.

Notably, and unusually for a porn film, both reviews pay tribute to the high standard of *Pirates*' storyline. When making porn films, as Edward Buscombe states, 'One way of supplying at least a modicum of narrative structure is to steal it from elsewhere' (2004: 27). This 'parasitic' pornographic custom is adhered to and exploited by *Pirates*. Clear echoes of *Pirates of the Caribbean*'s narrative appear in the film's plot, which chronicles the adventures of evil Captain Victor Stagnetti (Tommy Gunn) and his first mate Serena (Janine), newlywed couple Manuel and Isabella, and a heroic crew of pirate hunters led by the comically inept Captain Edward Reynolds (Evan Stone). In *Pirates*, Stagnetti's hunt for a magical Incan staff causes him to kidnap Manuel who, as a direct descendent of an Incan king, possesses an inherited power.

This is evidently drawn from the Disney version, where a similar kidnapping occurs because Captain Barbossa believes that Elizabeth (rather than Will) is Bootstrap Bill's child and so has the ability to break the ancient curse that he and his crew were placed under when they stole Aztec gold. For audiences already familiar with the Hollywood original there are, therefore, obvious correspondences between the narrative tensions and character motivations of the two films.

Pirates is, however, at its most unashamedly parodic in its interpretation of Johnny Depp's character in *Pirates of the Caribbean*, Captain Jack Sparrow. Played by Depp, Captain Jack is perhaps best described as idiosyncratic, a mannered performance which combines roguish sexuality with off the wall humour and anti-heroic qualities. In *Pirates* considerable effort is made to retain a great deal of the spirit of Captain Jack, but the porn film's habitual emphasis on sexual (rather than acting) performances can be thought to result in a key change that is the separation of appearance from characterisation. Whereas *Pirates*' villain Captain Victor Stagnetti owes much of his costume and look to Captain Jack (he also wears a bandana and black eye makeup, has long black hair, a goatee with two beaded braids, gold teeth and a leather pirates hat), it is the film's hero, Captain Jack Reynolds, who takes on Depp's lighter and more comic characteristics.

Similar to Depp's Captain Jack, *Pirates*' Captain Reynolds is portrayed as having a huge ego and as having embellished his own reputation; he is reliant on rhetoric rather than his skills as a captain. Early on in the film, Reynolds' arrogantly dictates his captain's log, in which he mythologises both his crew and himself. During this sequence his comically misguided voiceover description of what he believes to be first mate Jules' ability to motivate the male crew members 'by helping them improve their oral skills or perhaps even bible study', is undercut by a montage where she is seen having oral and straight sex with a variety of crew members and in a variety of positions. It is in such moments that, as Hunter says of *Lord of the G-Strings*, *Pirates* can sometimes be left 'hovering awkwardly between parody and porn' (2006: 322). For while, unlike many pornographic feature films, *Pirates* does, on the whole, manage to maintain a connection between coherent narrative and sex scenes, the parodic handling of a main character like Captain Reynolds does not always sit so easily when it comes to his own rather uncharacteristically 'solemn bouts' of hard-core sex (2006: 323).

THE *PIRATES* PHENOMENON GOES MAINSTREAM

It would seem fair to suggest, then, that *Pirates*' status as a hard-core version of a contemporary Hollywood film comes with its own difficulties to be negotiated. Not only is *Pirates* like and unlike mainstream cinema, it is also like and unlike other feature-length porn. Although perennial differences in industry and content mean that it still remains highly problematic to judge most porn by the standards of mainstream cinema (see Hunter 2012), a film like *Pirates* is clearly both playful and calculated in its response to the success of the Hollywood blockbuster *Pirates of the Caribbean*.

As already discussed, marketed to porn audiences, *Pirates* was advertised first and foremost in terms of its A-list sexual performers and sex scenes, with the added, secondary spectacle of special effects that helped its co-producers to emulate the visual style of the original film. But *Pirates*' investment in traditionally mainstream production values does not end there, and nor has its appeal. Not only was the entire film shot and mastered on High Definition, it also used a professional script, a sizeable cast that included non-sex roles, and a music score that was later made available as standalone Original Motion Picture Soundtrack. Furthermore, *Pirates* was initially released on a triple disc set: the first DVD contains the standard-resolution version of the film; the second contains the film in HD format and the third, standard-resolution, disc contains special features including behind the scenes, casting video, photo gallery, *Pirates* short, trailers, visual FX making of and cast biographies. With the inclusion of a wide selection of 'bonus' material and the upgraded audiovisual quality offered as part of this triple disc set – temptingly titled *Pirates Collector's Edition* – Digital Playground and Adam & Eve have sought to replicate the mainstream's common commercial strategy for using DVD extras to capture (and re-capture) audiences.

Finally, the print, design and gatefold presentation of the DVD box also signal that, as a total package, *Pirates* is committed to high-quality production values. Set alongside one another, the similarities between the box covers of *Pirates of the Caribbean* and *Pirates* are, no doubt, far from coincidental. Here, as

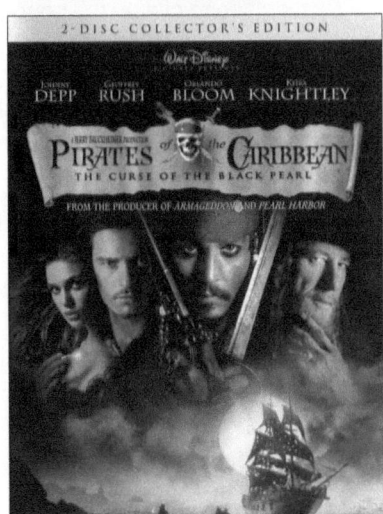

Fig. 15 and Fig. 16 *Pirates*' DVD cover (top) takes its inspiration from the design for *Pirates of the Caribbean* (bottom).

elsewhere, the porn film takes liberally from mainstream Hollywood, favouring the reproduction of some of the original's iconography over allusions to hard-core sex and sexuality which, on the front cover at least, remain limited to the generous bosoms and pouting lips of its female porn stars.

Ultimately, though, *Pirates* became more than just another hard-core version of a popular Hollywood film phenomenon. Indeed, *Pirates* was arguably a mainstream cultural phenomenon in its own right. In addition to using an extensive marketing campaign, high production values and adult media hype, Digital Playground and Adam & Eve also gave *Pirates* a 'mainstream' premiere, held at the Egyptian Theatre in Hollywood. With a full red carpet, gift bags, a pirate band, fire breathers and 'the feel of a XXX-rated 18th Century theme park', *Pirates*' premiere was staged in a similar, extravagant, style to those premieres typically held to celebrate the release of contemporary blockbusters (Digital Playground 2005b). (Interestingly enough, *Pirates of the Caribbean*'s world premiere really had taken place in a theme park, Disneyland California.) Because theatrical premieres are comparatively uncommon in the porn industry, this made *Pirates*' release a major event that attracted attention from the mainstream media. For example, the weekly entertainment magazine *Variety* featured a tongue-in-cheek article on this 'unusual' film premiere (Ron and Harris 2005: 19).

Pirates also received coverage from *Newsweek* in November 2005, when it received a record twenty-four nominations for *AVN*'s forthcoming 2006 award ceremony, called the 'Oscars of porn'. *Newsweek* compared *Pirates* to another successful Hollywood blockbuster, predicting that the film 'seems poised to pile up the honours the way *The Aviator* (2004) dominated this year's Oscars' (McGinn 2005: 8). This prediction proved to be accurate as not only did *Pirates* dominate *AVN*'s 2006 awards (where it won in eleven categories including Best Director, Best Special Effects and Best Video Feature), it subsequently won a variety of other major porn prizes, including Best Epic and Best Release at the 2006 X-Rated Critics Organisation Award Show (XRCO) and 2005 Viewer's Choice (plus five other award categories) at the Adult DVD Empire Awards.

As James F. English points out, the awards in the porn industry work in essentially the same way as the corresponding awards in the mainstream film industry, and in both cases they 'play a formidable role in establishing the symbolic and economic hierarchies in their field' (2005: 97). Too numerous to provide a complete list here, *Pirates*' many porn awards can be thought to function as a symbol of cultural prestige that directly links to the film's reported bestselling sales and rentals records (see Stanton 2006).

However, *Pirates*' most significant move towards mainstream cinema and audiences occurred in May 2006 when an edited version of the film received an R-rating from the Motion Picture Association of America (MPAA). The fact that *Pirates* had its hard-core sex scenes cut and there was actually still a film to watch is further testament, if not to the quality of either the acting or dialogue, to the presence of a storyline and characters. The precise nature of the relationship between the original XXX release and the R-rated version of *Pirates* must, unfortunately, form part of another study at another time. At present, and in the context of this final part of the discussion of *Pirates* as a mainstream cultural phenomenon, I wish only to call attention to the way that the R-rated version was used by its co-producers to generate more hype around the film and as an extended advert for the XXX original.

It is no secret that Digital Playground and Adam & Eve timed the release of R-rated *Pirates* to coincide with the theatrical release of the second instalment in the Hollywood trilogy, *Pirates of the Caribbean: Dead Man's Chest* (2006). Peter Lehman has argued that, in the adult industry, the pleasure (and profit) of 'selling trash in relationship to respectability' is one of the main, transgressive functions of parodic porn 'remakes' of Hollywood cinema (1996: 48). After having reportedly endured a difficult, six-month-long struggle with the MPAA in order to achieve an R-rating, *Pirates*' co-producers would presumably have taken particular pleasure from once again selling the film in relationship to the Hollywood franchise. Moreover, an R-rating meant that an even closer relationship could be established between the two. For the first time *Pirates* was able to occupy the same shelf space in legitimate stores and rental outlets as the original Hollywood film and, marketed and distributed to mainstream audiences, the boundary between 'trash' and 'respectability' had become well and truly blurred.

When interviewed, though, Joone suggested another transgressive function of the R-rated version that is equally as valuable. He commented that 'a lot of people will see the R-rated version of *Pirates* and then they'll want to see the adult version, just to see what they missed' (2006b). Without detailed audience research it is of course impossible to say whether or not audiences really have responded to the R-rated version in this way. But clearly, as Joone points out, *Pirates*' R-rated version can be viewed at one level as little more than a long and clever 'commercial' for the XXX original. So it is possible that, in this way, porn production and its audience crossover to the mainstream and vice versa.

At the time of writing, *Pirates*' assault on the mainstream is far from over. In the same way that Disney ensured that the box-office success of *Pirates of the Caribbean* meant that it became the first film in a series (with two back-to-back sequels, *Dead Man's Chest* and *At World's End*, released in 2006 and 2007 respectively and a fourth instalment, *On Stranger Tides*, out in 2011), Digital Playground has also followed up *Pirates*' success with the sequel *Pirates II: Stagnetti's Revenge*, released in September 2008. *Pirates II* uses many of the same central characters and continues the storyline of the first film. But ultimately, and in true blockbuster style, *Pirates II* aimed to outstrip the spectacle of the original, delivering audiences more special effects, more contract stars, and even bigger production values than before. In an industry where size is everything, the *Pirates* phenomenon reached epic proportions. Forty years after feature-length porn's brief challenge to Hollywood in the 1970s, *Pirates*' crossover appeal and marketability begins to suggest that, at the beginning of the twenty-first century, the era of the mainstream pornographic blockbuster might finally have arrived.

NOTES

1 Thanks to Darren Kerr for suggesting the title and topic of this chapter to me. Thanks also to Jacqueline Furby and Donna Peberdy for their comments.
2 *Butthole Pirates* actually features three outdoor scenarios based around a hitchhiker, a nude sunbather and a 'middle-aged businessman type' (Patrick 2005).

WORKS CITED

Buscombe, E. (2004) 'Generic Overspill: A Dirty Western', in P. Church Gibson (ed.) *More Dirty Looks: Gender, Pornography and Power*. London: BFI, 27–30.

Digital Playground (2005a) 'Digital Playground to Debut *Pirates* at VSDA'. Press release, 22 July. On-line. Available: http://www.piratesxxx.com/main.php?tab=news&newsid=830 (accessed 22 April 2008).

____ (2005b) '*Pirates* Premiere Unprecedented'. Press release, 14 September. On-line. Available: http://www.piratesxxx.com/main.php?tab=news&newsid=838 (accessed 22 April 2008).

____ (2005c) '*Pirates* Outselling the Competition'. Press release, 4 October. On-line. Available: http://www.piratesxxx.com/main.php?tab=news&newsid=841 (accessed 22 April 2008).

____ (2006a) 'Joone's R-Rated *Pirates* Releases Worldwide'. Press release, 10 July. On-line. Available: http://www.piratesxxx.com/main.php?tab=news&newsid=899 (22 April 2008).

____ (2006b) 'Joone's *Pirates* Sets Industry-Wide Sales Record'. Press release, 2 October. On-line. Available: http://www.piratesxxx.com/main.php?tab=news&newsid=931 (accessed 22 April 2008).

____ (2007) 'Digital Playground Goes Blu-Ray with *Pirates*'. Press release, 20 December. On-line. Available: http://www.piratesxxx.com/main.php?tab=news&newsid=989 (accessed 22 April 2008).

English, J. F. (2005) *The Economy of Prestige: Prizes, Awards and the Circulation of Cultural Value*. Cambridge, MA: Harvard University Press.

Gardiner, B. (2007) 'Porn Industry May Decide Format War'. *Fox News*, 22 January. On-line.

Available: http://www.foxnews.com/story/0,2933,245638,00.html (accessed 10 August 2008).

Hunter, I. Q. (2006) 'Tolkien Dirty', in E. Mathijs (ed.) *The Lord of the Rings: Popular Culture in Global Context*. London: Wallflower Press, 317–33.

____ (2012) 'A Clockwork Orgy: A User's Guide', in X. Mendik (ed.) *Peep Shows: Cult Films and the Cine-Erotic*. London: Wallflower Press.

Jay, Dr (2005) 'Pirates – Collector's Edition'. *Adult DVD Reviews*. On-line. Available: http://www.actiondvd.com/info.asp?product_id=STDV25853&rvw=2570&userid=0D00D26 8-BE69-4AD9-8D8F-29C3A2031FA1 (accessed 10 August 2008).

Kennedy, D. (2003) 'The Fantasy of Interactive Porn Becomes a Reality', *New York Times*, 17 August. On-line. Available: http://www.nytimes.com/2003/08/17/movies/17KENN.html?pagewanted=1 (accessed 10 August 2008).

King, G. (2002) *New Hollywood Cinema: An Introduction*. London: I. B. Tauris.

Kuhn, A. and T. Schatz (2007) 'The Classic Studio System', in P. Cook (ed.) *The Cinema Book*. Third Edition. London: BFI, 19–20.

Lehman, P. (1996) 'Twin Cheeks, Twin Peeks and Twin Freaks: Porn's Transgressive Remake Humour', in B. Braendlin and H. Braendlin (eds) *Authority and Transgression in Literature and Film*. Gainesville: University Press of Florida, 45–54.

LeRoy, N. (2005) 'Surrender the Booty'. *AVN*, November. On-line. Available: http://www.avn.com/movies/61985.html (accessed 10 August 2008).

Maltby, R. (2003) *Hollywood Cinema*. Second Edition. Oxford: Blackwell.

McGinn, D. (2005) 'XXX Blue, Spending Green', *Newsweek*, 28 November, 8.

O'Toole, L. (1999) *Pornocopia: Porn, Sex, Technology and Desire*. Second Edition. London: Serpent's Tail.

Patrick, R. (2005) 'Butthole Pirates'. *AVN*, June. On-line. Available: http://www.avn.com/gay/movies/59129.html (accessed 10 August 2008).

Pipe, R. (2005) 'Pirates'. *RogReviews*, July. On-line. Available: http:///www.rogreviews.com/reviews/read_review.asp?sku=3748 (accessed 7 July 2008).

Rich, F. (2003) 'Naked Capitalists', in G. Dines and J. M. Humez (eds) *Gender, Race, and Class in the Media: A Text-Reader*. Second edition. London: Sage, 28–60.

Richtel, M. (2007) 'In Raw World of Sex Movies, High Definition Could Be a View Too Real', *New York Times*, 22 January. On-line. Available: http://www.nytimes.com/2007/01/22/business/media/22porn.html (accessed 10 August 2008).

Ron, T. and D. Harris (2005) '*Pirates* Pic Unbuckled', *Variety*, 15 September, 19.

Rutter, J. (2005) 'Pirates'. *AVN*, December. On-line. Available: http://avn.com/movies/62399.html (accessed 19 September 2008).

Ryall, T. (1978) *Teachers Study Guide No. 2: The Gangster Film*. London: BFI.

Simpson, N. (2004) 'Coming Attractions: A Comparative History of the Hollywood Studio System and the Porn Business', *Historical Journal of Film, Radio and Television*, 24, 4, 635–52.

____ (2005) 'The Money Shot: The Business of Porn', *Critical Sense*, 13, 1 Spring, 11–40.

Stanton, T. J. (2006) '*Pirates* Reaches One-Year Milestone on AVN's Sales Chart'. *AVN*, 30 September. On-line. Available: http://www.avn.com/video/articles/5966.html (accessed 16 October 2008).

Sullivan, D. (2008) 'Digital Playground Adopts Day/Date Release Schedule for Blu-ray'. *AVN*,

9 June. On-line Available: http://www.avn.com/video/articles/30651.html (accessed 10 August 2008).

Warren, P. (2007) 'Digital Playground: *Pirates* Blu-ray 'Selling Like Gangbusters''. *AVN*, 28 December. On-line. Available: http://www.avn.com/performer/articles/846.html (accessed 10 August 2008).

Williams, L. (1990) *Hard Core: Power, Pleasure and the 'Frenzy of the Visible'*. London: Pandora.

FLUID EXCHANGES
Hard-core Forms and Aesthetics

CHAPTER NINE

FASHIONABLY LAID: THE STYLING OF HARD-CORE
Pamela Church Gibson and Neil Kirkham

The concept of 'clothes and pornography' might seem puzzling – the two do not, automatically, go hand in hand in the popular imagination. Linda Williams' (1990) conception of the 'frenzy of the visible' suggests that it is the very ability to see that to which we are not usually exposed that governs the aesthetics of the genre. Indeed, the exposure of various bodily parts and the visualisation of the sexual act – something that hard-core pornography requires in order to justify this self-same definition – would seem to suggest that clothes have no relevance within this form of entertainment, that they would simply *get in the way*. And on occasion they do. Some pornography purposely uses clothing to restrict the vision of the voyeur, teasing and gradually allowing the sight of what has been awaited, expected. But by and large, this is just a prelude – eventually the clothes will be shed and the body revealed. The work of Marcel Hénaff on the Marquis de Sade notes how nakedness is essential in the erotic in literature and on film, since 'the bodies being offered still need to give proof of their availability ... to get bodies undressed articulates both a demand for immediacy and submission; the naked body is a body acknowledged to be sexual (nakedness thematises desire) as well as a body without defences (nakedness confirms mastery)' (1999: 126–7).

Clothes are, in fact, extremely important within the narratives of hard-core pornography, since they help to structure and slow down the route towards orgasmic climax. Gradation, or the gradual unfolding of the sexual performance, demands that it be relatively swift – the scenes that litter hard-core pornographic films last, on average, for twenty minutes – but must not finish too precipitately. Both striptease and the slow removal of the clothes of the female performer help to prolong the spectacle – whilst, at the same time, her compliance means that the act itself does not last too long. And as with all film costuming, the clothes possess a second function within the diegesis, beyond their first, which is that of assisting the narrative. Whereas in traditional cinemas, clothing is used to indicate character, occupation and social status, here it is designed to stress the 'compliance' and 'availability' of the female performer.

However, the large-scale sub-genrification of pornography, over the last three decades, has led to some modes of expression that rely more heavily on clothing to stimulate and create the desire of the viewer. The modern, internet-driven sub-genre of 'non-nude pornography', for example, uses clothes in a similar way to its more explicit counterparts – as a tease – but extends this idea, continually and indefinitely. In many ways it is like the opening section of a normal pornographic scenario, yet repeated *ad infinitum*. This sub-genre is defined by conspicuously *clothed* bodies, wearing stereotypical outfits – cheerleader, dominatrix, secretary – or, perhaps, complex arrangements of underwear, including the phenomenon of the 'hand-bra', in which a part of the body itself, even on occasion another, differently-gendered and extraneous body, becomes, itself, a garment.

The work of Laura Kipnis (1996) on transvestite pornography, in which the male participants remain fully covered, albeit by women's clothes, raises interesting questions as to whether or not an image of someone who is not actually naked and openly displaying their genitals can be considered pornographic at all. Kipnis describes how, in her home city of Chicago, such material was in fact considered to be even more offensive than sadomasochistic pornography – something that ties into Walter Kendrick's suggestion that pornography is best defined as 'whatever representations a particular dominant class or group does not want in the hands of another, less dominant class or group' (1987: 92). Deploying Robert Stoller's definition of the genre as material 'that intends to produce a certain response – arousal – in its audience', Kipnis demonstrates that even images of the fully clothed body can be considered 'pornographic', something that suggests that such garments do indeed have a role to play in the construction of the genre (1996: 83).

To imply that examining the language of clothes or, more accurately, *costume* within the 'outlaw genre' of hard-core pornography will, in some way, present bizarre contradictions is both naïve and incorrect. Any informed perusal of fashion and dress, both global and historical, will remind us that the human body is never, ever, totally naked – it is always adorned and decorated in some way, in accordance with social and cultural traditions. No society, however primitive, is without bodily decoration of some kind – face or body painting, tattooing, scarification, ritualised jewellery, and particular arrangements of hair. These sign systems – as with the dress and accessories of more 'advanced' societies – offer encoded information; they proffer clues as to social, and sometimes marital, status. Within advanced capitalism, however, they can take on a further significance – the attempt at proclaiming an individual 'identity' rather than that assigned by society and, furthermore, the 'social status' on display here is often a *desired* social status; the adornment of the self is concerned with *aspiration*. At any given historical moment, the particular presentation of face and body – or their deliberate obscuring – informs us of the social hierarchy in place, of the beliefs, values and customs of a particular society. No writing on or clothing of the body has ever been in any way random – and the body is always a text on which there are indeed some inscriptions, which is encoded in some way. It is invariably 'cooked' rather than 'raw' (see Levi-Strauss 1994).

This chapter will examine the function of adornment and 'clothing' of the body within a genre too often seen as synonymous with simple nudity. It will consider sub-generic films situated within this most stratified and complex of genres and include a detailed case study of John Stagliano's 2002 film *The Fashionistas* – a porn film deliberately yoked to clothing, since it is set within what purports to be the fashion industry. Of course, anyone who has studied hard-core film pornography will know that, firstly, the performers are rarely completely naked – even at the very end of a scene. Secondly, generic conventions dictate that, as long as the genitalia of the female performers are on display and the sexual act can be clearly seen as taking place, any combination of footwear, skirts and tops is possible, permitted, even arguably encouraged.

FASHION PORNOGRAPHY, PORNOGRAPHIC FASHION?

Alistair O'Neill has reminded us that porn sets seem instantly recognisable, even to those possibly unfamiliar with the genre. When well-known photographer Steven Meisel used 'porn sets' as the backdrop for a Calvin Klein fashion shoot, there was an immediate outcry: 'The appropriation of this assemblage of imitation wood-laminate wall coverings and cheap peach coloured carpets ... caused widespread complaint; the poses of the models were ... deemed pornographic in the context of their constructed setting' (2004: 141). This shoot, of course, carefully exploited the visual trappings of hard-core precisely to provoke such publicity. Moves like this within the fashion industry are mirrored by some of those recent pornographic films that reference and use the world of fashion, and which deploy new and different conventions around dress. To those who do not pay attention to shifts within the hard-core industry, this may seem bizarre; they assume that there is nothing remotely 'fashionable' or 'stylish' about its products. Yet recently, attempts have been made to incorporate elements of fashion and style into the construction of the work itself. Titles such as *Pussyman's Fashion Dolls* (2001–05), *Tera Patrick's Fashion Underground* (2006) and Red Light District Video's *Fashionably Laid* (2004) engage with what their female performers are wearing in a slightly different way.

There are particular reasons for hard-core film-makers wanting to associate themselves with the world of fashion. The particular type of stylish beauty demanded of fashion models puts them, in the eyes of many, into a higher social and sexual category; most female porn stars conform – in the main – to conventional standards of what is 'sexy'. This can be seen through examining the fantasy scenario which lurks behind titles such as *Fashion Models Gone Bad* (2005). Obviously, the stars here in no way resemble the highly-paid models to be found within the pages of glossy fashion magazines, or on the catwalks of Paris, London, New York and Milan. There are sub-generic modes of pornography which do depict unusually thin, even anorexic models, but these are the exception. The bodies on view within the world of hard-core are far too fleshy for the world of fashion. Fashion models are unusually tall, notoriously and preternaturally slender with a dangerously low body-mass index and, of course, are invariably flat-chested. A supposedly fashion-based story or setting provides a novel opportunity for product differentiation in a market now swamped by thousands of titles; some of the films can cling to the most unexpected elements of dress in order to provide a distinctive edge, a new 'offer'. Among the more unusual of these might be that sub-genre which features bespectacled women, for example, *Specs Appeal* (2001–04) is a twenty-one volume series. And there is of course an entire sub-genre which features the tiaras traditionally worn by high school 'prom queens'.

By a strange, fascinating irony, at the very moment when pornography has looked to the world of fashion for both inspiration and a touch of 'class', the fashion industry itself is increasingly making use of the aesthetics, the titillation, and the overall feel of pornography – most notably in advertising shoots. Since the 1980s, the spectacular advertising campaigns shot by Herb Ritts and Bruce Weber for Calvin Klein men's underwear have provided a perfect example – the 'buff' bodies of overly muscular men wearing tight white trunks or jockey shorts, especially when blown up on ten-metre billboards, have ensured maximum publicity for the company, the product and, indeed, the underpant-wearers.

The Dolce & Gabanna magazine campaign of Spring/Summer 2007 went still further, showing group activities including an act that was deemed to simulate rape – the images were eventually banned for their use of overly sexual scenarios. The fashion industry is as desperate as the industry it references for novelty, for new ways of increasing consumption in a seemingly saturated market. The Spring fashion shows held in New York in 2003 for the 2004 season were particularly noteworthy in this respect. Designer Jeremy Scott's catwalk show 'Sexybition' featured pole dancers and a 'dungeon sex slave', and the Pierrot knitwear show was styled to resemble a porn shoot, with the designer as director and the models posed in various well-known tableaux. At the Betsey Johnson show the models were paraded down the runway wearing, in addition to the clothes, conspicuous labels – 'FLUFFER', for example.[1] Simon Donovan, the Creative Director of Barneys, the Manhattan high-fashion store, wrote in his column for the *New York Observer*: 'The hetero porno antics which dominated the first few days of Fashion Week were a mystery to us attendees ... we poofters and fashion chicks, when confronted with all this Bada Bing muff culture, could only stare at one another like terrified gerbils trapped in the headlights' (in Levy 2005: 24). This clearly indicates a significant disparity between the operations of these two industries, now nevertheless busily seeking to benefit from one another.

THE HARD-CORE 'WARDROBE'

Those of us who have argued, over the past ten years or more, for the acceptance of pornography within the academy, have invariably claimed that it is a genre, like any other, with its own generic codings and *mise-en-scène*. Furthermore, every genre has particular costume conventions; these include not only what David Bordwell and Kristin Thompson call 'costume props' (1980: 81), but also the particular styling, the hair and make-up of the performers. For 'costume' in cinema – like 'fashion' itself – does not stop at the neck; rather, it includes and is dependent upon hairstyling, make-up, jewellery and indeed all other forms of accessorising to fulfil its diegetic task. The generic conventions around costume within this particular genre are invariably used to suggest what has been termed 'the aesthetics of availability' (see Church Gibson 2011). Central here are the use of make-up and the styling of hair. Similarly, there are wider stylistic techniques and conventions employed in film pornography, hard-core or otherwise, that are often perceived as cementing the reputation of the genre as a 'low art'. The soundtracks of pornographic films, where the often overdubbed grunts and groans compete for attention with tacky scores are read in relation to other aspects of *mise-en-scène* such as the locations – bedroom, sitting-room, kitchen – and the acting, since many performers struggle to cope with even the most simple lines within the rudimentary dialogue also seen as characteristic of the genre.

One interesting aspect of costume in hard-core film pornography is the distinction between that found in narrative pornography – typified by the films of 1970s 'porno-chic' and the early 1990s 'couples pornography' – and the more commonplace non-narrative, or 'four-stroke' format. It is understandable that the former has more need for a 'sophisticated' wardrobe as it seeks to flesh out character traits in more detail than its narrative-free counterpart. Linda Williams (1990), whilst not focusing on the use of costume in any great detail, does note the importance of the shift in the appearance of 'Misty' in the film *The Opening of Misty Beethoven* (1975). A porno-chic film loosely based around George Bernard Shaw's 1913 play *Pygmalion*, *The Opening of Misty Beethoven* depicts the transformation of 'a poor, unsophisticated whore' into 'the most desired sexual performer of the international jet set' (Williams 1990: 136). In doing so, it charts her changing appearance: 'a vulgarly made-up, gum-chewing Misty, wearing a T-shirt with AMERICAN EXPRESS and MASTER CARD emblazoned on the front' is transformed into the elegant young woman in a green dress, whom we see at the film's conclusion, the narrative significance of which is noted by Williams (ibid.).

Of course, 'porno-chic' and 'couples-pornography' incorporates rather more by way of costuming, if only because in such films the performers spend more time *not* having sex. But characterisation is still a necessity in non-narrative hard-core films that do away with conventional storylines. In relation to the female performers in both these hard-core formats, a simple and identifiable personality trait should therefore be readily available to the viewer so that he or she can easily identify the sexual experience and presumed 'knowledge' of the actress they are watching. This is best exemplified by the way in which such films attempt to depict youth, inexperience or naiveté. *The Opening of Misty Beethoven*, like so many examples of the 'porno-chic' era, is an 'initiation' film in which a direct shift in the main female protagonist is seen, manifest in both appearance and sexual knowledge. In non-narrative initiation films, which have to incorporate this learning process within the sexual performance itself, a distinction is made between older, more experienced female performers who are often clad in the stereotypical uniform of the genre – high heels, stockings, suspenders – and younger actresses, who usually conform to a more 'everyday' aesthetic. Rocco Siffredi's *Initiations* series (1999–2006) for Evil Empire, owned by Stagliano, consistently conforms to this idea, using a contrast between highly sexualised costumes and, at times, deliberately dowdy forms of dress in order to distinguish the hierarchical structure which governs the performance of the initiatory scene.

Indeed, such a shift can also be seen to be at work within the narrative of *The Fashionistas* when we are shown, through costume and make-up, a transformation in Belladonna's character, Jesse. When we first see her at work in the Fashionistas' office, she is de-glamorised and sub-cultural in her style, with greasy hair, jeans and a shapeless sweatshirt. The scene in which she reveals her 'true self' in a provocative dance before the mirror in her apartment – tying her hair back, stripping off her clothes to reveal her underwear and, significantly, swapping her heavy boots for high-heeled shoes – displays and

THE STYLING OF HARD-CORE

reinforces all the important visual distinctions that prevail in hard-core films. These tend to show on the one hand a 'utopian', highly-sexualised female identity and on the other a 'normal', everyday naiveté.

Of course, such 'naiveté' is not always visualised as synonymous with 'normality' or inexperience. The stereotype of the sexually vivacious teenager is one that dominates particular sub-generic forms of pornography; whilst the industry is understandably careful to distance itself from any accusations of producing child pornography it is not scared to draw on the iconography of youth in depicting such traits in far older, adult performers. In such films, the high heels become trainers, the underwear a school uniform or a cheerleader outfit complete with long white socks, the long hair is put up in bunches and accessories can include lollipops, backpacks and pristine white knickers. The films of Max Hardcore (recently released

Fig. 17 and Fig. 18 Belladonna as Jesse before (top) and after (bottom) in *The Fashionistas*.

from prison after serving a sentence for obscenity) push these stereotypes to extremes, dressing clearly adult performers in a way that grossly over-emphasises both the construction and the iconography of what they are wearing. Interestingly, Hardcore applies the same ideal to the make-up that his actresses wear, layering it on in an overly naive, even childlike way and then smearing it over their faces as the performance progresses.

'THE EVERYDAY'

The American hard-core film industry, located in Van Nuys, California, is often referred to as 'the other Hollywood' and it is true that it shares a sense of the oppositional aesthetics that govern counter cinemas in the US. Like much independent and art-house cinema, it is often wary of conventional narrative structures and does not always seek to hide the artificiality of its construction. The recent rise in both explicit sexual representations and episodic, *hard-coresque* narratives in films such as *Romance* (1999), *Baise-Moi* (2000) and *9 Songs* (2004) are symbolic of the way that counter cinemas have arguably begun to modify their oppositional stances and merge with high-end pornography. This is, of course, not dissimilar to those moves within the fashion industry described earlier. Over the past decade the art-house has embraced pornography while, through such films as *The Fashionistas*, pornography has entered the art house.

There is little academic study of the role of costume as an indicator of 'realism' in contemporary independent cinema, American or otherwise. Sarah Street (2001) does attempt to redress the balance with her work on 'the embodiment of the real' in Michael Winterbottom's *Wonderland* (1999). Her template of addressing costume in relation to its ability 'to convey something of life "as it is"' (Street 2001: 73) and its 'authenticity' are useful as a way of assessing the manner in which hard-core film pornography uses costume as a visualisation of its 'realist vs. utopian' contradiction. For hard-core must be, somehow, both 'realist' in its aesthetic – it contains actions and visual representations that must be presented as actually 'happening' in order to meet viewer expectations – and at the same time, what Williams (1990) describes as utopian – the depiction of 'perfect' sex, where nothing ever goes wrong and everybody leaves satisfied.

This contradiction has been heightened by the rise, since the end of the 1980s, of the 'gonzo' subgenre, a type of hard-core aesthetic that stresses the realism and unpredictability of the sex that takes place. It was John Stagliano who did more than any other director to pioneer this mode of production with his series of *Buttman* videos (1989–). In these films, the Buttman character would stalk the streets of California, Rio and Barcelona searching for willing female participants; they, at all times, had to be seen to have been approached unawares. The *cinéma-vérité* style of Stagliano's earlier work is at odds with the pre-planned, scripted aesthetic of *The Fashionistas* in which the characters are told what to say and, presumably, what to wear. But the importance of costume is no less significant in the *Buttman* films than it is in his later work. For in gonzo hard-core, the viewer must be able to think that these 'actresses' are anything but; that they are 'real 'girls found by 'chance', who willingly partake in the sexual activities that follow. In short, the idea is that they are not paid actresses, they are amateurs – they are like girls on the street everywhere. As such, they must not be dressed like porn-stars and must therefore avoid the typical signifiers that such a profession brings. Stagliano would never, for example, find a girl on the street dressed only in high heels and underwear. The *Buttman* films were hugely influential in providing a counter-aesthetic to the burgeoning 'couples market' of the early 1990s (see Juffer 1998; O'Toole 1998) and all the gonzo directors within Stagliano's Evil Empire imprint follow a similar style of filmmaking.

Jules Jordan's work (formerly distributed by Evil Empire) is a case in point – the opening scene of *Flesh Hunter 3* (2002) sees the director walking the streets of Van Nuys, camera in hand, and coming across two apparently 'normal' young women. They are attempting to call their boyfriends in order to procure a ride home. Of course, Aurora Snow and Jenna Haze are not 'ordinary' young women; both of them had already made a considerable number of gonzo-style films. However, their 'everyday' appearance, seemingly unstyled and just off the street, belies this fact – as they are dressed in a way that any young girl might dress, one in boob tube and dungarees, the other in T-shirt and hot pants. These clothes – albeit revealing – are in tune with the overall aesthetic of the scene, the notion that Jordan has simply 'found' the girls and can then convince them to forget their boyfriends, return to his flat and engage in a session of prolonged sexual activity.

Interestingly, the first thing Jordan does when they arrive at his 'home' is to show them a collection of his own DVDs, normalising what is about to happen in a manner that a more contemporary audience may find disturbing. This is highly symbolic in that it signifies the gulf that exists between the genders in the gonzo 'narrative'. For Snow and Haze are playing roles that rely on the denial of their position within the industry; Jordan, however, is playing a part which reinforces his real-life role. The director is always a director,

Fig. 19 'The everyday': Aurora Snow & Jenna Haze in *Flesh Hunter 3*.

whilst the performers are always, initially, 'real women'. Of course, in order for this scene to work effectively experienced hard-core viewers must suspend their disbelief, for two well-known actresses are on screen, clearly role-playing. However, the ability of the viewer to behave in just this way is crucial to the successful functioning of the hard-core pornographic film. This gulf between characters is often, but not always, strengthened by the role that costume plays in the gonzo performance – many directors are positioned outside of the sexual act, filming it and therefore remaining fully clothed, although on some occasions, as is the case with this one, the director fulfils the role of the male performer. The contrast between the clothed director and the naked female performers establishes a hierarchy in which the former has control through the way that he directs the action, but also avoids displaying his own body and leaving himself open to objectification.

'CLOTHED' PORNOGRAPHY

The growth of the internet and its continuing dominance over the way in which illicit material of all kinds is now consumed has led to a further fragmentation in the sub-generic form of pornography. It is now the case that not only does the industry provide a specific product for every imaginable 'perversion', but that a continued exposure to internet pornography will lead the consumer, often unwittingly, towards a new activity, something that they may stumble upon, and then find to be more arousing and attractive than anything else.

The internet helped to fragment further the hard-core/soft-core distinction by adding a third layer to the explicitness of pornographic material. As we identified earlier, non-nude pornography comes in an assortment of forms, from single model sites such as those of *Kari Sweets* and *Next Door Nikki* to more voyeuristic material, based around 'candid' photography taken on the street or on beaches around the world. Non-nude pornography is highly controversial in that for a period it permitted images of underage models to appear online in a context that did not have to bow to the various international laws regarding the presentation of sexually explicit material; although this was amended by legislation in the UK, non-nude sites do tend to lean towards the depiction of younger, 'teen' models – the two cited above are examples of such a trend.

However, what is interesting in this context is the reliance of such pornography on the presence of clothes. Not only do these sites tease and stimulate viewers in depicting more and more flesh whilst never actually allowing them to see what they desire, the clothes become the very factor around which so many of these sites are designed. Each will contain a number of different photo or video sets, organised by differing elements of *mise-en-scène*, either by costume, or on occasion, location (such as on a beach, in a swimming pool or in the more domesticated setting of a kitchen or bedroom).[2] As such, the costume takes on a dual role. Firstly, it signifies the personality and particular, presumed sexuality of the model in this specific context. As with hard-core film pornography, the model can be depicted as a naive cheerleader, a girl-next-door or a powerful dominatrix. Secondly, the costume frames and fetishises the body in a particular way, emphasising a specific body part. In images that do not show those parts of the body that the voyeur presumably wants to see, we might question what exactly they *do* find stimulating about such material.

Clearly, one of the reasons that items of clothing are carefully incorporated into the hard-core sexual performance is to fetishise the female form in a manner pleasing to the eyes and taste of the viewer, the *heterosexual* male voyeur, presumed to be the main consumer of hard-core. Indeed, the more fetishistic the type of pornography the greater the role that clothing plays. To some extent, the mainstream heterosexual market has incorporated the aesthetics and iconography of sadomasochistic pornography, but modified in order to suit its own specific ends.

THE FASHIONISTAS – POLYMORPHOUS PERVERSITY?

The most famous example of such engagement – and of a 'fashion setting' – is perhaps Stagliano's film *The Fashionistas*, the plot of which incorporates both fashion 'labels' and their relationship to the S/M underground subculture. Conceived as a tribute to the director's close friend Bruce 7, who produced a number of S/M film series in the 1980s and 1990s, *The Fashionistas* clearly depicts the importance of clothing in hard-core spectacle. However, it also raises several interesting points about the relationship between these two industries, fashion and pornography, one expensive, glamorous and socially acceptable, the other more dubious in so many ways. The term 'fashionista' is used to mean someone – usually a woman – who obsessively follows and consumes, both visually and in reality, all the very latest fashion trends, regardless of whether or not they suit their body shape and physical type. In *The Fashionistas*, it is deployed simply to connote those working in the fashion industry, and it is also the name of the imaginary fashion house which Antonio (Rocco Siffredi), the rather implausible fashion designer who is the central character, approaches with his ideas for the incorporation of S/M design into their future fashion ranges.

The Fashionistas opens with a fashion show, which bears little or no relation to most catwalk shows, despite the desperate antics in the New York Spring shows for 2004 described above – the clothes are cheap and garish, while the 'models' in no way resemble the six-foot skeletal figures seen in most runway shows. At one point in the film, Antonio is in the offices of the fetish-based fashion label which provides the film with its title. He dons a pair of tight fitting latex trousers and models them for his fellow characters – and, it is presumed, the viewer. Clinging tightly to his body, Siffredi's crotch, legs and buttocks are overtly sexualised and displayed in a manner that challenges the usual doctrine of heterosexual hard-core film pornography, which dictates that male bodies should not be framed and fetishised in such a way. This is one of a number of ways in which Stagliano's film attacks the conventions of heterosexual hard-core. Siffredi's role as a fashion designer incorporates him into a different world – sophisticated and polysexual – from that of his own, more typical, non-narrative films; characteristic of these are series and titles such as *True Anal Stories* (1998–2004), *Animal Trainer* (1999–2009) and *Nasty Tails* (2005–07) also for Stagliano's Evil Empire company. These films do not overtly sexualise his body, but seek instead to emphasise and frame the size and potency of his erect penis. In *The Fashionistas* the sexuality of Antonio is questioned – but significantly never really challenged – by the gay designer Eddie. He is responding not only to Antonio's very involvement in the fashion industry, but also his willingness to wear the type of garments not usually seen on men outside the confines of sadomasochistic or certain modes of gay pornography. The fact that his wearing of these latex trousers attracts the attention of both male and female members of staff limits the homoerotic nature of the scene; nevertheless, it is still unusual to see the male body displayed in such an overtly sexualised way within a genre that sees being *not-homosexual* as its only real manifesto.

The Fashionistas – and its *Fashionistas Safado* (2006–07) follow-ups – has won a clutch of plaudits for the way in which it brings together those two, often polarised strands, of the heterosexual hard-core industry – non-narrative hard-core and the narrative-heavy 'couples' film. Its high production values – for it is shot, like the art pornography of directors Andrew Blake and Michael Ninn, on 35mm – its running time of over four hours, its credible, original score and lastly its narrative complexity distance it from the routine accusations levelled at hard-core films; namely, that they are short, repetitive and cheaply made. One aspect of its production values – the use of costume – is of particular relevance here. Unusually, the credits for the film feature a five-strong make-up and hair department, together with a 'costume department' with one overall designer (Ms. September), a wardrobe assistant and named, individual creators of latex fetish costumes. The majority of hard-core films do not stress the size or input of such departments; significantly, many have no fashion credits at all, and might simply state 'Make-up by Rebecca', as is the case in Michael Stefano's *Dual Invasion 3* (2005). In contrast, Stagliano's film takes the time to outline the care and attention that went into the visual construction of the work. This is because the film is attempting to distance itself from the bulk of films created within the porn industry, with their low production values and episodic non-narrative aesthetic. Significantly *The Fashionistas* is very much *about* clothes themselves and the way in which they can be used within a sexual context.

FETISHISM AND SADOMASOCHISM

In 'Maid to Order: Commercial S/M & Gender Power', Anne McClintock discusses the presence in Madonna's *Sex* collection of 'the theatrical paraphernalia of S/M: boots, chains, leather, whips, masks, costumes and scripts' (2004: 237). It is clear that *The Fashionistas* seeks to conform to these well-known S/M codes, through the way in which the performers are dressed and the complexity of the plot, which at all times stresses the consensual nature of the sexual act. There is, too, a narrative strand that directly comments upon the clothes themselves. It is true that sadomasochistic hard-core film pornography relies far more on paraphernalia and the iconography of dress than its mainstream heterosexual pornographic counterpart. As we have argued, whilst the latter does not – and cannot – sideline clothes entirely, it is still not unusual to see combinations of bodies *seemingly* shorn of all garments. S/M cannot do that. Its reliance on the fetishised body is absolute, adhering to Richard von Krafft-Ebing's early definition of fetishism as 'the association of lust with the idea of certain portions of the female person, or' – importantly in this context – 'with certain articles of female attire' (in Steele 1996: 11). For it is the image of the dominatrix (brandishing her whip, clad in high-heels, stockings, long gloves, corset and even a mask) that, for Freud, makes women 'tolerable sexual objects' and so averts the male fear of castration, which provides the sadomasochistic performance with its theatricality, its gender balance and, in turn, its significance (see Steele 1996: 15).

It is not surprising, then, that when *vanilla*[3] heterosexual hard-core films attempt to incorporate sadomasochistic practices, such paraphernalia is indeed present – but it is usually modified and arguably tokenistic. Christoph Clark's *Euro Domination* series (2004–06) for Evil Empire is a case in point – the female performers are clad in and surrounded by the usual collection of boots, chains, leather, whips, masks and costumes, but they are customised to appeal to the vanilla heterosexual viewer. Whilst masks will, on occasion, be left on throughout the scene, the other garments are organised so that they always allow both visual and physical access to the breasts, vagina and anus. This is in keeping with the fact that heterosexual hard-core pornography demands, if not nudity, then the visibility of both the sexual act and the usually covered parts of the female anatomy. Furthermore, although the female performers may at first be allowed to appear as dominant, they must eventually revert to a traditional position of submission.

The 'heterosexualisation' of the iconography of S/M is also seen within *The Fashionistas* through the character of Jesse, played by Belladonna. As a minor figure in the Fashionista organisation, she is responsible for creating the promotional DVDs that are sent to Antonio to promote the company's various designs. Within these discs she hides a series of S/M performances that include her as the submissive victim, clad in the requisite garments and chained to a metal frame. However, such behaviour and costume are kept separate from the main location of the film's narrative – we only see Belladonna in such clothing when appearing within the promotional material she creates for the company or in the Crevice Club, the underground S/M establishment where the Fashionistas group exhibit their designs. In her final, climactic scene with Siffredi, she divests herself entirely of such paraphernalia (aside from the chain on her vagina), performing free of clothes and so distancing the performance, even though it takes place within the S/M club, from any overtly sadomasochistic overtones. The fact that Stagliano cast Belladonna as his female lead is symbolic of the power she had attained within the industry in the preceding three years. But it is her appearance, her image, which is of particular interest here. This, unusually for a porn-star, has been consistently and drastically altered.

Beginning her career as a blonde, Belladonna has continuously amended her appearance in a way that does not fit the routine hard-core stereotype of 'shifting' simply in relation to the particular role being performed on screen. Typically, female porn-stars will retain a consistent overall image, selling themselves around a particular bodily feature – breast size, buttock size or, more usually, hair colour. In an industry that likes to pigeonhole both its female and male performers – the latter are routinely defined by the size of their penis, or in the case of Jules Jordan or Peter North, the potency of their ejaculate – it is highly unusual to find a star who constantly alters in physical appearance. However, Belladonna has constantly amended her 'look' through modifying her hair – bleached blonde in her early films, the jet-black bob that we see in *The Fashionistas*, a short crop and even, for a while, a 'skinhead' look.

Belladonna's mutating appearance emphasises the fact that, far from being static, the dress codes of hard-core films are susceptible to the shifts in fashion that govern other forms of visual representation. The idea that pornography never changes, that it retains a common and consistent visual iconography of lacy push-up bras, scanty synthetic-fibre knickers, suspenders, high-heeled shoes and garish make-up ignores the fact that it too can move with the times. The stereotypical female performer of the 1980s, with her big hair, big cleavage, basque and stockings would look ridiculous placed next to Belladonna and her streamlined, Brazilian-waxed contemporaries in their Victoria's Secret lingerie. Nevertheless, the 'aesthetics of availability' do mean that the make-up in hard-core, by and large, does *not* change in accordance with the rules of conventional fashion. Lips are usually pink and invariably glossed, nails are always long, and eyes are made up heavily in colours that bear no relation to 'this season's trends'. Even Belladonna, confrontational and shape-shifting as she is, conforms to these unwritten rules which govern the use of make-up in hard-core – even if she does sport a massive tattoo. What Belladonna's constantly shifting image does emphasise is that the body in hard-core film pornography can indeed be 'dressed' or adorned *without* the use of clothing or underwear. Her appearance alongside other stars such as Ginger Lynn, Jenna Jameson and Nina Hartley in Timothy Greenfield-Sanders' *XXX: 30 Porn-Star Portraits* (2004) collection emphasises this very fact. These pictures illustrate the differing forms of bodily modifications which always operate despite the seeming 'nudity', which communicate personality traits and define the wearer even when seemingly deprived of all 'costume' – here Belladonna is presented with a shaven head to accompany her trademark heart tattoo. Indeed, this tattoo, which she has had since the start of her career, in many ways defines the kind of performer she is – streetwise, aggressive, apparently knowing, often 'masculinised' in her sexuality.

CONCLUSION

Over the past decade, due to the combination of the wider availability of pornographic material online and the 'mainstreaming' of pornographic imagery in advertisements and popular music videos, the iconography of pornographic films, particularly in relation to dress, has become much more visible on the high street. There are cult labels such as 'Porn Star' who specialise in ranges of T-shirts and sweatshirts emblazoned with images of 'porno-chic' stars such as Ron Jeremy and John Holmes. But there are also much cheaper T-shirts, available everywhere, which blazon this very same career choice across the chest of the wearer, and others which indicate his, or her, sexual predilections and physical desirability. Typical T-shirt slogans include 'Porn star in training', 'Masturbation is not a crime', 'Nobody knows I'm a lesbian', '69' and, a favourite with young girls, 'All this and brains too'. Indeed, the very revealing clothes that any young women wear now are seen by some to conform to an imagined quasi-pornographic aesthetic. In 2005, an article by Janice Turner in the *Guardian* newspaper posited the idea that

> somehow in recent years, porn has come true. The sexually liberated modern woman turns out to resemble – what do you know! – the pneumatic, take-me-now-big-boy fuck-puppet of male fantasy after all.

The continuing dominance of 'celebrity culture' has certainly played a part here. For while the contemporary celebrities who are popular within the fashion industry – the Olsen twins, Kiera Knightley, Kirsten Dunst and Kate Moss, model extraordinaire – are slim and stylish, other celebrities who stare out at us from magazine covers have a different mode of self-presentation. The leading British luminary Jordan, born Katie Price, has published four autobiographies to date and has designed clothing ranges, including lingerie for supermarket chain Asda. Jordan was a 'glamour' model before her move into reality television and her rise to 'celebrity' status. Though she can 'shape shift' to some extent by varying the styling of her hair, her extravagantly-bosomed figure, the result of several sets of silicon implants, prevents too much variation. And in all her magazine shoots she usually sports hair extensions, fake fingernails, and pink lip-gloss. She looks, of course, exactly like a porn star.

The hidden has become the visible, the marginalised mainstream – yes, all the constituent elements of the 'looks' we have examined within this article can be easily obtained in a high-street shop near you.

NOTES

1. A 'fluffer' is the name given to the employee on a porn set whose specific task is to ensure that whatever male member he or she is tending is in a state of permanent arousal at all times.
2. It is this design that defines the importance of costume in non-nude pornography, for it is not the only technique available to the photographer who wishes to 'imply nudity' in his/her work. Although several methods include the use of clothes, props or accessories (hats, scarves, belts) other approaches are available that have no use for costume (shooting the silhouette, covering the body with other elements of the *mise-en-scène* such as location).
3. For those unfamiliar with the term 'vanilla', it means the display of sexual acts involving no artificial aids or role-play.

WORKS CITED

Bordwell, D. and K. Thompson (1980) *Film Art: An Introduction*. Reading, MA: Addison-Wesley.

Church Gibson, P. (2011) *Fashion and Celebrity*. Oxford: Berg.

Greenfield-Sanders, T. (2004) *XXX: 30 Porn Star Portraits*. New York: Bulfinch Press.

Hénaff, M. (1999) *Sade: The Invention of the Libertine Body*. Minneapolis: University of Minnesota Press.

Juffer, J. (1998) *At Home with Pornography: Women, Sex and Everyday Life*. New York: New York University Press.

Kendrick, W. (1987) *The Secret Museum: Pornography in Modern Culture*. New York: Viking.

Kipnis, L. (1996) *Bound and Gagged: Pornography and the Politics of Fantasy in America*. Durham: Duke University Press.

Levi-Strauss, C. (1994) *The Raw and the Cooked: Introduction to the Science of Mythology*. London: Pimlico.

Levy, A. (2005) *Female Chauvinist Pigs: Women and the Rise of Raunch Culture*. London: Simon and Schuster.

McClintock, A. (2004) 'Maid to Order: Commercial S/M & Gender Power', in P. Church Gibson (ed.) *More Dirty Looks: Gender, Pornography and Power*. London: BFI, 237–53.

O'Neill, A. (2004) 'Taste-Making: Indifference, Interiors and the Unbound Image', in P. Church Gibson (ed.) *More Dirty Looks: Gender, Pornography and Power*. London: BFI, 137–48.

O'Toole, L. (1998) *Pornocopia: Porn, Sex, Technology and Desire*. London: Serpent's Tail.

Steele, V. (1996) *Fetish: Fashion, Sex and Power*. Oxford: Oxford University Press.

Street, S. (2001) *Costume and Cinema: Dress Codes in Popular Film*. London: Wallflower Press.

Turner, J. (2005) 'Dirty Young Men', *Guardian*, October 22. On-line. Available: http://www.guardian.co.uk/theguardian/2005/oct/22/weekend7.weekend3 (accessed 1 April 2009).

Williams, L. (1990) *Hard Core: Power, Pleasure and the 'Frenzy of the Visible'*. London: Pandora Press.

CHAPTER TEN

SHORTBUS: HIGHBROW HARD-CORE

Beth Johnson

Whether mainstream or marginal, the realisation of a cinema of hard-core sex naturally provokes a questioning of screen cultures in association with notions of reality, desire, ethics and public/private permeations. This chapter provides a material interrogation of the American film, *Shortbus* (2006), directed by John Cameron Mitchell. Engaging with the artistic aims of the film, the contemporary social and cultural anxieties associated with sex and the *vérité*-style of shooting/screening sex employed by Mitchell, this chapter addresses the emergence of a cinematic culture in which hard-core sex acts are performed in order to progress sensory engagement with highbrow stories.

Historically, hard-core has been associated and understood in line with an explicit pornographic aesthetic – an aesthetic coded to arouse the filmic viewer by showing 'real' sexual performance on screen. Moreover, hard-core has traditionally been perceived as a discourse of autoerotic affect, that is to say, a discourse that induces irrational and repetitive arousal, provoking the body rather than the mind of the viewer. As Bill Nichols argues in *Representing Reality*: 'Pornography ... may involve social ritual but its representation favors viewer arousal more than understanding or analysis' (1991: 211). Showcasing and privileging the 'money shot', hard-core intentionally evidences a type of authentic pleasure in which the overwhelming convulsive and often compulsive pleasure of the body, can always be seen as hard, wet, willing and ultimately, orgasmic. Dominantly separated from emotional intimacy, hard-core sex on screen has frequently then been figured as 'base' and animalistic, in short, as a stimulating and salacious sub-category of the obscene. Arguably however, such readings have failed to address the polysemic potential of hard-core, focusing instead on the masturbatory *modus operandi* of the genre.

While often considered as a category distinct from 'regular' commercial cinema, hard-core does not stand alone, but must be figured as an important part of a larger popular and political social discourse about sex, sexuality and sexual representation. Often defined in contradistinction to soft-core, erotic and art film, hard-core occupies a populist yet contentious cultural space in the twenty-first century. The space that hard-core inhabits is undoubtedly and increasingly an important one. The advent of new digital technologies since the 1990s has meant that in the West hard-core not only dominates virtual spaces, but moreover, plays a key role in driving, organising and regulating the ways in which such spaces are being transformed, re-imagined, repopulated and read. As a result of such technological and societal transformations, hard-core has spilled over, adulterating previous aesthetic boundaries of 'film art'. While arguably retaining several of its 'realist' conventions, a new strand of hard-core film can now be classified as highbrow; an increasingly permeable space – a space in which previous delineations between heterosexual hard-core and homosexual hard-core, art and pornography, pleasure and pain, can co-exist.

HIGH-BROW HAPTICS AND 'THE SEX FILM PROJECT'

John Cameron Mitchell (2006) notes in his documentary 'Gifted and Challenged: The Making of *Shortbus*', the recent dominance of 'real' sex in European cinema. Mitchell opens his documentary in fact with the acknowledgement that while such real sex is figured in various ways in contemporary European cinema, it is dominantly presented as 'negative', that is, as both depressing and displeasurable. Indeed, twenty-first-century European 'real sex' films such as Catherine Breillat's *Romance* (1999), Coralie Trinh Thi and Virginie Despentes's *Baise-Moi* (2000) and Michael Haneke's *The Piano Teacher* (2001) can be held up as examples of such an argument and yet, it is ironically for this reason that such filmic texts have been culturally validated as filmic art rather than hard-core pornographic pictures. As Tanya Krzywinska points out in *Sex and the Cinema*, in various ways in recent (dominantly European) real sex films: 'the cinematic representation of real sex ... is sanctioned only on the conditions that certain signifiers of 'art' are present [...] The presence of such elements prevent the viewer from enjoying these films as simply erotic spectacle' (2006: 226–7).

Discussing his intentions regarding *Shortbus*, Mitchell explicitly states that one purpose of *Shortbus* is to 'frame and screen real sex in a positive way' (2006). However, Mitchell also makes clear his highbrow aesthetic intentions for *Shortbus*. Addressing the process of recruiting actors for the film, Mitchell notes that recruitment was undertaken via a web call for an artistic project – namely 'The Sex Film Project'. The call for actors was prefaced on the web with the following sentence: 'WARNING: This web site contains and discusses material which may not be suitable for all audiences ... LIKE ART.' Thus, we can see Mitchell purposefully positioning his project as an artistic and cultural one; a project that plays up to highbrow sanctions of legitimacy. Mitchell further notes that in order for actors to feel 'safe' while engaging in real sex for his 'Sex Film Project', he cast the actors first before creating the story entirely through collaborative workshops and improvisation sessions. Potential actors were also asked to construct a 'chart of attraction' noting which other actors they were most attracted to, thus creating a matrix of interconnection that formed a type of *vérité* aesthetic. In addition, Mitchell notes that he placed the camera at a distance from his actors allowing them to engage with the intimacies and space more 'naturally'. Captured on camera speaking to a potential actor for his project Mitchell is asked directly whether the film is 'to contain pornographic tropes, like close-ups of my pussy?' Mitchell answers as follows:

> No – pornography is something that there is no connection to in this film. The way it's shot, the purpose of it, the receiving it, it's just not anything to do with what we're doing with this film – which is hard for people to understand because that's the only example of American-made sex on film. (2006)

The fact that *Shortbus* is an American film, doing hard-core differently, is consciously acknowledged in the diegetic world of the film as well as in Mitchell's various press interviews. For the record, Mitchell admits to liking pornography but being dominantly bored by the 'same' unimaginative scenes. *Shortbus*, he notes, is different. Both the 'Shortbus salon' (a salon in which anxious New Yorkers meet, watch films, rant, fuck and flirt) and the city of New York are recreated and located as distinctive American spaces; places of freedom and ingenuity even while this hope in the 'land of the free' is mingled with contemporary anxieties. As Mitchell reminds us in a press interview: 'It's a patriotic film. It opens with the Statue of Liberty and this idea of the outcasts coming to this country – I mean, that used to be the real American value and it hasn't been mentioned for a few years' (in Lamble 2006). The salon is, as is made explicit in the film, a retrosexual space – a space in which the discursive language of sexual freedom (particularly the American bohemian sexual freedom of the 1960s) allows for a *beau monde* yet culturally diverse community of care, hope and support as well as a plurality of sexual perspectives.

Moreover, the community of Shortbus come together to 'let go', to wallow, to fuck, to laugh, to be themselves or someone else if they so desire, in essence to explore their own identities. Saliently, the diegetic salon hostess (drag artist Justin Bond), notes that the title of the salon 'Shortbus' refers to a colloquial term and is an American reference to a shorter version of the school bus, associated with 'special' kids and learning difficulties. Indeed, the salon can certainly be seen throughout Mitchell's film as a space in which those with seemingly impermeable individual 'difficulties' – often relating to love, intimacy and sex – can go to be permeated. Shortbus can, in these terms, be seen as a site of redemption, as a place where people can go to connect, a place where its members do not have to feel alone in the world, but can literally as well as figuratively, 'cum' together, or, at least, seek a connection.

Amidst the Shortbus community, the performance of self is recognised as a dynamic journey of sexual discovery, but also a journey of salvation. Again however, the filmic representation of sexual expression and experience as a significant part of a journey of self-discovery has a history of visibility in high art European real sex films such as Patrice Chéreau's *Intimacy* (2001) and Christophe Honoré's *Ma Mère* (2004). Moreover, other serious sex films based upon the quest of sexual discovery such as Nagisa Ôshima's *In the Realm of the Senses* (1976) and Victor Nieuwenhuijs and Maartje Seyferth's *Venus in Furs* (1995) are consciously, comically and often ironically referenced in *Shortbus* – adding to the highbrow hard-core ambience and aesthetic of Mitchell's film. Inside the salon (based on the real American Cine Salon[1]), for example, avant-garde 16mm art films are, we are told, projected and their aesthetic and cultural value discussed. Moreover, the salon appears to be a culturally heterogeneous environment – a utopian space of racial, sexual and age-based equality into which new members are invited to join based on existing member recommendations. The community of Shortbus can also be understood as a close community in the sense that all the members appear to know each other in some way. In addition, the members of the Shortbus community appear to genuinely and actively care about making positive the experience of others both within and outside of the salon.

Within this screen culture of shared intimacy and connection, the only character who is seen to make open and inappropriate responses to the voicing of shared anxieties and desires of others is Severin (Lindsay Beamish) – an unhappy New York dominatrix. Her name is of course a cultural nomination of hard-core comedy – specifically, an explicit reference to Severin von Kusiemski, a character in the novel *Venus in Furs* (originally published in 1870) by Leopold von Sacher-Masoch. Ironically, within Sacher-Masoch's novel, Severin (a male character) becomes infatuated with a woman named Wanda von Dunajew. This infatuation leads him to beg her to allow him to become her slave. As his master, Wanda must humiliate Severin, yet Severin describes his feelings during these dominating experiences as suprasensual engagements. This conscious highbrow reference to classical master/slave relations are particularly apt as our first view of Severin on screen is of her dressed in leather underwear and high-heeled black boots, angrily cleaning dildos in a hotel room which looks out onto Ground Zero. Her slave 'client' who is watching her, asks her about her sexual dominance or submission in 'real-life': 'Are you a top or a bottom?... in real life?' In response, Severin sarcastically informs her client that this is 'real life'. Rephrasing his question, he then states: 'Let me put it this way, do you think we should get out of Iraq?' Recognising that her client is both baiting her to punish him while simultaneously perhaps believing that if he is paying her to be his master he has a right to ask her about herself, Severin explodes in temper – whipping his ass with her cat o' nine tails and commanding him to 'Get on the fucking bed!' Severin's seeming and complete lack of pleasure in contradistinction to her client's, can be understood here as a source of displeasure rather than a perfect dominatrix/submissive pairing. Indeed, while Severin's 'john' interpolates a physical connection between himself and his mistress (via baiting her to whip him), the scene could arguably be read as a pivotal moment of disconnection and miscommunication for Severin. Indeed, towards the close of the film, Severin reveals that her 'real' desire is to give up her dominatrix work but continue living in New York. Severin wants, she confides, 'a home and a cat and to make art for a whole year'. Rather than having her cultural worth determined by her clients, Severin appears to want to redefine herself outside of the economic arena – and establish herself as a visual artist who attains inspiration from the city streets that surround her – her home amongst others who, like her, do not quite 'fit in'.

CARTOGRAPHIES OF COMMUNICATION: RE-MAPPING TECHNO-SEXUAL INTERSECTIONS

Fittingly, in line with such high art bohemian pretensions, Mitchell's film opens with a purposefully artistic virtual scale model of New York City, navigated from the air. The spectacle of the virtual model is not only visually impressive (appearing on first sight not as a computer-generated city model, but rather as a beautifully hand-crafted and highly detailed replica), but can further be understood as a means of narrative guidance and thematic focus and as a technological project of cartography – redrawing the map of modern-day intimacies. Indeed, such a vision makes visible from the off the significance of technology (a reoccurring thematic preoccupation throughout Mitchell's film) and the important and transformative intersections between technology, art and contemporary New York City life. Arguably, through this opening scene, Mitchell can be understood to situate the significance of contemporary screen

Fig. 20 Mitchell's virtual model re-imagines NYC's (sexual) landscape.

cultures, making visible perhaps the disparity between replication and reality. That is to say, the virtual replica of the city – and the fact that audiences may initially presume the virtual city depicted to be a tangible, real scale model of New York – calls into question the potential for new technologies to re-imagine and re-present the real in various ways. In addition, this opening vision could also be seen to purposefully highlight the significance of misconception – and could in turn be seen to consciously call into question contemporary expectations of screen cultures. In the realm of hard-core filmic expectations, such an opening is poignant but also playful – perhaps suggesting that Mitchell's intention is to utilise new technologies to re-present, re-frame and re-imagine habitual hard-core.

Following this virtual expose, the audience are then interpolated into a self-conscious and voyeuristic scene in which we are guided by the camera to peep through New York apartment windows. Inside three specific apartments, we are made privy to the sexual intimacies of the inhabitants via a litany of intercourse, masturbation and cunnilingus. Yet, pre-empting these habitual hard-core scenes, we are initially encouraged to view the naked body as de-sexualised. To the backdrop of jazz music, the camera zooms out from a close-up shot of an opaque rectangular window making visible a shabby, small and lived-in looking bathroom. Littered with toy cars, a snow globe and a burned-out candle in a wine bottle, our vision is jerkily guided to the figure of a naked male in the bath. Staring into space and with his arms resting on the sides of the bath, the white male bather is figured as thoughtful, honest and perhaps a little sad (his eyes are red and his face blotchy). Next, we see him holding a digital camcorder which he points at his semi-erect penis. This double frame is then refigured as the male's point-of-view through the digital screen and we see, in close-up, his penis bobbing about in the water before a stream of urine yellows the clear water. The male then briefly holds his penis in one hand moving it from side to side in a non-sexualised manner. The camera then reverts to its original framing position and we see the male continuing to film himself. This film on film makes for an intriguing scene; however, intrigue is arguably attained through the potential of the audience to consider the male's state of mind rather than the state of his penis. The male's actions appear deliberate, self-conscious and yet, these actions are coded as unthreatening. Moreover, the male does not sexualise the filmic text he appears to be making, but rather, appears to simply document, to de-sexualise his genitals. Poignantly, it is the staring eyes of the male that cause provocation in this scene rather than the display of his naked body. As such, the male's vision (and by proxy, the vision of the spectator), can be understood as self-reflexive – a meta-commentary that functions to subvert the notion of the naked male body, and in particular the penis, as a hard-core sexual and social spectacle.

Such a reading is particularly relevant in relation to the revelation of the male's identity. Later in the film we learn that the nameless man is called James (Paul Dawson) and that he lives in New York with his boyfriend of five years, Jamie (PJ DeBoy). The film that James is engaged in making throughout *Shortbus* is understood initially as a filmic love letter – a document through which James feels that he can make tangible his love for Jamie through the propagation of wordless images. Amalgamating footage such at that of himself in the bath, with the couple's previous home videos and photographic stills from their separate childhoods, James is seen on screen working to edit the texts into a 'final' filmic gift for his lover. The poignancy of James's filmic document is moreover increased when the spectator later learns that the film is planned as James's final gift to Jamie – a suicide note, a confession of his impenetrability and an illusion of togetherness that James has failed to make real. Via the process of filmic editing and selection, James utilises the medium of film to both document and deconstruct the couple's reality via a conscious reassembly of their experience, time and space. The filmic text produced then, like the mode of documentary itself, can be understood as a site of social change and contestation in which technology, rather than flesh, is relied upon as a type of connective tissue.

The power of looking is also made explicit through the palpable positioning of not only the camcorder, but of cameras and binoculars in Mitchell's film. Severin, we are shown, carries her Polaroid camera everywhere, taking pictures without permission of 'inappropriate' moments in which her subjects have become emotionally permeable or at least, exposed. Situated in the 'Pussy' room at Shortbus for example, Severin snaps a photograph of Sofia (Sook-Yin Lee), a couples counsellor who has just admitted to the female inhabitants of the room that she is 'pre-orgasmic'. In essence, what Sofia is admitting to here is the fact that she has never had an orgasm, neither alone, or with her husband. The irony and pain of this admission is not lost on Severin who is, like the other women in the room, aware of Sofia's position as a Manhattan sex therapist. Sofia's unmasking of her pre-orgasmic status is met by advice, pathos and the unexpected and momentarily blinding flash of Severin's camera. The spatial relationship between these two women further signifies both their distance and proximity. Severin is situated on a high shelf near the ceiling of the Pussy room. Sofia is sat cross-legged on the floor, forming part of a conscious and sharing circle of women. Severin's choice to sit outside of and above the circle connotes her purposeful separation from the polite 'pussies' in the room. Metaphorically however, this spatial distance could also be read as an acknowledgement of her own impermeability and refusal to articulate or share her real desires. Despite this, Severin's choice to situate herself in the Pussy room could be seen as a masochistic act – an act in which she forces herself to look at the opening up of others – an opening up that we can infer Severin silently desires. It is, after all, such emotional moments of openness, of explicit exposure, that Severin consistently tries to capture. Interestingly however, Severin is seen in her diegetic world to give all of the pictures she takes back to her subjects once she has inked or etched her thoughts onto the various portraits. Indeed, this act of giving back the image to the people could be read as an overt and politically informed act – a gift from Mitchell to his audience. It is, as such, worth noting here that the act of reimagining hard-core, making it real, giving it back to the people, was both a nominated challenge and aim of making *Shortbus*.

Fig. 21 Severin's visual art: emotional moments of exposure.

RE-FRAMING VOYEURISM: PERSPECTIVE, PARTNERSHIPS AND POLITICS

A further politicised act of looking in *Shortbus* concerns voyeurism. However, again, this practice is refigured and reframed by Mitchell as a soft, intelligible and protective rather than hard-core, aesthetic activity. While the term 'voyeurism' refers to the pleasure of looking at others while remaining unseen, and thus connotes a dominantly devious or deceptive visual practice, the voyeurism represented in Mitchell's film is situated as benign. While viewers are, from the outset of *Shortbus* given a sense of voyeuristic privy (forced to look, via the camera, into the apartments of unsuspecting characters), voyeurism is also figured in the filmic diegesis. After watching the character James in the bath (as described above), we next see him setting his camera up on the living room floor of his apartment. As in our previous introduction to him, James remains naked, positioning his white towel on the floor in front of his apartment window. Initially lying on his back as if preparing to engage in yoga, James rolls backwards and uses his hands to support his back, ultimately positioning his genitals directly above his face. Softly-lit and framed from a low angle, James goes on to slowly autofellate. On climaxing however, James does not moan or express pleasure but rather, is seen to breakdown and cry. Vastly at odds with dominant responses to climax in other hard-core films, spectator responses to this scene are potentially complex. James's tears intermingled with the liquid ejaculate on his face signal a form of generic leakage. James's self-fellation is indeed a cinematic and sexual spectacle yet his tears, his isolation, his breakdown immediately following his climax quickly renders the scene as sorrowful, serious and sensitive.

Furthermore, this reading is almost immediately further complicated by a change in perspective – suddenly placing us outside of James's apartment and in the apartment of another man who is watching James through binoculars. The voyeur is a young male named Caleb (Peter Stickles) who justifies his voyeuristic action later in the film by nominating 'I work from home, I'm a proof-reader and I don't have cable'. This is an interesting, slightly ludic and yet seeming explicitly honest comment which can be read of many levels. Firstly, Caleb does indeed seem to live his life through watching a relationship that he appears to read as the truth or 'proof' that love really exists. What's more, the 'love' that Caleb sees in James and Jamie's relationship, is wholesome, and seemingly exemplifies Caleb's own American dream. The specificity of the James/Jamie pairing as an 'American dream' is further developed in an entertaining and droll *ménage à trois* involving James, Jamie and Ceth (Jay Brannan) – a young sensitive man who the pair met at Shortbus. At James and Jamie's apartment (and watched through binoculars by Caleb), the three guys engage in a sexual daisy chain – James laid on his back on a raised box with Ceth positioned above him while Jamie is rimming Ceth and masturbating. The spirit of the daisy chain is one of pleasure and fun; however, the scene takes on an increasing ludic yet political aesthetic when Jamie begins to sing the American national anthem loudly and rousingly into Ceth's anus. At this time, in this apartment, amidst the laughter of the guys, the 'land of the free' of which Jamie sings seems to really exist. Yet it is worth noting that while Jamie's singing (joined by the others using erect penises as pretend microphones), ends climactically with his loud and proud rendition of 'the land of the free and the home of the brave', none of the men actually sexually climax. The chain is instead overcome by the humour and genuine playful fun of the moment.

In opposition to the fun of this three-way experience, Caleb, alone and watching the events, is distressed and perturbed. Confronting Ceth, Caleb makes an impassioned plea for him to 'leave them alone!' noting that they are perfect together as they are. Significantly however, Caleb the proof-reader knows this is in fact untrue, for through his voyeurism he has seen the flaws and faults in the punctuation of their relationship. He knows that however much James and Jamie love each other, James will still not, after five years, allow Jamie to penetrate him. But rather than being understood to pose a threat to one or both of his voyeuristic subjects, Caleb is seemingly positioned as some sort of guardian angel – protecting the couple and driving away outside threats to their relationship. Caleb's next physical intervention comes after following James to his place of work to find him attempting to commit suicide in the pool where he ironically works as a life-guard. Dragging him out of the water, Caleb saves James's life in an effort to guard the relationship that he so ardently believes in. Despite this and in line with hard-core conventions however, voyeurism in *Shortbus* nearly always leads to sex. Unlike hard-core though, the sexual acts are not immediate and nor are they figured as straightforward penetrations. Rather, the eventual sexual engagements pre-empted by voyeurism in Mitchell's film, lead to intimate permeations, to real experiences of connection.

Releasing himself from hospital after his suicide attempt, James goes to Caleb's apartment to recover. Caleb watches James sleep, gently holding his hand. On waking, Caleb ask James why when he has 'so much', he would want to end his life. In response James tells him that he used to work as a hustler – performing pleasure on a daily basis. This, James confesses, is why he will not let Jamie penetrate him. His 'johns', James notes, 'treated him like shit'. This experience was, we can infer, a painful and destabilising one for James; a necessary but difficult means of survival. Revealing to Caleb he is terrified that Jamie's love for him will never truly permeate his sadness inside, James, in spite of himself, actually begins to open up and share his fears. Their intimacy and honesty with one another following this conversation leads, significantly, to penetration. More specifically, James allows Caleb to penetrate him and permeate the barrier or mental block that functions as a hangover from his scarred past. While the audience has a hard-core view of James and Caleb's intimacies, the sex is not coded as frenzied or orgasmic, but rather as sensual, meaningful and healing. The aesthetic of equality here can be seen via a change in the camera position. Interestingly, a 90-degree shift takes place in order to show the audience that even while James is underneath Caleb being penetrated, he is not being positioned 'beneath' him.[2] This act of permeation is thus positioned as an act that is truly 'felt' and a penetration of the senses, rather than a fuck that is performed.

TECHNOLOGICAL ANXIETIES IN THE REALM OF THE SENSES

Indeed, this opening up of the body is connected to James locating his inner strength in an effort to live more happily and honestly in the world. The notion of 'penetrating the senses' is, of course, associated with artistic hard-core, specifically Oshima's infamous film *In the Realm of the Senses*. As in *Shortbus*, practices of voyeurism in Oshima's film interpolate emotional intimacy, sexual desire and sensory engagement. Moreover, Oshima's film is explicitly referenced in *Shortbus*. To be specific, 'In the Realm of the Senses' is the name given to a pink vibrating love egg that Sofia inserts into herself at the salon in order to try and overcome her pre-orgasmic anxieties. Giving over control to her husband, Rob (Raphael Barker), Sofia entrusts him with the remote control for her ironically-named love egg. Sadly, Sofia's hope does not come to fruition. Rob misplaces the remote and it is found by others whose sporadic and comedic pressing of various buttons move Sofia's body so violently that she headbutts, elbows and punches other salon members. Disappointed, pre-orgasmic and angry with herself and her husband, Sofia's frustration boils over. Pulling a plastic model leg ornament off the salon wall, Sofia walks outside, removes the egg from her vagina and smashes it into pieces. Eventually stopping, Sofia bows her head, hunches her shoulders and begins to cry before walking away. This is both a highly comic and tragic scene explicitly signalling the shattering of Sofia's hopes and desires. More significantly however, this scene demonstrates that *Shortbus* is not reductive in treating sexual anxieties as problems that can be easily overcome. Arguably, the failure of Sofia to experience an orgasm, coupled with the attempted suicide of James and the isolation of sex worker Severin, function to acknowledge sexual and social anxieties concerned with sex, satisfaction and sensory permeation.

More specifically, the failure of Sofia's contemporary technology – the vibrating love egg – to 'work', calls into question the link between the

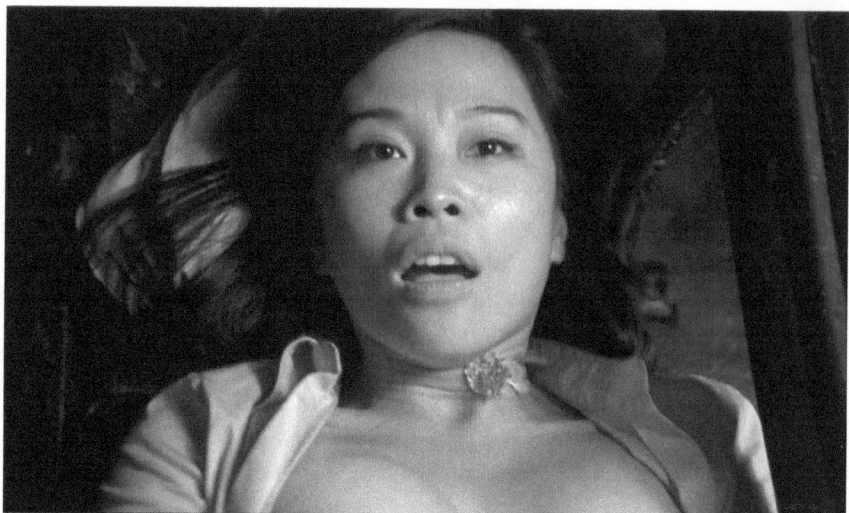

Fig. 22 A pre-orgasmic Sofia.

contemporary commodification and mass dissemination of technologies promising and rendering 'natural' orgasmic pleasure. One of the hard-core elements of Mitchell's film is arguably then its acknowledgement of real human destabilisation, real anxiety, induced by perfect and endless images of pornographic pleasure. In this way, *Shortbus* can be understood to acknowledge the contemporary and often contentious 'place' that hard-core inhabits in popular culture as well as making visible new technologies of pleasure that have helped to shape the ways in which sexual pleasure could, or more probably, should, be performed. Ultimately, *Shortbus* is dominated by the themes of technology and misconnection. Indeed, the irony of the mass of technologies that promote connection is, as Mitchell illustrates, also perhaps part of the problem of misconnection. Connecting technologies – digital video, the internet, the camera, the vibrating love egg – all inhabit complex positions in Mitchell's film. These technologies stress the possibility of connection, of pleasure, and yet can also be seen to function as the source of contemporary anxieties when people feel that they have failed to live up to, or connect with others, in spite of the endless possibilities. As the film draws to a close, it is in fact a visible disconnection – a black-out experienced by the whole of New York City – that functions as a catalyst to bring all of the characters back to the Shortbus salon.

The new darkness of the city makes visible the over-reliance on connecting technologies in contemporary society. The black-out brings to light the power of haptic human interconnections that can only be made face-to-face. It is amidst this darkness, that 'real' connections finally take place. Sofia opens herself up to an experience with a couple whose lovemaking in the orgy room she has previously admired. James and Jamie return to Shortbus together – the truth of James's previous impermeability, exposed and acknowledged allowing them to move on and partake in an equal relationship. Ceth and Caleb see each other in a new light and make a connection. Severin seems to genuinely enjoy the company and connections of others in a different and positive way. Sofia finally cums. The lights of the city come back on. The backdrop to all this is a salon party, a finale over which Justin Bond, dressed in a Grecian style gown (mirroring the situation of the Statue of Liberty at the beginning of the film) presides. Crooning 'Everybody Gets it in the End', Bond's performance is accompanied by an energetic and spirited marching band. Salon members smile, laugh, cheer, sing along, scream and dance. Knowing looks are exchanged between the main characters, Severin, Rob and Sofia and James and Jamie, recognising, we may infer, the significance of this shared and hopeful experience. In this finale, the power and energy generated by honest and real connection can, Mitchell illustrates, fuse disparate desires and create a contemporary culture of increased understanding in which we can all 'get it in the end'. While there is undoubtedly what Linda Williams nominates as an 'orgasmic imperative' (2008: 288) projected in *Shortbus*, the final figuration of this orgasmic imperative is refigured and re-framed. Sofia's orgasmic achievement 'in the end' of the film is represented not with a money shot but through a close-up of her face, contorted, exhilarated and softly-lit. The aesthetic employed here, while climactic, is anything but affectively arousing. Rather, this finale makes visible the significance of community, active sensitivity and soulful connection. The lyrics of Bond's song are poignantly revealing, relaying the difficult and challenging core experiences of the film's protagonists and their quest for a pleasure that permeates the skin – that touches the soul. Bond sings: 'We all bear the scars yeah, we all feign a laugh, we all cry in the dark, get cut off before we start, but … we all get it in the end.' Indeed, this is a song about the human experiences, human anxieties, human disconnections that affect and connect us all. Such a serious approach and aesthetic appears again to be at odds with traditional hard-core, yet, it must not be forgotten that the experience of orgasm is situated as central to re-connection in Mitchell's film.

The orgy of the orgasmic/highbrow ends optimistically demonstrating the sensorial success of Mitchell's incisive yet sexually explicit engagements with his characters/actors on the 'Sex Film Project'. Sofia's sublime orgasm (achieved through her ability to finally let go of the hard-core physical ideal), marks a change of status in which the orgasm comes through an opening up of her mind rather than just her body. The ending of *Shortbus* thus exhibits the displacement of the singularity of hard-core physical arousal, instead, appropriating in its place, the significance of intellectual arousal via a penetrating highbrow aesthetic. The salon is alight with hope, diversity, orgasmic energy and euphoria. It is a euphoria that likely infects the filmic audience as we are explicitly reminded of our own implication and participation in the construction of this highbrow hard-core vision. Forced to recognise the closing down of our own voyeuristic experience, one line of diegetic dialogue seems hauntingly apt, specifically Bond's assertion to the then-Shortbus newcomer Sofia, 'voyeurism is participation'. We too then, it is finally revealed, have actively engaged in, connected with, and contributed to Mitchell's 'Sex Film Project'.

NOTES

1. Mitchell states: 'The place that most directly inspired the film is a place called Cine Salon, which is run by the guy who passes out condoms in the movie during the sex show. At Cine Salon they would show experimental short films and then hand out food. And then at the end of the evening, in the same space, not a big apartment and filled with about 30 or 40 people, sex would break out. It was fascinating that sex was a part of the whole evening' (Foley n.d.).
2. I would like to express my thanks to Dr. Greg Tuck, Senior Lecturer in Film Studies at UWE Bristol, for drawing my attention to this aesthetic detail at the SCMS Conference 2010.

WORKS CITED

Foley, J. (n.d.) 'Shortbus – John Cameron Mitchell's interview', IndieLondon. On-line. Available: http://www.indielondon.co.uk/Film-Review/shortbus-john-cameron-mitchell-interview (accessed 13 March 2010).

Krzywinska, T. (2006) *Sex and the Cinema*. London and New York: Wallflower Press.

Lamble, D. (2006) *John Cameron Mitchell (Shortbus)*, David Lamble/Claudesplace.com Interview. On-line. Available: http://video.google.com/videoplay?docid=1695377531690680469# (accessed 12 March 2010).

Mitchell, J.C. (2006) 'Gifted and Challenged: The Making of *Shortbus*', DVD Extra on *Shortbus*.

Nichols, B. (1991) *Representing Reality: Issues and Concepts in Documentary*. Bloomington and Indianapolis: Indiana University Press.

Sacher-Masoch, L. and G. Deleuze (1989) *Masochism: Coldness and Cruelty: Venus in Furs*, trans. by Jean Mc Neil. New York: Zone Books.

Williams, L. (2008) *Screening Sex*. Durham and London: Duke University Press.

CHAPTER ELEVEN

HOMESPUN: FINNPORN AND THE MEANINGS OF THE LOCAL

Susanna Paasonen

100% Finnish girls show all their abilities to the hungry camera team. But that's not all! Genuine Finnish Santa Claus visits the set a couple of times to check out the sucking and fucking skills of these youg [sic] Finnish beauties … Witness a dissolute mating ritual at Tampere's Viikinsaari. Watch as a horny couple, to the horror of elderly folks, fuck their way in Suomenlinna.

Rich in promises of hard-core action performed and recorded in specific geographical locations, this introduction to Radical Pictures' *Finnish Fuck Film* (2007) is exemplary of how the meanings of 'the local' are played out in Finnish porn production (also known as 'Finnporn' or *suomiporno*). Through recognisable settings and details, homespun execution and semi-amateur performances, the films invite their viewers – Finnish viewers in particular – into affinities based on familiarity. This chapter provides a brief overview of porn production in Finland and investigates the ties between the local origins of the films and their claims for authenticity. Based on a broad sample of contemporary Finnporn, it considers four films – *Pure Porn* (2001), *Fucked in Finland* (2004), *Finnish Fuck Film* and *The Magic Birds* (2008) – and addresses the role and function of things Finnish in them. The main concern is how regional and national origins become tied to notions of realism and how these ties structure particular relationships between the viewers and what is depicted on screen, such as national culture, identity, imagery and gender politics.

FINNISH PORNOSCAPE – A BRIEF OVERVIEW

The Nordic countries enjoy a certain pop cultural reputation as havens of sexual liberalism and accessible pornography. Denmark was the first country to decriminalise audiovisual hard-core pornography in 1969, followed by Sweden two years later. Both countries became central European producers and distributors of pornography: Lasse Braun's production company Beta Film gained wide fame with their Super 8mm porn loops produced in 1966–77 that were also distributed in North American peepshow parlours. The Swedish Private Media group, built around the first full-colour hard-core magazine *Private* (est. 1965), also grew into one of the largest European adult entertainment companies (see Di Lauro and Rabkin 1976; McNeil *et al.* 2005; Lane 2000; Smith 2005). These developments, along with the already established practice of screening Danish and Swedish films (both art-house and documentary films featuring some degree of nudity) in North American sex film theatres, helped to establish persistent connections between Scandinavia and pornography (see Williams 1989; Wyatt 1999; Kulick 2005).[1]

However, despite the reputation for liberalism, during this period the relevant legislation governing pornography did not change in Finland, Norway or Iceland. In Finland, a 1927 law regulating offences against 'sexual discipline and decency' – that is, regulating the production, import, export, advertising and distribution of pornography – was not replaced until 1999. This facilitated both easier access to hard-core pornography and a rise in local productions (see Jyränki 2007; Paasonen 2009). From the 1970s to the late 1990s, local porn production consisted mainly of print magazines: although films were made since the 1980s (often abroad), they received little attention (see Korppi 2002). Whilst legislation remained fairly strict – and became stricter with the 1987 video law banning the production and distribution of all material forbidden to under 18-year-olds – public attitudes towards pornography have been, and remain, more positive in Finland than in the other Nordic countries. According to surveys, women as well as men are interested in hard-core pornography and it is in mundane use particularly among the younger generations (see, for example, Haavio-Mannila and Kontula 2001; Anttila 2004; Sørensen and Knudsen 2006; Kontula 2008).

The new millennium witnessed something of a porn trend in Finland, facilitated by these transformations in legislation, new technologies of production and distribution (such as online porn) as well as an increased visibility of pornography in the mainstream media (see Nikunen *et al.* 2005). Female porn performers and producers, most centrally Rakel Liekki, Mariah, Laura Sade and Emilia, Laura Lee and Sabina of the ELS Productions, helped to redefine Finnish pornography as an arena of female agency and exploration. These women had years of experience working in the industry and their public image was largely that of savvy, intelligent and independent entrepreneurs (see Nikunen 2005; Nikunen and Paasonen 2007). Numerous films by women – like Mariah Production's *Mariah Pornfolio* (2004), *Filthy Passion* (1999), *Showtime* (c.2000) and *Truth or Dare* (c.2000), ELS Productions' *Best of ELS* (2002) and *ELS Behind the Scenes* (2004) or Laura Productions' *Bonneville* (c.2004), *Ironsteel* (c.2005) and *Sneaking on My Sister* (2006, shot on HDV) – have tended to approximate the style, feel and production values of international hard-core pornography. Aimed at broader international distribution, these films have generally been void of Finnish language or any specifically local references.

In the early 2000s, women ran up to two-thirds of Finnish film porn production (see Korppi 2002) yet the trend was short-lived: both Liekki and Mariah have since retired from the industry, and Laura Productions, operating primarily online, remains the most successful of the current female-run companies. The market for Finnporn remains small and profits are thin, particularly since broader distribution is difficult to achieve. Local film production relies on a handful of active producers (Radical Pictures being the most notable one) whose films continue to be identifiable by semi-amateurism, small budgets and homespun aesthetics. Due to the small-scale production and the central role of women, Finnporn has been framed as 'fair-trade' in the sense that it lacks the kinds of exploitative work practices associated with the industry internationally. In a further analogy to locally grown consumables, Finnish performers are often defined as 'organic' (*luomu*) in the sense of not having gone through cosmetic surgery and having relatively little work experience in the field. This has helped to frame domestic porn as more ethical and 'authentic' than its foreign competitors – and also as more 'real' in its semi-amateur execution.

It is noteworthy that the internationally-oriented aesthetic and economic strategies of Mariah, Laura or ELS Production differ from those of other Finnish production companies that highlight the national origins of their products as a form of branding and promotion. Many DVDs come with little Finnish flags connoting nationality and film titles make references to the country in question, as in the Radical Pictures titles *Fucked in Finland, Finnish Fuck Film, Finnish Teens Fuck* (2005), *Teen Pussies from Finland* (2005), *Teensex from Finland 1* (2006) and *2* (2007), *Finnish Teens 1* (2005) and *2* (2006), *Real Finnish Porn 1* (2005) and *2* (2006), *True Finnporn 1* (2005) and *2* (2006), *Girls from Finland* (2006) or *Domestic Heat 1* (2006) and *2* (2006). Like Radical Pictures, Kullervo Koivisto (of KKCane) decorates his titles, including *Finnish Girls 1* (2005), *2* (2006) and *3* (2006), with a small Finnish flag. Considerable emphasis is laid on the national origins of the female performers in particular. Through its repeated commodification, the figure of the 'Finnish Girl' has been construed as an object of desire that is both reachable and recognisable as a semi-amateur girl-next-door. Unlike women considered porn stars (for instance, Mariah, Rakel Liekki, Jamina or Candy) selling titles with their own names, 'Finnish Girl' is a more anonymous term referring to a contingent group of young female performers. Finnish Girl is then a brand crafted and developed by the production companies – a sexualised fantasy figure connoting amateurism, youth and familiarity.

HOMESPUN AND 'AUTHENTIC'

Due to legislation, it was largely up to Swedish companies to distribute porn shot in Finland and/or featuring Finnish performers before (and some time after) the year 1999. These films were marketed with promises of local girls – both in titles with an all-Finnish focus (*Finnish Amateur Action/Finsk amatör action* (1998); *Finish* [sic] *Nights* (2000); *Finnish Giant/Finska Gigant*, (c.2000) or *Go Finland!/Heja Finland!* (c.2000)) and in ones with more of a pan-Nordic approach (*Nordic Debutantes 2* (1997); *North Sucks/Norden Suger*, (c.2000) or *So Hot up North/Het så in i Norden* (c.2000)). Many of these films were shot in Denmark and Sweden while the Finnish performers spoke Swedish or English. The styles of the individual films range from amateur porn to glossier mainstream hard-core action. Regional specificity is manifested through language and accent, as well as the overall packaging and framing: *Go Finland!*, for example, starts with a spinning Finnish flag and the cover of *Mariana* (2002) comes with an emblem stating 'Made in Finland'. Further local marking is achieved through clothing, décor and other forms of material culture. *Finnish Amateur Action*, yet another film with a large Finnish flag decorating its cover, starts with a shot of a man jogging in a shell-suit, a piece of clothing iconic to the semi-rural and/or suburban post-recession Finland of the 1990s. The sexual acts in this film take place inside a wooden house of the kind seen in abundance in the Finnish countryside. Such references to the local cultural landscape became more accentuated as films catered to a specifically Finnish (rather than Nordic or international) audience in the 2000s.

Whilst Finnporn was an unknown category a decade ago, it has since become a staple niche that is distributed on DVD locally and on the internet globally (as both pay-per-view and torrents) available to all. In most cases, however, the films are not dubbed or subtitled and they remain understandable only to a Finnish-speaking audience (to the extent that dialogue actually plays a central role in understanding and experiencing such films). The films make use of local performers, vernacular language and cultural codes that set these products apart from their international competitors. As Merja Lind (2000) has pointed out, such a multilayered coding of 'Finnishness' has been equally central in porn magazines and their narrative elements. The sense of the regional, the homespun and the familiar are key factors in the films' marketing and assumed appeal to audiences. *Fucked in Finland*, the very first film by Radical Pictures, is shot exclusively indoors and most of the scenes are set in the same bedroom. The performers address the camera directly and interact with the cameraman, creating a feel of familiarity and directness. The back cover of the DVD frames the action as both domestic and amateur:

> 100% genuine Finnish production where no time is wasted on chit chat. See how Finnish blokes fuck beautiful girls first time in front of the camera. The first timer girls will surely remember these fuck sessions in the next millennium!

The promise of ingénue women involved in porn for the first time is repeated on the cover of one title after another. Closely tied to the Finnish origins of the performers and producers, codes of amateurism and inexperience give rise to a broader assemblage of 'realness'. This is clearly illustrated by Radical Pictures' online introductions to their titles:

> Are you bored with fake acted basic porn? So were we and so we made this genuine home sex video. It is 100% real thing where all mouning and groaning is for real and the drops of swet are true. See how finnish [sic] people truly fuck! (*Finnish Amateurs 1*, 2005).

> – This material is over the top
> – It is completely finnish, all girls and boys are finnish
> – Models do not act. The action is for real and girls cum genuinely [sic]
> (*Finnish Teens 1*)

In a rhetorical move characteristic of the marketing of gonzo, reality and amateur porn, the titles claim to show the reality of sex rather than fictitious, acted, scripted or stylised variations of it. In contrast to 'fake acted basic porn', these films are framed as real, raw and authentic.

Similar framing is used in the promotion of Finnporn more generally and it also seems to play an important role in its reception, judging from online discussions of domestic porn. A discussant on the forum topic 'Masturbation', for example, associates his interest in Finnish porn with being bored of 'the eternal "oh fuck, ooh, ahh, fuck my fucking ass with your fucking big cock, oh yeah..."' as iterated in US productions (Azor 2008). For their part, the discussants on the *Elitisti* forum (a 'popular-elitist film zine') remain more suspicious of the pleasures, production values and professionalism of Finnish porn making. This is evident in the opening questions of the thread, asking: 'Is it really so that Finns have no idea as to how make porn? At least all the stuff I've seen has worked mainly as social porn... Has anyone here ... looked "closely" into domestic productions? Can anything be found among all the crap?' On pondering these questions, others participants reminisce about some 'fresh', 'spontaneous' and 'real' performances, noting that some of Radical's female performers are 'pert' and the films are 'pleasantly stripped-down in their audiovisual expression' (see Elitisti 2006). Nevertheless, the overall tone remains sceptical.

On yet other forums, Finnporn is repeatedly critiqued for its lack of quality: 'I'm not too interested in Finnish porn production already for the simple reason that the films and the women tend to be pretty awful', 'Finnporn suuuuuucks to no limit' (see City 2008) and 'Finnporn equals some fat white broad moaning on some mattress with a hood over her head and some hairy dude slapping her ass with some cunt-leather chain!' (see Basso 2002). This line of critique is encapsulated in a review of the film *The Magic Birds*: 'Finnporn reminds one mainly of pimply asses, shaky camera, corny lines and poor quality' (Paroni 2008). All these comments do, in different ways, set Finnporn apart from general or mainstream pornography and characterise it as homespun, semi-amateur and 'raw', yet they also give different meanings and values to its special characteristics. Rawness is considered both a virtue and a fault (although rarely at the same time), depending on what is identified as desirable or 'good' pornography. The films themselves involve a broad play with the local, particularly when it comes to locations, dialogue and cultural references. This works to construct specific relationships between the films, their performers/producers and viewers that can be found appealing, off-putting or both. In addition to being homespun, the films are markedly domestic and 'homely'. When anchored in identifiable Finnish locations (e.g. cityscapes, landscapes, buildings, monuments, cars or trains), they gain a further sense of realism.

GETTING UP CLOSE

Finnish Fuck Film/Kotimainen pornoelokuva starts with a sequence shot on a lakeside island, Viikinsaari, near the city of Tampere. The very first shot displays a cruise boat with a large Finnish flag swaying in the wind, hence verifying the title's promises of domestic origins and focus. Other scenes are shot on location in the Suomenlinna fortress (a UNESCO World Heritage site) as well as the Ferris wheel at the Linnanmäki amusement park. All in all, the sense of the regional is played out at the levels of language, locations and props to excess: in two of the scenes, performers are dressed in a Santa Claus costume (since, according to tourist bureaus and vernacular stories, Santa is Finnish and resides on the Lapland fell of Korvatunturi).[2] The regional is equally present in minor quotidian details such as shoes and clothes – or even the

Fig. 23 What's in Santa's bag? Tony Scorpion and Jatta in *Finnish Fuck Film*.

plastic bag of the grocery market chain, Prisma, wrapped around 'Santa's' penis in an oral sex scene. Local references are ironic and over-the-top, yet also the very fabric that Finnporn is made of.

In one sequence in *Finnish Fuck Film*, a couple are having sex on a rock by the lake as a storm begins: rain starts pouring down and their random possessions are blown over by gusts of wind that also threaten to turn over the camera's tripod. The couple simply gets up and finds another location, and the filming continues despite the rain and visibly chilly weather. This solution is motivated by a low budget and tight shooting schedule, yet it also works to produce a sense of the recognisable to those familiar with Nordic summer conditions. Similarly, in *Pure Porn: Cock-hawks from the Woods/Silkkaa pornoa: metsikön munahaukat* (2001), a couple is performing outdoors on a ski-jumping judges' platform as they notice some passers-by taking an interest in their activities and decide to leave. This is also the end of the episode, midway into the scene. Such impromptu improvisation feeds into and supports a specific form of pornographic realism, namely the promise of authenticity and directness (in the sense of the non-manipulated and that which has truly taken place) that is central both to pornography as a genre and Finnporn as one of its niche subcategories.

My argument is not that these films would facilitate some easier form of identification with the characters or scenarios depicted. In fact, identification may be too large and loose a term for describing the dynamics and experiences of pornography that entail much more random and shifting moments of recognition and arousal. The films do not generally involve one large narrative but consist of independent scenes featuring different performers in varying positions and places, simply having sex. *Fucked in Finland* exemplifies such stripped-down modality: episodes start as the actors enter (or are seen as already being in) a room and as the sexual acts have reached their climax, the episode ends and another begins. There is hardly any dialogue and no first names are used. Whilst this may be an extreme example – *Pure Porn*, for instance, contains some minimal narrative framing (a man picks up a female hitchhiker in two scenes; a couple hooks up; a man reminisces past sexual adventures when waiting for his date to arrive) – there is little in the films to go on in terms of background or motivation. Overall, character construction and the development of narrative, central to classic analyses of identification within film studies, remain only marginal concerns: there may be no central character, the focus may be shifting and the viewer is constantly invited to assume the position of an outside observer.

As Laura Marks (2002) notes, both optimised visibility (of sexual acts, body parts and bodily fluids) and a distance (in terms of identification) between the viewer and the bodies on the screen are characteristic to pornography as a genre. In Finnporn, the sense of distance is further heightened by their explicitly performative style: actors look directly at the camera, address the viewer, talk with the production team and follow their orders and suggestions. While the films are 'in your face' and 'up close' in detailed depictions of sexual acts and the bodies performing them, they do not invite the viewer into an intimate proximity with the characters on the screen by the means of identification. Rather, the modality remains laconic, stripped-down and observational – similar to those of reality television or gonzo porn. This version of *cinéma verité*, together with the heavy reliance on vernacular material culture and the overall unpolished style of the individual performances, invests the films with an unsettling quality, particularly for the Finnish viewer. It is this sense of the recognisable and the direct that can arguably give rise to awkward moments of discomfort and embarrassment as much as arousal.

Consider, for example, a scene in the porn comedy *Little Dick's Lessons of Life/Pikku-Kallen oppivuodet* (2002) where a couple are seen having sex in the woods next to an outhouse while a swarm of mosquitoes circles and bites the performers. The scene is not only about hard-core heteroporn but equally about ironic references to local vernacular culture. It may be experienced as sexually arousing but arousal is tied into, framed and conditioned by this particular landscape. Instead of identification, the homespun realism of Finnporn enables and encourages forms of recognisability, familiarity and hence overall accessibility of the performers, spaces and acts recorded that may even be felt as getting 'too close'. Such affinities or engagements may involve characters, objects, acts or sounds. The viewer, sharing the codes of vernacular language and local references, is simultaneously an 'insider' (in the sense of 'getting it') and an outsider in the sense that the scenarios are always performed for them as an implied recipient.

NATIONAL PORNOGRAPHY

Similar to *Finnish Fuck Film*, the scenes in the film *Pure Porn* are shot mainly outdoors, with performers driving through the Finnish countryside and performing sex in recognisable environments, such as the ski-jump towers of Lahti, which had hosted the winter sports world championships the same year. One of the scenes is shot in Aulanko, a lakeside hill near Hämeenlinna, which has been considered one of Finland's 'national landscapes' since the national romantic movement of the late nineteenth century. Aulanko has been promoted extensively for tourism and reproduced in scenic photographs to the point of becoming an iconic location (see Eskola 1997a; 1997b). In the film, a couple – Rakel Liekki and Jari – meet up in the Aulanko Jugendstil gazebo, engage in sexual acts in the stone fortress, and perform on the platform of the 1930s sightseeing tower overlooking the lake. Shots of oral sex are intercut with pans of the scenery, tying the acts firmly into the landscape and its multiple symbolic layers. Similar panoramic shots of Aulanko have been used to promote national sentiment, for example as illustration to the lyrics of the national anthem (see Eskola 1997a). The film mixes the conventions of pornography (loitering around Aulanko, Liekki is licking a large pink lollipop the shape of a penis, dressed in a girly mini-skirt and long socks) with the conventional pleasures attached to this location (such as sightseeing or watching ducklings). The combination of hard-core action, iconic locations and their historically accumulated symbolic layers results in something approximating a 'national pornography'.

The Magic Birds, directed and produced by Kullervo Koivisto (who is best known for his *Finnish Girl* series mentioned above) involves a different, yet equally knowing step in the direction of 'national pornography'. The film also stands apart from other domestic productions in its narrative and *mise-en-scène*. Set in a mythical past a thousand years ago preceding the systematic rule of the Swedish crown, the film depicts a wintery landscape inhabited by a tribe of violent Amazon warrior women. These Amazons are named Magic Birds (*Uivelot*, as the title goes in Finnish) after a species of duck (smew, to be exact) that they use as inspiration for both their black and white make-up and stylised mode of communication (through bird-like cries and sounds). The Magic Birds are renowned for their cruelty as well as their habit of enslaving men and treating them 'worse than domestic animals'.

The film opens with shots of the women on the icy terrains of Lake Saimaa dragging a shirtless male sex slave behind them in a sledge, accompanied by a voiceover narration that outlines the narrative framework. Aesthetically, and in its vaguely early medieval costumes and décor in particular, *The Magic Birds* is reminiscent of fictions that draw on the Finnish epic *Kalevala*, such as Kalle Holmberg's 1982 television series *The Iron Age*. Compiled of folklore

Fig. 24 The Magic Birds on the iced-over Lake Saimaa.

poetry by Elias Lönnrot, *Kalevala* has been an important cultural element in the building of Finnish national sentiment and identity since its first publication in 1849. As a kind of mythical origin story, it continues to influence ways of imagining Finnish culture. For example, Louhi, the matriarch ruler of an evil and cold land, Pohjola, as depicted in *Kalevala*, was one of the central characters of *The Iron Age*: the shores of Pohjola were decorated with bodies of men and Louhi possessed impressive magical powers over weather, healing and even heavenly bodies. Like Louhi, the Magic Birds represent cruel matriarchal power: they are insatiable, aggressive and devoid of feminine softness.

With its explicit referencing of national mythology and its canonised representations, *The Magic Birds* was intended for international distribution and it was in production for five years. The finished version, however, remains something of a patchwork with less than thirty minutes of higher quality footage set in the mythical past, shot on the wintery lakeside and featuring performers in quasi-historical garb and fantasy make-up. In contrast, most of the film, spanning more than an hour, follows the homespun mode of Finnporn under the headline 'the Magic Birds of today'. Set in the contemporary, it depicts young sexually active women making their presence and heritage known. The more homespun scenes are mostly stripped of excessive make-up or stylised acting. Despite their drastically different style, these scenes are also saturated with culturally specific references: sequences are shot in a summer cottage, sauna and lakeshore, all locations invested with symbolic meanings – the stuff that Finnish summers are made of. This landscape is partly depicted as experienced through the eyes of a foreign man (Tony Scorpion) in search for contemporary Magic Birds. (He is referred to simply as 'the Foreigner' and his alien status is verified by English language, as well as his recurring cries, such as 'Mamma mia!')

In one notable montage sequence, the camera first shows a lakeside ship about to dock, then cuts to shots of a small fox scratching its jaw in the grass, a middle-aged couple getting dressed after swimming in the nude, the calm surfaces of Lake Saimaa in the soft rays of the midsummer evening sun, birch leaves and a country road. All this is accompanied by an accordion sing-along of the popular World War II-era song, 'Life in the Trenches' ('Elämää juoksuhaudoissa'). The song is deeply melancholic; describing a soldier's longing for home, lost love and the uncertainty of life, and efficiently glues the shots together into a nostalgic cavalcade of all things Finnish. As the montage sequence continues and the location changes to that of a dancehall, the sound becomes diegetic. In the following shots, people are gathered outside the hall, enjoying drinks and dancing, an old man is holding a pint of beer, dressed in a blue-and-white sweatshirt with the word 'Finland'[3] written on the front, some ducks have gathered at the shore, the moon is full over the lake and people on the dance floor do the 'letkajenkka', a popular group dance of the 1960s. As the music continues, the camera shifts to the lakeshore where a young woman, dressed in skimpy Magic Bird garb, circles a campfire. The sequence is short – less than a minute long – and shot over a couple of hours as the midsummer sun turns into blue twilight. Since the montage serves no clear function in terms of the narrative or sexual action, its main motivation is to provide a series of quick yet rich references to popular Finnish iconography and to embed the mythological Magic Birds in this cultural landscape.

STRONG FINNISH WOMEN

Female sexual insatiability is a central recurring theme in pornography: in porn, female desire, sexual performance or orgasmic potentiality seems to know no bounds. As Linda Williams has shown, the figure of female insatiability dates back to literary pornography and it has been given comical, threatening as well as positive meanings (1989: 175–82). In the 2000s, this figure is mainly positive and associated with promises of sexual accessibility and abundance (see Kangasvuo 2007). On Finnporn DVD covers, women 'can't get enough' (*My Film*, 2002), 'nothing is sacred' to these 'young horny pussies' (*The Magic Birds*), 'hardy porn prima donnas keep the male actors trembling with fear in their place' (*Behind the Scenes*) and 'sex-loving horny insatiable women give all in the most extraordinary acts… As these lusty ladies get their hands on a man, they dance the horizontal mambo with furious raunchiness' (*Best of ELS*). In a recurring theme, the male actors are framed as being at the mercy of insatiable women ready to do anything for their own sexual satisfaction. This theme is obviously taken further in the 'historical' sequences of *The Magic Birds* where ruthless Amazons keep men as sex slaves. The voiceover explains that the rule of the Birds came to an end centuries ago, the tribe almost died out and men gained their basic rights. Nevertheless, the narrator explains, the legacy of the Birds is still alive among the Finnish female population. Or, as the back cover of the DVD exclaims, 'oh pity the man who is left at the mercy of the Magic Birds of today'.

In addition to the generic conventions of pornography, the theme of female dominance and insatiability in *The Magic Birds* can also be read as a take on a particular national gender mythology involving strong Finnish women and weak Finnish men. In other words, by following the hyperbolic depiction of gender differences, sexual desires and pleasures characteristic to porn in general, it also references specific national gender imagery. Film scholar Anu Koivunen has traced the development of this gender imagery featuring strong women and weak men back to Finland's agrarian history, traumas of World War II, male alcoholism and the *Kalevala*. According to Koivunen, this imagery has been mapped out and reiterated since the 1930s in a range of fictions, commentaries and public debates. Narratives on the 'strength' or 'power' of Finnish women have been anchored in 'a past, pre-modern, agrarian world' and, through references to the *Kalevala*, a 'mythical timelessness of repetition and monumentality' (2004: 12). Through such performative reiteration, this story has gained particular power and become a 'foundational fiction' used in making sense of gender in the Finnish context. In *The Magic Birds*, this gender imagery is not only made explicit but hyperbolic: the men are literally held captive and enslaved in cages while the women rule the land and use their dominant position as they choose.

The fact that *The Magic Birds* was finished and released (locally) on DVD owes much to one supporting performer, Johanna Tukiainen, seen briefly topless in the first part of the film. In the spring of 2008, Tukiainen – head of the erotic dance group 'Dolls' – made public some of the erotic SMS messages that Ilkka Kanerva, the Minister of Foreign Affairs, had sent her. After publicly lying about the communication, and having been found out lying, Kanerva had to resign. For her part, Tukiainen became a national celebrity (albeit one with considerably low cultural status) and her newly found fame helped to sell *The Magic Birds*. The evening papers made headlines of Tukiainen's participation in the film: a video of her practicing smew-like bird sounds and following the director's instructions on location was viewed more than million times, becoming the most popular video of the year on the website of the newspaper *Ilta-Sanomat*. The same paper published a tongue-in-cheek review of the film's trailer, comparing it to both *The Iron Age* and Erik Blomberg's classic 1952 film *The White Reindeer* (featuring a young woman turned into a man-killing reindeer) under the title 'Man is a sex slave to the Magic Birds'. The review also noted that 'if Ilkka Kanerva had had the opportunity of watching *The Magic Birds*, he would have mapped the field of action through the eyes of a preying Magic Bird tribe-member, rather than his own masculinity' (Manninen 2008), thereby linking Tukiainen and her actions to the cinematic landscape of dominant women and oppressed men.

Both the release of *The Magic Birds* and the controversy over the case of Tukiainen and Kanerva coincided with a debate on 'women's sexual power' initiated by Henry Laasanen's (2008) book of the same name (also mentioned in the *Ilta-Sanomat* review). According to Laasanen, women's sexual power is one of the unnoticed social forces: women control access to sex (the sex in question being unquestionably heterosexual) and men have to pay for sex one way or another while also suffering from performance anxiety and role expectations. This variation of the discourse of 'strong Finnish women' with sexual powers and weak Finnish men suffering from the consequences, as presented by Laasanen, gained some popular attention. The very public incident of Tukiainen and Kanerva was used repeatedly as reference to and further proof of Laasanen's arguments: it was sexual desire that caused Kanerva's downfall, while sex was Tukiainen's main asset.[4] In these instances, the national mythology of strong women and weak men became explicitly sexualised (in contrast to the more traditional variations emphasising maternal power). The markedly excessive and fantastic imageries of *The Magic Birds* draw on, and contribute to, the stories told about Finnish gender relations – from national mythologies and their displays across the field of media to debates on gender equality and heterosex. But by drawing on the national gender imagery of strong women and weak men, the film also builds it into a sexualised spectacle that, in its excessiveness and explicit artificiality (in terms of stylised acting, make-up, clothing and the guttural cries of the Magic Birds) also reads as parody of this very imagery. Indeed, the voice of the male narrator outlining the story betrays some amusement, as if drawing quotation marks around it all.

However, as an attempt at 'national porn', *The Magic Birds* is knowingly attached to multiple layers of culture in ways that are not merely ironic or parodic. There is a certain seriousness to the film that renders it disturbing as it oscillates between stylised references to the *Kalevala* in the framework of hard-core heteroporn, and scenes that follow the aesthetics of semi-amateurism (with young women urinating in train bathrooms, exploring the pleasures of sex toys or entering a 'porn cave' of the rural town of Imatra). Displaying particular kinds of gendered bodies – such as blonde young women or seemingly drunken men – *The Magic Birds* also gives shape to collective bodies through the 'syntaxes' of national gender mythology and pornographic hyperbole.

LOCAL PORN FOR LOCAL PEOPLE?

In *Intimate Citizenship*, Ken Plummer discusses the circulation of intimacy as different kinds of 'flows': between the local and the global, sameness and difference. With this, Plummer refers to the ways in which 'local cultures pick up, and usually transform the many features of personal life displayed around the globe' and how 'certain stock images of sex, marriage, bodies, and gender roles ... are packaged and marketed in efficient and predictable forms' (2003: 119; 121). Such a dynamic is evident in Finnporn. Local aspects and references can be subdued (as with ELS or Laura Productions), manifest, heightened or even fetishised (as in the 'Finnish Girl' series, *The Magic Birds*, *Pure Porn*, *Fucked in Finland* or *Finnish Fuck Film*). Yet the films also follow the generic codes and conventions of porn in their depictions of sexual acts, arousal, pleasure, body parts and fluids that repeat from one film to another across linguistic and cultural borders.

Like the seemingly contradictory and parallel, yet mutually inseparable flows of globalised intimacies addressed by Plummer, the category of porn is simultaneously bulky and diverse, incredibly repetitive and notably divergent in terms of its aesthetics and production practices (involving studio systems, cottage industries and random sex radicals alike). In the Finnish context of small-scale production, terms such as 'porn industry' or 'porn star' seem rather grandiose. Since international distribution remains a challenge despite online platforms, Finnish films have mainly a local audience. The films are rich in references to local scenery (landscapes, monuments, buildings and so forth) and material cultures of everyday life. These can be seen as attempts at branding Finnporn to an international audience through touristic vistas and local colour, yet I would argue that they involve more of a knowing and marked attempt at catering porn to Finnish viewers. Paraphrasing the BBC comedy *The League of Gentlemen* (1999–2002), the pleasures involved in such 'local porn for local people' expand from sexually explicit action to mundane details, phrases and cultural references that fail to translate to those more unfamiliar with the cultural landscape. As argued above, the proximity between Finnporn and its viewers is not one of identification inasmuch as shared codes, recognition and familiarity that work to strengthen the films' claims of homespun authenticity and overall realism. This involves a particular modality unsettling in its familiarity as mundane details, bodies and objects draw the Finnish viewer close, and possibly even a bit too close for comfort.

NOTES

1. Such tenuous associations are evident, for example, in the naming of Caballero's popular film series *Swedish Erotica*, beginning in the 1970s. Starting with Super 8, and competing with Braun's productions, these all-American films, spanning some 120 titles and featuring major porn stars from John Holmes to Seka, migrated to VHS and DVD and became the most widely sold adult film series ever. However, the films are connected to Sweden by name only.
2. The same shots with Santa are also used on the cover of other Radical Productions titles, *Edestä ja takaa – nämä tytöt jakaa* (freely translated as *From the Back or Front, These Girls Give*, 2008) and *Ja taas nussitaan* (*And Let's Fuck Again*, 2007), while shots from Suomenlinna also decorate the cover of *Naidaan vaan* (*Let's Just Fuck*, 2007). Such recycling of the same scenes in a range of titles is standard practice in pornography but it is also telling of the small production volume of Finnish companies and their aim to capitalise on their scarce supply of products. For similar reasons, scenes in most Finnish porn films include camera flashes as they double as photo sessions for online and print media.
3. 'Suomi' sweatshirt: the design was modelled after those worn by the Finnish track and field athletes of the past decades and it has been popular for decades. In this sense, it embodies both nostalgia and national sentiment.
4. I stumbled on this connection rather abruptly myself as a journalist from the Finnish News Agency phoned me to ask 'whether Tukiainen has sexual power' while making a news item on the theme for national distribution. The connection was also picked up on Laasanen's blog.

WORKS CITED

Anttila, A. (ed.) (2004) *Lapsuuden muuttuva maisema: puheenvuoroja kulutuskulttuurin seksualisoinnin vaikutuksista*. Helsinki: STAKES.

Azor (2008) 'Re: Finnporn online?' *Itsetyydytys.org* [discussion list], 25 October. On-line. Available: http://www.itsetyydytys.org/keskustelu/index.php?topic=38649.0 (accessed 27 March 2009).

Basso (2002) 'The best porn star', *Basso* [discussion list], 5 February. On-line. Available: http://www.basso.fi/keskustelu_aihe.php?v=13435s (accessed 27 March 2009).

City (2008) *Citypress Oy* [discussion list], 28 July. On-line. Available: http://www.city.fi/keskustelut/view.php?id=52240&total=62&offset=0 (accessed 27 March 2009).

Di Lauro, A. and G. Rabkin (1976) *Dirty Movies: An Illustrated History of the Stag Film 1915–1970*. New York: Chelsea House.

Elitisti (2006) 'Domestic porn', *Elitisti* [discussion list], 17 July. On-line. Available: http://www.elitisti.net/forum/index.php?showtopic=4647 (accessed 27 March 2009).

Eskola, T. (1997a) *Teräslintu ja lumpeenkukka: Aulanko-kuvaston muutosten tulkinta*. Helsinki: Musta taide.

_____ (1997b) *Kuva Aulanko = Aulanko Revisited*. Helsinki: Musta taide.

Haavio-Mannila, E. and O. Kontula (2001) *Seksin trendit meillä ja naapureissa*. Helsinki:

WSOY.

Jyränki, J. (2007) 'Pahennus, julkinen tila ja siveellinen tapa – epäsiveellisten julkaisujen säätely – ja käsitehistoriaa Suomessa', *Oikeus*, 36, 1, 75–100.

Kangasvuo, J. (2007) 'Insatiable Sluts and Almost Gay Guys: Bisexuality in Porn Magazines', in S. Paasonen, K. Nikunen and L. Saarenmaa (eds) *Pornification: Sex and Sexuality in Media Culture*. Oxford: Berg, 139–49.

Koivunen, A. (2004) *Performative Histories, Foundational Fictions: Gender and Sexuality in Niskavuori Films*. Helsinki: SKS.

Kontula, O. (2008) *Halu & intohimo: tietoa suomalaisesta seksistä*. Helsinki: Otava.

Korppi, T. (2002) *Lihaa säästämättä: 30 vuotta suomalaisen pornobisneksen etulinjassa*. Helsinki: Johnny Kniga.

Kulick, D. (2005) 'Four Hundred Thousand Swedish Perverts', *GLQ: A Journal of Lesbian and Gay Studies*, 11, 2, 205–35.

Laasanen, H. (2008) *Naisten seksualinen valta*. Helsinki: Multikustannus.

Lane, F. S. III (2000) *Obscene Profits: The Entrepreneurs of Pornography in the Cyber Age*. New York: Routledge.

Lind, M. (2000) '"Aina löytyy antaja panomies Pentille": suomalaisuus seksilehdissä', in H. Salmi and K. Kallioniemi (eds) *Pohjan tähteet: populaarikulttuurin kuva suomalaisuudesta*. Helsinki: Kirjastopalvelu, 132–65.

Manninen, T. (2008) 'IS arvioi: Mies on uivelonaisen seksiorja', *Ilta-Sanomat*, 13 March. On-line. Available: http://www.iltasanomat.fi/viihde/uutinen.asp?id=1520755 (accessed 27 March 2009).

Marks, L. (2002) *Touch: Sensuous Theory and Multisensory Media*. Minneapolis: University of Minnesota Press.

McNeil, I., J. Osborne and P. Pavia (2005) *The Other Hollywood: The Uncensored Oral History of the Porn Film Industry*. New York: Regan Books.

Nikunen, K. (2005) 'Kovia kokenut domina ja pirteä pano-opas: Veronican ja Rakel Liekin tähtikuvat pornon arkipäivästäjinä', in K. Nikunen, S. Paasonen and L. Saarenmaa (eds) *Jokapäiväinen pornomme: media, seksuaalisuus ja populaarikulttuuri*. Tampere: Vastapaino, 208–33.

Nikunen, K., S. Paasonen & L. Saarenmaa (2005) 'Anna meille meidän… eli kuinka porno työntyi osaksi arkea', in K. Nikunen, S. Paasonen and L. Saarenmaa (eds) *Jokapäiväinen pornomme: media, seksuaalisuus ja populaarikulttuuri*. Tampere: Vastapaino, 7–29.

Nikunen, K. & S. Paasonen (2007) 'Porn Star as Brand: Pornification and the Intermedia Career of Rakel Liekki', *The Velvet Light Trap*, 59, 30–41.

Paasonen, S. (2009) 'Healthy Sex and Pop Porn: Feminism and the Finnish Context', *Sexualities*, 12, 2, 586–604.

Paroni (2008) 'Film Review: *The Magic Birds*' David Krokett [discussion list], 28 April. On-line. Available: http://davidkrokett.org/forum/viewtopic.php?f=9&t=1499 (accessed 27 March 2009).

Plummer, K. (2003) *Intimate citizenship: Private decisions and public dialogues*. Seattle, WA: University of Washington Press

Smith, C. (2005) 'A Perfectly British Business: Stagnation, Continuities, and Change on the Top Self', in L. Z. Sigel (ed.) *International Exposure: Perspectives on Modern European Pornography, 1800–2000*. New York: Rutgers University Press, 146–72.

Sørensen, A. D. & S. V. Knudsen (2006) *Nuoret, sukupuoli ja pornografia Pohjolassa – Loppuraportti*. Copenhagen: Nordic Council of Ministers.

Williams, L. (1989) *Hard Core: Pornography and the 'Frenzy of the Visible'*. Berkeley: University of California Press.

Wyatt, J. (1999) 'Selling "Atrocious Sexual Behavior": Revisiting Sexualities in the Marketplace for Adult Film in the 1960s', in H. Radner and M. Luckett (eds) *Swinging Single: Representing Sexuality in the 1960s*. Minneapolis: Minnesota University Press, 105–31.

CHAPTER TWELVE

REEL INTERCOURSE: DOING SEX ON CAMERA
Clarissa Smith

This chapter focuses on the performances of the sexual body in pornography. In much theorising of pornography, seemingly any woman will do – she's merely a hole for penetrating – if there are any distinctions offered it is to focus on body types – is she blonde, busty, young – rather than the physicality that a star might make available to her viewers. While feminists opposed to pornographic production have made public the labour of the woman in the porn film they have done so in very particular ways – woman as victim, as drugged, trafficked and/or abused. The body of the porn star is thus too often understood as just meat, to be penetrated, categorised, rescued. This chapter explores the ways in which the presentations of actual sexual interactions in pornography may signal an alternative logic of filmic production centred on the spectacular body. I address questions of acting, performance and presentation of 'real' sex as it is expressed via the bodies of two popular actresses. Rather than view sex as an inert property of the filmic process I examine the sex scene as performed through actors' bodies, with the potential for carrying dense and significant meaning (see Baron and Carnicke 2008: 16) even if performed for that most graphically realist of genres. In exploring the ways in which two porn actresses – Eva Angelina and Allie Sin – express sexual abandon, desire, authenticity and pleasure through their bodily presentations and styles, I argue there may be more to a porn actor's performance than simply being there and doing sex for the camera to record.

'MORE REAL THAN JUST ACTING'[1]

The idea that pornography is a document – the facsimile of a contemporaneously occurring event – is one shared by porn producers, consumers and critics. Thus *Deep Throat*'s (1972) star Linda Lovelace,[2] agreed her performance was genuine, 'Right! It's me and that's what I can do, and how I really am' (in Helfrecht 1973). So began a long tradition of women claiming that appearing in pornography was a natural outcome of their own sexual proclivities. Demonstrating 'the born-to-be [a] porn star' (Paasonen and Saarenmaa 2007: 25) phenomenon, contemporary star Eva Angelina tells an interviewer:

> I actually wanted to shoot porn. I started shooting my own movies when I was 14, stealing my parents' little Handi-Cam and ran with it. (She laughs) I was always very sexually active. It [wanting to get into porn] was always more of me turning 18 so that I could really shine. (Pipe 2008)

In spite of Linda Williams' (1989) seminal work *Hard Core* which sought to establish pornography as a cinematic form, pornographic film continues to suffer from comparisons with cinema, indeed for some commentators the idea that porn can be considered cinematic in any sense is an anathema. According to George P. Elliott pornography is 'the representation, without aesthetic or sociological justification, of sexual acts with an intrusive vividness' (in Kendrick 1997: 206). Henry Clor observed it 'depicted [sex] in great physiological detail' (in ibid.). Jean Baudrillard claimed pornography offers a 'sham vision ... reveal[ing] the inexorable microscopic truth of sex' (1990: 31). Each of these focuses on the extreme visibility of filmed sex and are emblematic of the approaches to pornography which understand it first and foremost as a record of doing sex, a kind of documentary.

Anti-pornography feminist Andrea Dworkin wrote that pornographic images 'document a rape, a rape first enacted when the women were set up and used; a rape repeated each time the viewer consumes the photographs' (1981: 137). Pornography captures a 'live' event and holds it for us (the viewers) as something to be endlessly repeated through playback. *Deep Throat* was described by Andrew Sarris as a 'joyless repetitious documentary on the latest oral-genital techniques in the Kingdom of Pornalia' (in Smith 1973: 53) neatly capturing the oscillation between the real and the fantastic that pornography tries to maintain.

Even where producers might attempt more than a documentary form – the depiction of two or more people fucking – as in, for instance, the recent hit full-length porn movie *Pirates* (2005) (inspired by the Bruckheimer franchise *Pirates of the Caribbean* 2003–), this only highlights its inadequacy as filmic art. *Pirates*' attempts at sustained narrative, plot, dialogue and CGI pale next to those of its inspiration and all that seems to be remembered of it are the 'atrocious acting, mispronounced lines [and] anachronistic tattoos on women performers' (Williams 2008: 5). Such criticisms are entirely recognisable, especially the one about acting – because everyone knows that porn stars cannot act, even Lovelace could only claim she had learned her lines and delivered them adequately (1973: 90). Yet, of course this is to equate acting with speaking and perhaps performance in a body genre, such as pornography, is about more than lines being spoken with feeling.

The picture of pornography as a document of sex which utilises the cinematic technologies of camera and film, lighting and editing but which fails to achieve the necessary complexity of narrative and emotional import of *cinema* has recently been made less sustainable by the appearance of feature films which include demonstrably occurring sexual intercourse: movies such as *Intimacy* (2001) and *9 Songs* (2004). In the French films *Romance* (1999) and *Baise-Moi* (2000), the exploits of the female protagonists and their serial sexual encounters sparked considerable debate about the politics of 'art-house pornography'. For many critics, the films' claims to explore sexuality were simply a smoke-screen disguising their true intent – to sneak porn past the censors.[3] Explicit shots are not new to art-house cinema and shock headlines are certainly nothing new to filmmakers: the furore surrounding these films, however, suggested that their directors had done more than broken a convention of explicitness. In particular, they demolished the established mainstream conventions of re-creating sexual activity so that it is identifiable by viewers as a specifically *cinematic* achievement – bodies lit and filmed to emphasise their 'sexiness' while denuding them of their corporeality. Both *Romance* and *Baise-Moi* eschew the illusions of erotic display in favour of 'real sex' performed by porn stars.[4] The anticipated audiences for these films were not 'porn' audiences but art-house for whom this imagery might be recognisable as 'new', 'challenging' and 'extreme'. To this end, both films used penetration and other sexual activity as a form of special effect, a spectacular visual display of bodies in motion.[5] Whilst there is some acknowledgement of the 'dynamic trading' between 'legitimate and illegitimate cinemas' (Kryzwinska 2005: 224) critical discourse cannot accommodate the 'pornographic' attributes of real sex in cinema such as its intense physicality, its singularity of focus and its greedy use of onscreen time.

For instance, both Tanya Krzywinska and Linda Williams argue for the ways in which 'real sex' is contextualised and legitimised in mainstream cinema through the rhetorics of 'true' cinema: narrative, plot and cinematography all combine to produce more than the rather puerile 'what-you-see-is-what-you-get' (Krzywinska 2005: 226) performances of hard-core. As Krzywinska observes:

> By being placed in a psychosexual context, the spectacle of 'real' sex is given an emotional and philosophical colouring very different from the more superficial and immediate spectacle of the real found in hard-core cinema. The inclusion of a psychosexual dimension, borrowed in part from melodrama, makes the designation of the 'real' a relative and complex affair, an aspect that is underlined in the way such films play reflexively at the interface between the body-mechanics of sexual performance and its staging for cinema. (2005: 227)

Thus the specific excesses of 'real' sex are tamed by more respectable narrative dimensions. In other words, so long as these people talk before and after their sexual congress, viewers will be expected to do more than feel physically moved by what they have seen.

In her book-length study, *Screening Sex*, Williams cogently argues that sexual content *can* have purpose and meaning for its viewers, that sex on film can express interests and desires with radical intent. For example, the specifically politicised intentions of Catherine Breillat's inclusion of unsimulated sex in *Romance* – her intent to expose the exploitative relations inherent in heterosexuality through extended sexual scenes – is acknowledged and appreciated by Williams. However, this is through reference to the cinematic elements of scripting, voiceover, camera position and the inclusion of the 'non-pornographic' prop, the condom (2008: 277). Despite her intentions 'not to parse the good sex from the bad, or to determine which graphic sexual representations have gone 'too far' or 'leave nothing to the imagination' (2008: 23), Williams seeks to differentiate between *pornographic* 'hydraulics of sex' (2008: 5) and cinematic 'psychological revelation' (2008: 304).

She argues that even as films such as *Intimacy* feature the leads in 'sustained grappling' there is a division between pornographic film and such representations, not least because *Intimacy* does not go in for 'the hypervisible penetration and spraying ejaculate of the money shots of hard-core pornography' (2008: 273). Both Williams and Krzywinska are determined to retain some sense of difference in the production of art-house hard-core and its despised relative, pornography. By focusing on directorial intentions, editing, lighting and other technical features, both authors can reclaim these films as *art* pornographies, a branch of legitimate cinema.

In effect, Williams manages to sideline the specificity of many of the films she looks at – sex performed for record by the camera – in favour of an approach which examines how that record is *made*. Sex becomes an inert property of the filmic process rather than an interaction between actors. The excess of presenting real sex is just another directorial choice, a part of a wider narrative purpose and perhaps a kind of play with the conventions of film. The possibility that the use of actual sexual interactions might signal an alternative logic of filmic production centred on the body is sidelined and questions of acting, performance and presentation of 'real' sex are occluded.

Thinking about whether or not porn stars act requires borrowing from mainstream film studies which have their own problems with the notion of acting. Walter Benjamin suggested that film actors be considered an inanimate stage prop, simply bodies to be placed according to the director's wishes exactly as if they were a table or chair in the *mise-en-scène* (1968: 227). Cynthia Baron and Sharon Marie Carnicke observe that while film actors have been credited with physical grace and 'skilful virtuosity' both of which 'emphasise [actors' contributions to] spectacle, action or display more than character and narrative' they are denied any 'true acting skill' (2008: 12). Film acting is 'received acting', that is,

> performance in which the representation of characters does not arise from the agency, talent or labour of actors, but instead through the costuming, make up, lighting, framing, editing and sound design choices made by other members of the production team. (2008: 12–13)

Baron and Carnicke challenge this perception arguing that performance and acting are deserving of more sustained and rigorous attention. Given that their book-length study pays no attention to the disreputable cinematic form that is pornography, it might go entirely contrary to common sense to say that their insights could be useful for thinking about the ways in which pornography makes use of its star performers, but that is exactly what the remainder of this chapter will attempt. As already stated, I suggest that there may be more to a porn actor's performance than simply *being* there and *doing* sex for the camera to record.[6]

DO PORN STARS ACT?

If movie actors should be considered little more than props, this goes more than double for the porn actor. If there is often little perceived difference in 'proper' cinema between, as Dirk Eitzen puts it, 'that's a "real" person crying and that's an actor crying' (2005: 195), in pornography which sells itself as a document of 'real sex', there is seemingly no perceived difference between a 'real' person having sex and an actor having sex. Online videos are advertised with a personalisation which maintains the lack of separation between reality and performance – 'Come see my first ever boy/girl anal'.[7] Insertion shots are proof that the real thing is happening and lend an air of reality to all other action. Male pleasure can be documented by demonstration of a 'hard dick' and 'popping' on cue, the 'money shot', ejaculation, the *sine qua non* of pornography – although, as Williams points out, the money shot is not just evidential it is a 'rhetorical figure that permits the genre to speak in a certain way about sex' (1989: 94).

As numerous commentators, from Eva Angelina, through Louis Theroux to Linda Williams, have observed, men in pornography simply have to produce an erection – 'Get your dick hard on cue and pop when we tell you to'[8] – to 'star' in a porn film. The male star does not *act*, he is simply a prop for the performance produced by the female star. Emily Shelton's examination of the 'homosocial cult' of star Ron Jeremy takes Jeremy's long pornographic career more seriously, seeking to understand the nature of his popularity. She suggests that

> Ron Jeremy is a star because porn's predominately male audience likes him and will see his movies on the strength of his name. As a sort of open dirty secret, he is both amusing and reassuring, a naughty inside joke of contemporary pop culture. And while he may appear to be the exception to the rule, a flabby anomaly in a mass of muscular macho men, his generic ubiquity reveals him to be ... an unthreatening 'everyman' with whom male viewers may comfortably identify. (Shelton 2002: 132)

Shelton's account stresses the ideological work done by the flabby everyman and in this sense her focus on his function for the male audience replicates work on stardom in cinema where physical beauty and attractiveness are considered central to the star persona (see Lovell 2003; McDonald 2004). Paul McDonald suggests that studies of spectatorship saw 'the actor as a figure, an object to be looked at' and that this is replicated in star-studies which ignores individual performances by an actor favouring instead a focus on the '"meaning of the performer" but not paradoxically, the meaning of performance' (2004: 24; 25).

As in film discourse, so in discourses on pornography there is constant reaffirmation of the centrality of the body and how it looks over any consideration of how individual actors might *move* their body in their scenes. Hence Jeremy is not considered for what he does on screen, how he has sex – he is just a *cock*. This might be appropriate for thinking about some presentations of the male co-stars where they are often seemingly disembodied penises but cannot suffice when it comes to female actresses especially when in films marketed on her name as 'star'. Mainstream star studies do accept that different stars convey different meanings to their audiences but no such diversity is understood to exist in pornographic production. Pornography's singular (and, according to many, ideological) intent to arouse the viewer means it hardly matters who performs what and how and to whom, occluding any understanding of expressivity. Thus even as there is acceptance of the particular corporeality of pornography there is no consideration of the movements, dispositions and gestures underpinning such physicality. Where it might be noted that a film includes, for example, fellatio and anal penetration, this seems to signify nothing more than an observation of content. More than this, the notion that pornography serves an ideological function in relation to women *as a class* has prevented asking questions about how stardom works in porn. Feminist analysis which focuses on the 'lies' being told about women in porn has understood the female star as standing in for *all* women. Moreover, as Elizabeth Bell notes, the star 'cannot escape the physical materiality of their work' (2006: 155) and there is the significant problem of the loss of reputation or social standing for the female star. In fact, what we see now in the newly industrialised forms of pornography is a range of branding strategies including the promotion of star performers and here the star precisely does *not* represent everywoman – she is highly individuated in order to speak to particular aesthetic and erotic tastes and interests and offering – through her name and her brand – guarantees of quality and expectations of performance (see Biasin and Zecca 2009).

In what follows I shall briefly look at the performances of two actresses, Eva Angelina and Allie Sin.[9] McDonald suggests that too often the minute actions of the actor are not examined for what they might reveal of the character's involvement with the circumstances of the narrative (see 2004: 32). What might it mean to think about the minute actions of the porn actor? Not to search for signs of consent: to judge whether 'their professed pleasure [is] an authentic pleasure' (Smaill 2009),[10] nor to sternly note their endurance of 'uncomfortable, if not dreadful, sexual positions in their performances of pleasure' (Bell 2006: 155); I want to demonstrate the ways in which these actresses are differentiated by more than the colour of their hair, size of their breasts or positions of their tattoos.

TECHNICALLY PROFICIENT ALLIE SIN

Allie Sin (aka Naughty Nati) has girl-next-door looks and a range of instantly recognisable tattoos. Her hard-core career began in 2004 when she was 19, and has been interrupted by 'relationship difficulties' with her minor rock star boyfriend. Her specialities are fellatio and anal sex but her style doesn't always meet with universal approval, as in this review by online critic, Gram Ponante:

> Everything from the better-than-average packaging to the cover art has High Expectations written all over it, so I was a little let down when the first scene revealed itself to be nothing more than a well-shot bathroom romp with the

tight Allie Sin. It's not that Sin isn't as compact a sex machine as anything our laboratories can produce, but when I hear 'Exile on Main Street' and 'old strip joint', I expect a sloppy, desperate hoedown that makes up in enthusiasm what it lacks in technical proficiency. Sin, on the other hand, is nothing if not technically proficient. (Ponante 2006)

Ponante's disappointment that Sin offers a technical performance but without the necessary enthusiasm was interesting to me, given that it separates performance into two constituent parts – technique and gusto. Shot and cut by 'Jack the Zipper', *Blacklight Beauty* (2005) mixes gonzo with a post-punk video aesthetic to recreate a grungy nightclub setting in which various women indulge in sex with strangers (one scene includes a rather sinister clown). The film has received favourable critical appraisals because of its innovative use of music and its particular representational style. Although a series of sexual vignettes, the film has a kind of narrative coherence centred on the possibilities of sexual interaction in the quasi-private spaces of public places. The scene which interests me is the opening vignette structured around the meeting and sexual liaison of Sin and an unidentified male in the nightclub toilet.

Fig. 25 Allie Sin in *Blacklight Beauty*.

The ten-minute scene opens on Sin who throws come-hither-looks over her shoulder to a presumed male as she walks towards a building. The camera follows her from the point-of-view (POV) of the stranger and retains this perspective through approximately three quarters of the scene. Sin leads the way into the building. Although no words are exchanged, her seductive looks to the guy/camera make clear her invitation; cut to her in the toilet as she exposes her breasts and pulls her g-string across to show her genitals, as she does this she gazes at her potential lover, a cool and appraising yet clearly inviting look. A short section follows in which the camera moves from POV to look down on the couple as the man fondles and slaps Sin's breasts; she grips his cock. Her eyes are mostly closed, he rubs his thumb across her lips and into her mouth for her to suck. The music obliterates any vocals. About two minutes into the scene the camera switches back to POV and Sin's out-of-focus body moves in closer to the lens and then down to fellate the man. A four-minute section focuses on Sin's face as she fellates the man, her body is held tightly crouched so that her face is almost the only visible part of her and her heavily-lashed eyes gaze up into the camera.

This is both a demonstration of skill and a performance of sexual play: throughout this scene Sin maintains full eye contact with the camera/male as she slowly and very deliberately moves her mouth back and forth, swallowing the penis, knocking it against the flat of her tongue and teasing it with the tip. Her lips slide over the penis in a smooth movement and as she pulls back to the tip, a hint-of-a-smile plays at the corner of her mouth. As her head bobs slowly back and forth, her gaze does not falter, demanding a response. At intervals the screen goes black replicating the closing eyes of the pleasured male. As his eyes open, Sin is still looking up – 'see me as I watch your pleasure'. Sin pulls her head back, her mouth disengages from the penis and smilingly and gently she presses her teeth against the glans, her gaze maintained. She playfully bites down the length of the penis, then, she pops it back into her mouth. Again she resumes her slow and languorous sucking of the penis.

The scene cuts to a side view of Sin and she presents her ass to camera, the man plays with her bottom, strokes her and licks her until he enters her from behind. They continue to fuck and Sin opens her mouth and closes it, the music covers her sounds, her eyes close and open in seemingly involuntary movements of pleasure as she thrusts back onto the man's penis. Occasionally she looks over at the camera but her gaze is mostly not engaged, it is a look that seemingly does not recognise the camera or the watcher, she is too absorbed in the physical sensations of the moment. The music cuts away and we hear them whisper to each other, both moan. The scene ends without ejaculation.

Although there is no 'money-shot' in this scene there are the other staples of the porn menu: oral and vaginal penetration, a little cunnilingus, stroking of the breasts and so forth, but I think there is more to note in this scene and in particular in relation to the segment which focuses on Sin's face. Sin's body effectively disappears in this segment, her hands move slowly and unobtrusively and rather than energetically performing oral sex – as the reviewer quoted above would have expected in a gonzo production – Sin offers a very restrained set of movements. There is no throat-fucking, no attempted gagging, Sin controls the action with a very light touch of her hand round the penis. The slow bob of her head is a seductive and sensual movement and her gaze is a knowing acknowledgement of the effect she is having. The slow, half-smiles are playful and teasing and when she appears to go to bite the penis it is marked by an archness that underscores the sense of power and control she has. This muted mode of physical interaction is contrasted with the more frenetic style of the subsequent penetration scene where Sin gives herself and her body over to the physical sensations of fucking and being fucked.

Despite the proliferation of pornographies online and across other delivery formats, Laura Kipnis's observation still holds true that

> There's zero discussion of pornography as an expressive medium in the positive sense – the only expressing it's presumed to do is of misogyny or

social decay ... One reason for this lacuna is a certain intellectual prejudice against taking porn seriously at all. Those who take pornography seriously are its opponents, who have little interesting to say on the subject: not only don't they seem to have spent much time actually looking at it, but even worse, they seem universally overcome by a leaden, stultifying literalness, apparently never having heard of metaphor, irony, symbolism – even fantasy seems too challenging a concept. (2006: 119)

In the Sin scene I have just described, the blow-job is depicted as an extended seduction, a power-play which does not require dominance but does enact submission to the pacing and technique of the performer. It stands in quite marked contrast to the claims that fellatio is an attack on women's very subjecthood (see Hardy 1998). In the various Sin vehicles I have viewed (some twenty scenes varying in length from three minutes to forty), her performance style is surprisingly restrained. Sin's repertoire has included anal, double penetration, gagging – the staples of gonzo – yet her 'responsive' style is muted: she does not do exaggerated gestures, pouting lips, groans or loudly vocalising her pleasure. This is particularly marked in facial scenes where she closes her eyes and, often her mouth too, and maintains a very placid expression while her partner(s) ejaculate(s) on her face complicating the picture of bukkake as a 'humiliation ritual' and the 'glory of seminal expression' (Moore 2007: 74; 75). Comments on fan sites draw attention to this and evaluate her performances in terms of responsiveness/professionalism:

> No kidding. All the videos I've seen of her she always seems disinterested in what's going on. "Gee, there's a 12-inch cock in my ass. Yaw..." (Dial_Tone)
>
> That's true! I find her really boring ... on other way, I think she does porn only for the money ... And maybe she's too lazy or too stupid to simulate or even to answer questions... (alliknow)
>
> She talks, she laughs, she even moans a little (bleary_eye)
>
> What? She even MOANS?!? Wow, that's a first! (Dial_Tone). (In Peachy 2006)

Her seeming lack of responsiveness is a source of some debate: is it simply that she is a boring performer or is it a measure of her cynical pursuit of money? Is it, heaven forbid, an indication that she *is* bored? It is, of course, impossible to definitively decide this from textual analysis of, or subjective response to, the scenes themselves. Anyway, are these the only questions to pose? Given the signs of Sin's popularity evidenced elsewhere on the web which make clear her fans' satisfaction with her performance of sensuality, lust and gratification, perhaps this is a style of response Sin has adopted as her signature in contrast to the more enthusiastic and excessive responses performed by other stars.

E FOR EVA!!!

Eva Angelina is the 25-year-old star of numerous gonzo shorts and full-length movies including the award-winning *Upload* (2006) and *Sleeping Around* (2008). Famous for wearing her spectacles during her scenes, Angelina is an attractive brunette with a wide, bright smile and laughing eyes. Her private life is documented on bulletin boards and porn sites, including details of her mother's mental illness, a boyfriend's suicide and Angelina's two career breaks from porn – once at the behest of a boyfriend and the second to have a baby. In candid non-porn promo videos she is chatty, witty and laughs a lot especially when describing her work and its ups and downs (no pun intended). Directors credit her with an impressive work ethic and dedication to 'getting things right, not always found in the industry' (Alexander n.d.). Colleagues regard her as a professional. These are elements of her persona which circulate around her performances; not only does she have an impressive pair of breasts, tattoos and a 'lovely ass' but she is regarded as a proficient by her peers and colleagues and, as her MySpace page testifies, is held in some affection by her friends and fans. But is she an actress?

I looked at a number of scenes featuring Angelina including a group sex pickup in the Bang Bros film *Fuck Team Five: The Afro Fuck* (2008), her features *Upload* and *Sleeping Around* and an all-girl 'attack' on Angelina from the compilation DVD *E for Eva* (2007). Although most of these can be loosely categorised as gonzo porn, each operates with a different 'representational rhetoric' (Naremore 1988: 36) of 'real' sex. The web offers a fantastic array of pornographies, there is no sexual taste that is not catered for and whether one celebrates or laments this state of affairs there is no doubt that it is inappropriate to speak of a singular form of sexual representation online. But even as that plenitude may be acknowledged in the listing of particular forms (for example, gonzo, twink, ethnic, BDSM) and features (anal, oral, fisting, gagging and so on), there is a flattening of the performance styles with which these forms and features may be associated. For example, most commentators will acknowledge gonzo as a marketing term promising a ring-side view of the sexual action.[11] Its particular *verité* trope is that of the amateur porn production with close-up filming, a rough and ready hand-held style and little evidence of formal plotting.[12] It also has an emphasis on rough sex: there is no pretence of romance, little gentleness and because scenes are often up to twice as long as those in more respectable forms of porn, the sexual action can seem more like an endurance test for viewers as well as the protagonists.

In the scene from *E for Eva*, Angelina is brought into a room gagged and trussed up in a black bag, three women help her out of it and then proceed to lay siege to her body. A description of this scene is very difficult because so much happens there is not enough space here to explain it all. The women paw at Angelina's body, a variety of sex toys are used on her, including two large dildos, a vibrator and, during much of the scene, Angelina fellates a large black strap-on wielded by one of her co-stars. The scene is clearly premised as coercive: Angelina's arms and legs are bound with black tape, she is slapped, gagged, choked and literally forced to orgasm. In the final minutes of the sequence, Angelina screams, shouts and laughs her orgasm as one woman grinds a vibrator against her clitoris, another bites and squeezes her breasts and the third slaps her face.

'Coercive' has particular resonances in discussions of pornography with arguments hinging on the possible compulsion of women in both the production and consumption of porn. For example, many feminists suggest that women's participation in porn is not a matter of free choice but rather produced or forced by current cultural and economic contexts and further, that porn consumption by men and the effects of that consumption create the conditions in which women's sexuality is produced as subservient to men's interests (see Dworkin 1981). Pornography's potential to eroticise sexual violence and to feed its prevalence in real life is of particular concern to anti-porn commentators, moralists and legislators alike but that is because they view pornography as a carrier of 'messages' and 'arousal' as the means or mechanism by which those messages are received. They have no time for the idea that there are sensuous *affects* in pornography, they recognise only *effects* made all the more pernicious by sensation.

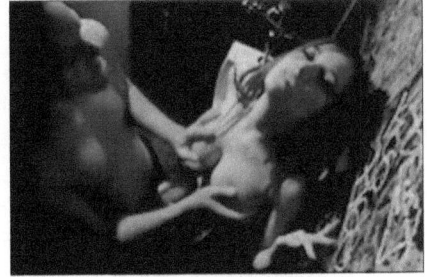

Fig. 26 Eva Angelina in *E for Eva*.

Of course, the girl-on-girl attack on Angelina appears counter-intuitive to normative notions of healthy, pleasurable sexuality – from the moment she is dragged into the room in the black bag, we are under no illusions that this is going to be a loving encounter characterised by mutuality. But then this is not ordinary, 'normal' sex or even an approximation of it – this is spectacular, hyperbolic, performed sex – it is sex as endurance sport. This is the kind of sex that fans have come to expect from Angelina and it is characterised by her willingness to go beyond the limits that other women might endure. And coercion in this scenario is a narrative motif which enables that demonstration of 'endurance'.

A key trope of gonzo porn is the performance style perhaps best described as 'down and dirty' and characterised by an expressive enthusiasm which echoes its reference to Hunter S. Thompson's description of gonzo as marked by 'total commitment, total concentration and a mad sort of panache' (Websters 2008: 507). Even as it professes to a rough and ready unscripted sequencing there is a high level of symbolic, even ritual action in gonzo and its actors are required to demonstrate their embodiment of excess, especially an authentic discovery of the extremity of their physical limits. Thus, gonzo does not just feature fellatio, it invariably has a demonstration of throat-fucking and gagging, sometimes to the point of vomiting.

Angelina is a consummate gonzo performer, throwing herself into her scenes: she moves her body with enthusiasm; she caresses her own breasts, squeezes and pulls her nipples, moves her hands over her body with strong, fluid movements, giving the sense that she enjoys her own body and offering up its pleasures to the viewer. Angelina expresses sexual abandon through her body – this might seem like an obvious point to make when describing a pornographic scene but Angelina goes the 'extra mile'. Her style is determinedly 'strong': when fucking she 'bucks and writhes', she matches her partner's strokes and thrusts with her own. She explains her popularity in terms of this bodily authenticity:

> I think my whole thing is that I'm very enthusiastic. I have a lot of energy and a lot of sexual chemistry to go around. People can see that and you can totally tell I'm having fun. I want to be there; I'm not just thinking about the dollar signs. (In Cherry n.d.)

Many of Angelina's scenes do not appear to be overdubbed, body parts slap against other parts, squelching, sucking and friction noises mix with a range of exclamations, declamations and instructions suggestive of the physicality of all-in wrestling. During her scenes, she grimaces, grits her teeth, screws up her eyes and gasps; loud, racking grunts and groans escape from her mouth, as she smiles and often demands more. There is nothing sedate or 'ladylike' about her moans of pleasure, her vocals make clear the physical exertion she is engaged in. She ends her scenes covered in sweat, her hair damp, make-up smudged, her breath ragged but she is always smiling. The reviewers love it: 'Her oral skills are awesome, she gags and sucks with such enthusiasm you'll wish a politician [could do] his job as passionately as she does hers' (Blanco 2008).

Central to this enthusiasm in Angelina's films is the sound: Angelina produces what John Corbett and Terri Kapsalis describe as a 'frenzy of the audible', her moans, grunts and shouts are 'the "release" of sound, the vocal expression of an inner state' (1996: 103). Corbett and Kapsalis take the view, as a corollary of the money shot, that sound is a 'kind of truth claim' for the 'fact' of sex having taken place:

> As evidence of the truth of her orgasm and the truth of his/her ability to bring her to orgasm, the listener is offered the sound of uncontrollable female passion. Sound is used to verify her pleasure and his/her prowess. (1996: 104)

This takes them into a number of questions around identification and subjectivity – what position does the listener take up in relation to the sounds of female orgasm? – but interestingly they do not leap to the conclusion that the viewer takes up 'a sadistic listening position', instead they wonder whether this enables 'the listener to identify with the vocalising woman' (1996: 109). Here then they are not so much concerned with whether or not these sounds are realistic, whether they are directly analogous to the sounds 'real' women make when they orgasm, but how they might show 'female sexuality as out-of-control and excessive' (1996: 106).

How sound and visuals might contribute to an individual viewer's pleasures cannot be absolutely deduced from examination of just the text – that is a question requiring other forms of analysis – but in the case of Angelina's bellowing, the vocals certainly amplify the intense corporeality of the scene. In the scene I have just described I would suggest that the sound is not just about orgasm but is integral to the particular symbolism of gonzo – there is not a narrative progression, expressed in sound, from arousal through to orgasm. Rather Angelina bellows, screams and exclaims throughout and her vocalisations are accompanied by her fellow performers' exhortations and instructions as well as the slaps and slurps of the various bodies and the buzz of the vibrator, providing a soundscape, a cacophony of sensation. Descriptions of porn often ignore the role of sound or focus on the inadequacy of the vocalisation or the profanity of the dialogue. It is easy to see why, generally the grunts and groans, swearing and exclamations do not seem to serve any narrative purpose but that is to assume that only words have some special force. Alison Landsberg (2010), drawing on sound scholarship, has suggested there may be particular affective pleasures made possible for viewers via what she terms the 'aural visceral' which 'produces specific kinds of cognition and knowledge' and 'compels us to respond'. The repeated use of expletives –'shit', 'fuck' – and inchoate grunts and groans are then perhaps not so redundant – as invocations of the effort involved here, they call for viewers to recognise the demands of gonzo on the body of the performer and her flair in enduring them.

That this is a performance style Angelina consciously adopts is made clear in the various interviews she gives which detail her preparations for her scenes and is underscored in the 'realist' presentation of another scene I want to look at here – from *Fuck Team Five: The Afro Fuck*. This is an offshoot of the successful Bang Bros franchise featuring a couple of men going in search of girls who will have sex with them in the back of their van. The premise is that the pick-ups are 'real' people, 'civilians' not porn veterans.[13] In *The Afro Fuck*, the gender dynamic is reversed: Angelina is on the beach in Miami with two friends – both porn veterans – Jaydean and Ashlynn; they meet up with a group of 'ordinary guys'. After some conversation, involving much boastful talk from the men and plenty of laughter from the women, Angelina *et al.* challenge the guys to come back to their room and make good on their claims. They head back. The scene is interesting because in its camaraderie and good-humoured banter it fractures its own illusion that this is a genuine hook-up. The conversation is at times almost inaudible but there are points at which the unscripted dialogue illustrates the scene as a piece of 'work'. It exceeds its reality quotient because the girls, particularly Angelina, constantly make ironic references to the work duties and operations of a porn shoot.

Shortly after getting into the apartment the girls require the boys to strip: much laughter ensues as the men reveal their penises, mostly flaccid and some adorned with copious amounts of pubic hair (in this age of *de rigueur* waxing, how strange to see these styled *au naturel*!). Trying not to giggle, Angelina says: 'You guys better get your shit hard … cos … like … You guys're in *our* world now, cos y'know we don't fluff the dudes before we shoot!' Whatever pertains in 'real world' relationships where women might be responsible for their man's arousal, here in the professional space workers take responsibility for their own preparedness! Throughout the scene, shot in real time and on a single camera, Angelina and her friends are laughing, joking, commenting on the various guys, their manoeuvres – 'He's found the clit right now, he's been practicing in the mirror!' – and the speed with which most of the males orgasm. As well as moaning and making sounds of pleasure, Angelina comes over all dictatorial 'If you nut in me … I'll shoot you dead … you pull it right out if you feel it cumming … I'm Cuban, I'll get real Cuban on your ass!' and, drawing attention to an evidently pre-arranged quota, turns down one guy's attempt to penetrate her with 'I already got my two guys in … here, I'll blow you though!' Incidental asides, along with instructions from the cameraman to give him a better view, make this a comic scene to watch[14] and highlight its contrivance.

As the scene draws to a close, Angelina cries out 'Come on you guys! NUT! NUT! NUT!' and exclaims 'Your dick is not hard, we can try all day to get this thing in me, its just gonna pop out!', hardly the most flattering of comments and drawing attention to the requirement of male performers for this kind of scene. The film ends with an assessment of each man's oral skills and, as the winner receives his friends' team-spirited congratulations, the girls laughingly comment:

What a day!
Wow! … Interesting!
Hey, it is what it is!

The Afro Fuck is fascinating in its presentation of the gang-bang as a team activity, and in its fracturing of the boundary between business and pleasure.

Its *verité* mode highlights the fun of the group interactions, the humour of mixing professionals with amateurs. The filmed sex is again a kind of sport but here the players are not equally matched and, therefore, Angelina is not called upon to demonstrate her staying-power or athleticism. The film also highlights the seriousness of pornography as a business: making sure there is plenty of action and getting it all on digi-film. It is that combination which stands in contrast to Angelina's intense and energetic demonstrations of sexual pleasure in her more dedicatedly professional performances.

How far Angelina's performances are appreciated by her viewers requires other kinds of research, the kind of research which takes seriously her appeal to her fans and which would explore how satisfied or dissatisfied viewers, who seek out her performances, are with the ways they get to see her. How they measure and talk about her expressiveness, her sensuousness, her physicality and so on. How far her performances fit with their expectations of a scene's embodiment of what they are attracted to in Angelina.

The contrasts I've offered here illustrate that 'sex acts', far from being interchangeable, are not performed by every porn star in identical ways. How to sum this up? A story has just caught my eye that demonstrates the particular problem I have been concerned with in this chapter. In an article in a UK daily newspaper – the *Daily Mail* – 'mother of two', Olivia Lichtenstein was commissioned to watch and write about her experiences of adult TV channels. She opines:

> If it wasn't so pathetic, it would be laughably absurd. Imagine receiving a work schedule which demands that on Monday you're a lesbian and Tuesday, a dominatrix, while on Wednesday you're a passive maiden half raped by a strong man.
>
> You wear leather, you wear lace, you take part in the euphemistic game that is 'water sports' and you claim to love it all. These poor women must lose all sense of themselves. (2009: 23)

This patronising account of women who appear in pornographic media conforms to the stereotype of them as simply 'props' to producer's demands and viewer fantasies highlighting the particular issue of denying women in pornography any agency or intentionality in their work. As part of the overall refusal to accord pornography any complexity (see Kipnis 2006) there is a refusal to acknowledge the authenticity of actresses' claims to enjoy their work. Particularly there is a refusal to acknowledge the specific social world which constitutes pornographic production or indeed its consumption: the porn actress is assumed to take part in practices that are experienced as degrading and unnatural, there is no acknowledgement of her professionalism, talent or skill.

Work on participants in extreme sports has highlighted the ways in which there are very different understandings of the vocational habitus that characterises, for example, competitive bodybuilding or its polar opposite, ballet, demonstrating that the requirements for specific body types, regimes of discipline and training, expectations of hard work and mental toughness 'impact on the ideals, aspirations and conduct ... influenc[ing participants'] perception and understanding of risk, pain and injury' (Probert et al. 2007: 273). The pleasures and dangers of any job of work or leisure pursuit are not absolute; they are socially and culturally bounded and may be understood quite differently by those within the particular milieu to those outside such work. Hence Lichtenstein's pronouncement that 'these "actresses" are the battery hens of the sex industry – performing what any sane person would see as horrible and degrading acts for the cheapened pleasure of others' (2009: 23) is oblivious to the ways in which a porn actresses may well challenge the conception of their work as inherently degrading. As Anne Probert et al. indicate in relation to athletes:

> Risk may be construed ... as an essential, routine part of activity ... a sensation which can be embraced and valued ... a means to test skill and self-mastery ... and/or an element ... to be managed, minimised and downplayed. (2007: 273)

Angelina and Sin are not only women who have sex on camera, they are performers, sexual athletes. They are also multi-faceted social beings capable of self-determination and agency, influenced not only by their 'pornographic' habitus but also by the broader social world of which they are a part. We have yet to formulate ways of understanding or theorising participation in pornography beyond simplistic notions of the abuse and harm or agency and liberation of such work. To insist, as a recent *Guardian* article did, that 'The sex bits of porn are so mechanical – and so completely interchangeable' (Dowling 2008: 55) is patently false. It homogenises practices, values, motivations and philosophies, which are then mapped on to the performances and ultimately the performers themselves. The presentation of real sex for camera is not simply documentary evidence of harm nor can it be reduced to representations of the unruliness of desire.

NOTES

1. Williams (2008: 275).
2. Lovelace was the stage name of Linda Boreman, later Marchiano.

3 See, for example, comments from John Beyer of the National Viewers and Listeners Association (now Media Watch UK) in 'FilmFour in Porn Accusation' (BBC News 2000).
4 In *Romance*, Rocco Siffredi; in *Baise-Moi*, Karen Lancaume and Raffaela Anderson.
5 The films are very different and their treatment in critical circles reflected this: where *Romance* was given considerable academic attention, *Baise-Moi*, with its insertion shots, seemingly unmotivated physical connections and extended sexual scenes, was not and this points to a particular problematic in the ways in which filmic sexual performance has been understood. *Baise-Moi* did not just cause problems for critics; audiences also found the film difficult to categorise. Martin Barker et al. found in their audience research that *Baise-Moi* presented its viewers with particular conundrums, including the film's proximity to porn, its ability to stimulate arousal, and the 'realism' of its rape scene (2007: 7). The precariousness of *Baise-Moi*'s status as porn or not porn opens up the possibilities of thinking about screened sexual activity as not simply another visual rhetoric in the director's armoury.
6 As I use the term 'performance' I am aware of Elizabeth Bell's critique of the tendency to try to 'rescue' porn via 'performance' and the legitimacy it derives from the idea of performance in other spheres of human activity including sports. According to Bell this notion of performance takes its place amongst three other usages of the term in relation to pornography: that it a) offers 'real sexual activity', b) is variously evaluated for its competence, taboo-busting or consent, and c) recognition of the 'tense relationship between the *real* and the *representational*' (2006: 153–58; emphasis in original). Bell is critical of the tendency of the multiple perspectives on pornography 'to serve their [own] political ends, variously highlighting sex, erasing sex, or replacing sex in their use of the word *performance*' (2006: 153; emphasis in original). I confess my guilt, but would suggest that a focus on specific performances can be used to begin to unpack the ways in which screened sex is offered to viewers and the affects and responses it gives rise to.
7 Eva Angelina at evaangelinaonline.com.
8 Eva Angelina in *Fuck Team Five: The Afro Fuck* (2008).
9 Chosen because there is a lot of online discussion about these women and their sex scenes and online commentaries referenced their very different styles. I should also say that I like them both, feeling a connection to them in much the same way as I do to other popular culture figures whose work I find amusing, interesting or affecting.
10 I make no claim to understand their motivations in appearing in their various films and I have not chosen films that can be assessed for their similarity or pretensions to 'proper' filmic art (see Paasonen and Saarenmaa 2007).
11 Not so much that every bodily flaw is visible (see Richtel 2007).
12 John Stagliano of the *Buttman* franchise (1989–) claims gonzo does have plotting (see Pipe 2002).
13 Bang Bros have been caught out having 'faked' the scenes in their amateur girl pick-ups: using professionals rather than the girls-next-door they claim. Newspaper *Local 10* 'learned in an undercover investigation, the women are actually paid performers, and the incidents are all set up in advance. Ox Ideas producer Olivier Caudron told a *Local 10* producer that the women are paid $700' (no longer available on the newspaper's own

site but reproduced at NASIOC 2006).

14 I have found my own response to this scene – being amused – is shared by others but interestingly, amusement is not a response supported by the binary oppositions of much porn theorising.

WORKS CITED

Alexander (n.d.) 'Eva Angelina, Action Hero', *XCritic*. On-line. Available: http://www.xcritic.com/columns/column.php?columnID=208 (accessed 4 April 2009).

Barker, M., K. Egan, R. Hunter, E. Mathijs, M. Selfe and J. Sexton (2007) *Audiences and Receptions of Sexual Violence in Contemporary Cinema*. London: BBFC. On-line. Available: http://www.bbfc.co.uk/downloads/pub/Policy%20and%20Research/Audiences%20and%20Receptions%20of%20Sexual%20Violence%20in%20Contemporary%20Cinema.pdf (accessed 4 April 2009).

Baron, C. and S. M. Carnicke (2008) *Reframing Screen Performance*. Ann Arbor: University of Michigan Press.

Baudrillard, J. (1990) *Seduction*, trans. Brian Singer. Montreal: New World Perspectives.

BBC News (2000) 'FilmFour in "Porn" Accusation', *BBC Entertainment*, 17 October. On-line. Available: http://news.bbc.co.uk/1/hi/entertainment/976437.stm (accessed 4 April 2009).

Bell, E. (2006) 'Performing "I do": Weddings, Pornography and Sex', in K. E. Lovaas and M. M. Jenkins (eds) *Sexualities and Communication in Everyday Life: A Reader*. London: Sage, 145-164.

Benjamin, W. (1968) 'The Work of Art in the Age of Mechanical Reproduction', in *Illuminations*, trans. H. Zohn. New York: Harcourt, Brace and World, 217–51.

Biasin, E. and F. Zecca (2009) 'Contemporary Audiovisual Pornography: Branding Strategy and Gonzo Film Style', *Cinema & Cie: International Film Studies Journal*, 9, 12, 133-150.

Blanco, Z. (2008) 'Shane's World Shows You How to Create a Legend: Eva Angelina!!', *Adult Maven*, 1 September. On-line. Available: http://www.sin20.com/sidebar/sinfinder.php?terms=anal.sex,DVDs,movies,pornstars,reviews&nid=6419&selfurl=/news/evalution-eva-angelina&urlname=http://www.adultmaven.com/articles/4415/1/Shanes-World-shows-you-how-to-create-a-legend-Eva-Angelina/Page1.html (accessed 15 January 2009).

Cherry, M. (n.d.) 'Eva Angelina Sizzling Hot!', *Xtreme*. On-line. Available: http://xtrememagazine.com/index.php/eva-avangelina.html (accessed 5 April 2009).

Corbett, J. and T. Kapsalis (1996) 'Aural Sex: The Female Orgasm in Popular Sound', *The Drama Review (TDR)*, Autumn, 40, 3, 102–11.

Dowling, T. (2008) 'Is that a spanner in your pocket…', *Guardian*, 15 November. On-line. Available: http://www.guardian.co.uk/film/2008/nov/15/opening-shots-porn-films (accessed 5 April 2009).

Dworkin, A. (1981) *Pornography: Men Possessing Women*. London: Women's Press.

Eitzen, D. (2005) 'Documentary's Peculiar Appeals', in J. D. Anderson and B. F. Anderson (eds) *Moving Image Theory: Ecological Considerations*. Carbondale: Southern Illinois University Press, 183–99.

Hardy, S. (1998) *The Reader, The Author, His Woman & Her Lover: Soft Core Pornography and Heterosexual Men*. London: Cassell.

Helfrecht, D. (1973) 'Linda Lovelace: An Interview With the Sexsational Star of *Deep Throat*', *The Daily Girl Interview*, September. On-line. Available: http://www.lindalovelace.plazadiscounts.com/page24.html (accessed 5 April 2009).

Kendrick, W. (1997) *The Secret Museum: Pornography in Modern Culture*. New York: Viking.

Kipnis, L. (2006) 'How to Look at Pornography', in P. Lehman (ed.) *Pornography: Film and Culture*. New Jersey and London: Rutgers University Press, 118–29.

Krzywinska, T. (2005) 'The Enigma of the Real: The Qualifications for Real Sex in Contemporary Art Cinema', in G. King (ed.) *The Spectacle of the Real: From Hollywood to Reality TV and Beyond*. Bristol: Intellect, 223–34.

____ (2006) *Sex and the Cinema*. London: Wallflower Press.

Landsberg, A. (2010) 'Waking the Deadwood of History: Listening, Language and the Aural Visceral', *Rethinking History*, 14, 4, 531–49.

Lichtenstein, O. (2009) 'The tawdry truth about those adult TV channels (...Jacqui Smith look away now)', *Daily Mail*, 31 March, 22–3.

Lovelace, L. (1973) *Inside Linda Lovelace*. New York: Pinnacle Books.

Lovell, A. (2003) 'I went in search of Deborah Kerr, Jodie Foster and Julianne Moore but got waylaid...', in T. Austin and M. Barker (eds) *Contemporary Hollywood Stardom*. London: Arnold, 259–70.

McDonald, P. (2004) 'Why Study Film Acting?: Some Opening Reflections', in C. Baron, D. Carson and F. P. Tomasulo (eds) *More than a Method: Trends and Traditions in Contemporary Film Performance*. Detroit: Wayne State University Press, 23–41.

Moore, L. J. (2007) *Sperm Counts: Overcome By Man's Most Precious Fluid*. New York: NYU Press.

Naremore, J. (1988) *Acting in the Cinema*. Berkeley: University of California Press.

NASIOC (2006) 'bangbus gets busted', *NASIOC* [discussion list], 1 July. On-line. Available: http://forums.nasioc.com/forums/archive/index.php/t-1037449.html (accessed 4 April 2009). Original: 'Porn Bus Shoots Sex On The Move', Local 10, 18 November 2004.

Paasonen, S. and L. Saarenmaa (2007) 'The Golden Age of Porn: Nostalgia and History in Cinema', in S. Paasonen, K. Nikunen and L. Saarenmaa (eds) *Pornification: Sex and Sexuality in Media Culture*. Oxford: Berg, 23–32.

Peachy (2006) 'Allie Sin/Gwen aka NaughtyNati', *PeachyForum* [discussion list], 1–18 August. On-line. Available: http://peachyforum.com/forums/p/86096/274425.aspx (accessed 4 April 2009).

Pipe, R. T. (2002) 'John Stagliano Interview'. *RogReviews*. On-line. Available: http://www.rogreviews.com/interviews/john_stagliano.asp? (accessed 4 April 2009).

____ (2008) 'Eva Angelina Interview'. *RogReviews*. On-line. Available: http://www.rogreviews.com/interviews/eva_angelina_08.asp (accessed 4 April 2009).

Ponante, G. (2006) '*Blacklight Beauty* Review', *Porn Valley Reviewed*, 21 August. On-line. Available: http://www.gramponante.com/reviews/2006/08/blacklight-beauty.html (accessed 4 April 2009).

Probert, A., F. P. Massey and S. Leberman (2007) 'The fine line: an insight into 'risky' practices of male and female competitive bodybuilders', *Annals of Leisure Research*, 10, 3-4, 272-290.

Richtel, M. (2007) 'In Raw World of Sex Movies, High Definition Could Be a View Too Real', *New York Times*, 22 January. On-line. Available: http://www.nytimes.com/2007/01/22/business/media/22porn.html?pagewanted=2&_r=1&adxnnl=1&ref=media&adxnnlx=1219309445-jze5RZO4FSzxWfuoz846DQ (accessed 22 May 2008).

Shelton, E. (2002) 'A Star is Porn: Corpulence, Comedy and the Homosocial Cult of Adult Film Star Ron Jeremy', *Camera Obscura*, 17, 3, 115–46.

Smaill, B. (2009) 'Documentary investigations and the female porn star', *Jump Cut: A Review of Contemporary Media*, 51. On-line. Available: http://www.ejumpcut.org/currentissue/femalePornstars/index.html (accessed 14 March 2010).

Smith, R. (1973) *Getting Into Deep Throat*. Chicago: Playboy Press.

Websters (2008) *Commitments: Webster's Quotations, Facts and Phrases*. San Diego: Icon Group International.

Williams, L. (1989) *Hard Core: Power, Pleasure and the 'Frenzy of the Visible'*. Berkeley: University of California Press.

____ (2008) *Screening Sex*. Durham: Duke University Press.

CHAPTER THIRTEEN

POWER BOTTOM: PERFORMATIVITY IN COMMERCIAL GAY PORNOGRAPHIC VIDEO

John Mercer

> There's zero discussion of pornography as an expressive medium in a positive sense... That it might have more complicated social agendas, or that future historians of the genre might produce some interesting insights about pornography's relation to this particular historical and social moment – these are radically unthought thoughts. (Kipnis 1999: 163)

Laura Kipnis's comments in *Bound and Gagged* are a useful starting point to contextualise the observations that will be made in this chapter and have, to a large extent, informed the agenda of my research into gay pornography and the associated issues that I have been attempting to address for several years. My interests, and the focus of this study, lie in the attempt to account for the relationship between iconography and culture, and in particular how the distinctive iconography of gay pornography reflects and inflects gay culture.

It has become almost customary in work on this subject to acknowledge the problems associated with academic enquiry into pornography, and whilst it is largely superfluous to rehearse once more the reasons why such problems exist, it can scarcely be denied that debate around pornography in a popular or an academic context has often been characterised by hyperbole and sweeping generalisations and (with a few notable exceptions) has too often failed to engage with the manifest textual content of the material itself.[1] It strikes me that this is an issue that must be addressed in order for a thoroughgoing engagement with porn and its influences and effects to take place and this continues to be my primary objective. Moreover, following the advent of the internet and the enhanced accessibility as well as the sheer volume of pornography that it has made available in ways that were unimaginable previously, the necessity to understand, account for, contextualise and explain this ubiquitous but still relatively unspoken aspect of contemporary culture becomes all the more urgent.

The focus of my research has been mainstream commercial gay pornography. It is important here to make a distinction between gay porn aimed at a mass market audience and material that is aimed at specialised interest markets. The notion of the mainstream, of course, raises a set of issues and questions concerning norms of behaviour and conduct and the normative desires that such mass market material produces. This is a subject that Mark Jancovich has written about with regard to heterosexual pornography:

> Constructions of the mainstream tend to present it as an entirely passive object which is only ever associated with conservatism, and hence as a place where nothing interesting ever happens. This position also suggests a sense of over-familiarity in which the mainstream is supposedly not worthy of examination because it is presumed to be all too well known and obvious. In debates over pornography ... interest is almost always in the 'transgressive' because mainstream pornography is assumed to be an essentially known entity which does not change... Rather than a stable, unchanging, homogeneous and known entity, this category itself may act to repress and contain the heterogeneity and contradictions involved within it. In other words, accounts of this figure rarely bother to subject this category to detailed analysis, but merely rely on, and reproduce, taken for granted assumptions instead. (2001)

As Jancovich notes, the mainstream and mainstream taste, far from being neutral and immutable, is of particular significance due to a number of factors ranging from its discursive hegemonic power to its status as the 'default' position from which those objects or phenomena that fall outside of its ambit can be defined as 'non-mainstream'. Indeed the very notion that there might be such a thing as a 'mainstream' gay pornography to a large extent may seem a contradiction in terms to the uninitiated. However, gay pornography emerges from a highly developed and sophisticated industry with an ever expanding and increasingly segmented market catering to tastes and interests that range from the highly specialised to the relatively conventional.

It is equally important to acknowledge the considerable provenance of gay pornography and its representations. As Thomas Waugh (1996) has previously observed in his exhaustive study of homosexual erotica, *Hard to Imagine*, the history of gay pornography is as extensive as its heterosexual counterpart. With the advent of the technologies of photography and cinema, representations of gay sexuality were recorded and circulated from the infancy of both media. Consequently, the history of gay pornography mirrors (albeit on a sometimes smaller and more artisanal basis) the development of heterosexual pornography. Therefore in parallel to the emergence of the cinematic pornography discussed by Linda Williams in *Hard Core* (1990), during the 1970s and early 1980s a small but significant gay pornographic cinema emerged. However, it was the emergence of VHS technology that facilitated an exponential growth of the gay pornography industry.[2]

By the mid-1980s the home video market for gay pornography was well established and with it came the emergence of a group of companies that dominated the production and distribution of commercial gay pornography, including Falcon Studios, Catalina and HIS Video. The successes of these studios brought with them the establishment of a range of generic expectations within gay video pornography, a paradigm of narrative tropes, iconography, and most importantly for my research, a range of types. These types, that I call 'prototypes', combine and conflate a range of physical attributes, characterisation, performative characteristics and iconography, and my research has been largely concerned with constructing a taxonomy that accounts for their construction and deployment. The paradigm of types that were established during this period of the gay pornographic industry are of key significance both to the understanding of their own contextual moment, and also to understanding the dominant representations of contemporary gay pornography.

In a chapter on the phenomenon of the gay porn star I have previously observed that

> the types that populate the world of gay pornographic video are organised according to a variety of criteria. With the absence of gender difference as a discourse to organise and categorise behaviour, performance and role in gay pornography, a plethora of codified types emerge. The pre-eminent form of categorisation concerns itself with sexual performance and sexual role: performers who are assigned the 'active' *Top* role in sexual encounters and those who are categorised as 'passive' *Bottoms*. This form of organisation and assignation of roles is based on predetermined assumptions about the nature of gay sexual practice and normative conduct, assumptions that are based largely on the agendas and perspectives of the producers of gay pornography. (Mercer 2006: 152–3)

During the 1980s and into the 1990s this dichotomy between the active and the passive is made explicit through representation. The classic porn top is the most recurrently deployed type in commercial gay pornography of the period. Drawing on the iconography of hegemonic masculinity, the top eroticises the signifiers of an authentic, macho masculinity. The top is discursively positioned through narrative, *mise-en-scène* and performance as a 'real man' and a man of action rather than words, and this is emphatically reiterated in iconographic and performative elements that are repeated over and over again with relentless regularity.

Set up in opposition to the classic porn top, the prototypical porn bottom is identified during the same period through a distinctive iconography, paradigm of discourses and performative characteristics. The classic porn bottom, perhaps more apparently than the classic top, draws on the classical Greek ideals of man/boy love. The porn bottom is frequently discursively positioned as the younger and less experienced partner in a sexual encounter. The iconography of the bottom emphasises youth – smooth, hairless, boyish bodies, often devoid of the overdetermined muscular definition that characterises the top – fair skin, boyish looks and blonde hair are the characteristics that recur. The body types that typify the porn bottom equally draw on classical precedents: the sleek and statuesque Adonis or Kouros of classical sculpture and the lithe and boyish Ephebus.

The classic porn bottom is often socially located within the domestic sphere; in the home, the luxurious domestic setting, the poolside and, of course, the bedroom. The specific location of the porn bottom emphasises the passive, receptive and sexually available qualities that are characteristic of the prototype's signification. The classic porn bottom belongs in the domestic arena, he is passive, always sexually available, he is young, his body is smooth and lithe, and he acts as a catalyst for the generation of discourses of romance and idealised domesticated fantasy.

Perhaps the clearest examples of the conjunction of youth, passivity and the situation of the domestic sphere in the iconography of the prototypical porn bottom can be found in the presentation of the performer Kevin Williams – probably the best known of gay porn bottoms of the 1980s – the star of such releases as *Big Guns* (1987), *Bare Tales* (1987) and *Out of Bounds* (1987). In many ways Williams is a transitional figure as, in the early stage of his career as a porn performer, his signification very clearly conforms to the prototypical ideals of the classic bottom, and in fact his representation is its epitome. However, following a ten-year hiatus Williams returned to the porn industry in 1998, with much pre-publicity hyperbole on the part of Falcon Studios, as an older and far more aggressive bottom performer.

In this latter incarnation Williams was instrumental in defining the role of the 'power bottom', which will be discussed subsequently. In a photo shoot appearing in *Men Magazine* in 1986, Williams' youthful looks and petite physicality are evident. In the images he is pictured in a domestic setting lying on a bed, his buttocks bared, assuming a posture that self-consciously references the stylistic vernacular of heterosexual glamour photography. Such idealistically passive images were to become a recurrent mode of representation for both Williams and the many other porn bottoms of the era.

The conjunction of youth, domesticity, innocence and sexual availability in Williams' signification is most effectively exemplified by the promotional pack shot for *In Your Wildest Dreams* (1988).[3] The video concerns the business of an escort agency that caters to the specific fantasies of its clients. Williams' fantasy is a training coach who will dominate him and the prototypical top, Chad Douglas, fulfils his wish in this regard. In the cover image for the video, however, the inference is that it is the lithe and youthful Williams, located in a luxurious domestic setting, that is the wildest dream of the viewer. Williams' youth and sexual desirability is foregrounded in the image by recourse to an almost hysterically overdetermined *mise-en-scène*. The setting for the image is dark, though we can observe a fire in the background, connotative both of sexual passion and domesticity. Williams is depicted semi-recumbent on a fur rug, sporting white briefs and surrounded by white soft toys.

The excessive *mise-en-scène* of the image, drawing on a wealth of sub-textual references, combined with William's posture, smooth body and coy glance at the camera, encourage us to read him as a male ingénue, seemingly unaware of his own sexuality. Within this context the video's title has another connotation that further draws on the signifiers of youth and inexperience played with in the image: that of the adolescent wet dream. Whilst this mode of representation was to continue throughout the remainder of the 1980s and is still in evidence in contemporary gay pornography, during the 1990s the term 'power bottom' emerged in promotional copy and video reviews. This term seems to identify the presence of a new prototype within gay pornography.

THE 1990s AND THE EMERGENCE OF THE POWER BOTTOM

The power bottom is of interest as a prototype that can be seen to have emerged during the late 1990s, and also as a construction that problematises the already established categories of sexual performance and role play that gay pornography of the 1980s deals with. The term was first used (as far as I can determine) to describe a newer more aggressive performance of the bottom role typified by the performer Tristan Paris. Appearing as the cover model for the July 1998 edition of *Adam Gay Video XXX* Showcase, Paris is described with the strap-line: 'TRISTAN PARIS Falcon's New Power-Bottom – He Can Take Whatever You've Got!' In the cover shot for the magazine, Paris is presented as the epitome of the clean, healthy, outdoors all-American boy-next-door – characteristics that could fit relatively easily within the broader discourses of the classic porn bottom. Paris's signification as the prototypical power bottom is most clearly identified through his performance and deployment in specific texts.

An example is Jocks Studios' video *Phoenix Rising* (1999). In this film Paris is presented as the off-the-rails nephew who disrupts the domestic harmony of Jason Branch whilst staying with him in his home in Phoenix, Arizona. Branch is the viewer's point of identification in the video: an affluent, sexually attractive, classic porn top, in a stable relationship with a younger man. Paris, by contrast, is constructed as wilful, promiscuous and sexually predatory. On arrival at Branch's home, Paris seduces workmen cleaning the swimming pool and encourages them to leave their work and engage in sexual play, which he orchestrates. In the scene Paris is not the passive recipient of the worker's attentions but the director of their sexual encounter, instructing them using a litany of expletives.

The scene culminates in all of the workmen fucking Paris at his demand. 'Uncle' Jason is told that work cannot continue on his house whilst the bad nephew Paris is around, and angered he returns home to confront his troublesome young relative. In the meantime, Paris has left the familiar domestic arena of the classic bottom to pick up a muscular blue-collar top at a cruising ground, returning to Branch's home for sex. The scene that ensues depicts Paris' enjoyment of the rough sex he receives at the hands of his pick-up who fucks him repeatedly in a variety of positions in the lounge. Throughout the sequence Paris demands that his trick fuck him harder: he is once more in control of the sexual situation. After returning home to witness this lengthy spectacle, Branch decides that he will teach his nephew a lesson and the scene is set for the 'punishment' of the power bottom. Blindfolded, Paris is lead into the garage where three muscular and immensely endowed black men are waiting. Under Branch's instruction Paris fellates all three of the men and once his blindfold is removed proceeds to have anal sex with each one, yelling his demand that they fuck him harder and alternating between partners. Finally 'Uncle' Jason fucks the insatiable Paris.

This narrative illustrates that rather than being presented as a passive, sexually receptive figure located in the domestic arena, the power bottom prototype can be seen as an autonomous sexual adventurer. The power bottom is not only available as a figure to be fucked, he actively pursues men and initiates sexual encounters: the power bottom orchestrates sexual situations that will result in him getting what he wants, which is usually a well-endowed, prototypical top who will satisfy his need for anal sex. The power bottom is distinguished in his sexual encounters by his aggressive performance of the 'passive' sexual act both by the ways in which he is seen as controlling the sexual play and frequently by his self-consciously aggressive delivery. The potential for destabilisation of the passive/active hierarchies of gay porn performance here are clear and, within the narrative context of several videos in the mid-1990s, an attempt to retain order is made through the recurrent use of the theme of the 'punishment' of the power bottom. However, during the late 1990s and early years of the twenty-first century, a rather less fixed and more fluid notion of gay male sexual roles increasingly emerges in gay pornographic video.

CAESAR: THE POWER BOTTOM PAR EXCELLENCE

The performer Caesar offers perhaps the most startling example of the prototypical power bottom. Whilst being clearly identified in a discursive and performative sense as a bottom, the power bottom Caesar has the physical characteristics, iconography and performative qualities that are more usually associated with the prototypical top.

Appearing as the cover model for the September 2001 edition of *Torso* magazine, Caesar is hailed unequivocally as a bottom through the strapline 'Caesar Confessions of a Trophy Bottom!!!' However his physicality, his distinctive iconography, his pose in the image, and yet more significantly his performance and deployment in the context of specific texts, questions an orthodox reading of the performer as a classic porn bottom – the smooth, lithe, boyish physique of the young Kevin Williams or Tristan Paris here is substituted by bulky, solid, defined muscle. Though hairless, Caesar's is the body of a man and not a boy.

Furthermore, Caesar's body is marked with tattoos, both a traditional symbol of a particular form of macho manhood and also an indicator of class. This sense of class, though only alluded to in the majority of cases, becomes a key aspect of Caesar's signification as prototypical power bottom. Caesar, we are to infer, is a blue-collar working-class man, a 'real' man, a man's man who enjoys sex with other 'real' men. In the video *Hail Caesar* (1999), Caesar is presented as the epitome of the urban gay male in charge of his own destiny and actively pursuing sexual adventure. *Hail Caesar* has a simple narrative structure, presenting a series of sexual encounters that, we are to believe, constitute a week in the life of the power bottom, linked together by Caesar's narration. On Monday Caesar spies on his 'pool mate going at it', on Tuesday he has an encounter with his 'army buddy Andrew' offering the opportunity to 'worship his big cock'. On Wednesday Caesar 'jacked with' his 'buddy Mark and his fuck buddy Kyle'. After this sequence he tells us that 'On Thursday I got my ass fucked good by my pal Tom'. In each of these encounters, although Caesar is located in the domestic arena of his own apartment and he adopts an exclusively bottom role in all of the exchanges, his aggressive performance of the bottom role, his incitement for his partners to fuck him harder and his orchestration of the sexual play, all signify Caesar's insatiable desire to be fucked and his pleasure in getting fucked. The narrative of the whole piece here is not structured around the top's goal of achieving a climax through fucking the bottom but rather the pleasure that the power bottom derives from being used.

In the video *Caesar's Hardhat Gang Bang* (2000) our understanding of Caesar as sexual adventurer and the active pursuer of tops is emphasised further. In the video Caesar's car breaks down on a construction site, he is told that it will take three hours for a mechanic to arrive. Caesar notices that the eight construction workers on the site (all either Hispanic or black) are involved in the sexual initiation of a younger colleague. The prospect of a sexual encounter with these prototypes of machismo is more than Caesar can resist, and he offers himself as the object of their attentions rather than the young initiate, allowing each man, in groups or individually, to have sex with him. In this video the dynamic of the group sex scenario, often revolving around the use of a single classic bottom is altered. The discourse of sexual abuse or degradation that is invoked to add extra frisson to the scenario is dispersed by Caesar's complicity. Caesar wants the construction workers to aggressively fuck him and it is him and not they who is structured as the primary recipient of sexual gratification in the video.

CULTURAL CONTEXT AND INSTITUTIONAL CHANGE

The power bottom emerges, I would argue, as a consequence of a range of institutional and cultural factors and his significances are equally various. Firstly, the advent of the internet has largely resulted in the fracture of the gay porn industry and the major studio's sphere of influence. Rather than a handful of gay porn studios, there are now hundreds of different producers catering to both mainstream and niche interests. Therefore the normative standards of desire that the major studios largely constructed can be and have been challenged. This proliferation of the gay porn market has, it seems, created conditions in which the very notion of the mainstream, and the mainstream sexual tastes that the old binarism of the top and the bottom are predicated upon, can be called into question.

This is evidenced not just by the growth of gay pornography, but also by the extent to which the representations and fantasies offered by the traditional market leaders have changed during the course of the past ten years or so. For example, the emergence of Titan Media, whose status as market leader is largely based on an iconography of hyper-macho masculinity – the very physical characteristics that the porn of the 1980s had almost completely eradicated. Titan's significant influence on the industry has in turn paved the way for the emergence of Hot House and Raging Stallion, both studios utilising older, hirsute models engaging in sexual scenarios that include sadomasochistic fantasies, and the rebranding of Colt Studios with high-profile releases focusing on the perennial sexual interest in bodybuilders. Even Falcon Studios, who for the majority of the 1980s and 1990s had established and maintained the iconographic and stylistic hegemony that had prevailed in the gay porn industry, have since widened their range of models to include older performers and some degree of racial diversity that had been conspicuously absent during the heyday of the mid-1980s and early 1990s.

Secondly, the emergence of queer politics, which in itself questions normative sexuality and articulates the possibility of more fluid and disparate sexualities, perhaps plays a part in the emergence of the power bottom. The extent to which this can be evidenced, however, is open to question as the established gay porn industry has a legacy of conservatism and has been slow to acknowledge cultural changes. This is most vividly illustrated by the well documented and consistently reactive responses of Falcon Studios, the undisputed market leader during the 1980s and 1990s, to almost every significant development – from the introduction of safer sex practices (including mandatory condom use in video shoots) to the shift from VHS to DVD as the dominant format and the possibilities of the internet.

Thirdly, the power bottom is of interest because of what this may say about changing social and sexual mores, as well as the potential implications surrounding sexual conduct and sexual health that result from the deployment and emergence of this particular prototype – these are the issues that will be discussed for the remainder of this chapter. Since the late 1980s gay porn has espoused the orthodoxy of safer sex practice (it should be noted that mandatory condom use was only introduced well into the AIDS crisis. All of the major producers were very slow to respond to this issue). Nonetheless, safer sex practice and mandatory condom use has become part of mainstream gay representation in gay porn. The power bottom's iconography and deployment, however, is concomitant with an increased use of fetish and more extreme sexual practices in mainstream gay porn representation and the emergence of the barebacking phenomenon.

BAREBACKING: TREASURE ISLAND MEDIA

Few cultural developments have caused more controversy within the gay community than the subject of barebacking, which became identified as a gay sexual fetish from the late 1990s onwards. Barebacking refers to not just the practice but the eroticisation of unprotected anal sex. It is a highly divisive issue within the gay community, as well as within the medical community, as the implications of this form of sexual conduct are significant and additionally pose huge challenges for health agencies who have invested immense physical and emotional resources since the advent of the AIDS crisis in the communication of the safer sex message. The cultural factors that lie behind the emergence of this phenomena are complex, ranging from improvements in HIV treatments and an increasingly sexualised gay culture based on the perceptions that HIV is now a manageable condition to what has been described as 'safer sex fatigue' and require much more detailed consideration than it is possible to provide within the context of this chapter.[4] Nonetheless the apparent radicalism of this sexual practice, especially in the cultural and political climate that has prevailed post-AIDS, has inevitably meant that barebacking as a phenomenon would inevitably lend itself to pornographic representation.

It is therefore no surprise that bareback pornography has emerged as a new subgenre of gay porn. The first and still the most prominent producer of such material, Paul Morris and his company Treasure Island Media have become synonymous with the phenomenon and an emergent barebacking subculture. Morris himself is a highly eloquent commentator on his creative practice as a pornographer and the cultural and political agendas that lie behind his work – not least because of the huge amount of controversy and negative press his videos have attracted. Morris has argued that bareback pornography (and by inference bareback practice itself) has emerged to some extent in response to the rigid and desexualised orthodoxies of safer sex practice that are enshrined in mainstream gay pornographic representation. In a roundtable discussion conducted at the University of California, San Francisco in 1999, Morris notes:

> I see myself as sort of being an iconoclastic pornographer, and that's only because what I'm doing or what I make is rejecting the sort of codified rules that said in porn, over the last decade and a half, that ... had nothing to do with the nature of the sexual activity, it just removed the pornographic representation of sex away from the original function of porn, which was to give the viewer a sense of the original erotic sexual heat. (In Sheon 1999)

In a paper delivered at the World Pornography Conference in 1998 his argument is emphasised:

> In the last ten to fifteen years, representation of dangerous or even just unusual practices have all but disappeared and porn has been dominated by a nearly universal acceptance of broad strictures that allow not only for very little danger, but also set stringent limits on the types of acts that can be depicted and the types of people who will be allowed to perform. And today, while gay sex is in the midst of a second 1970s, porn is mired in the strict conformity and conservativism of a new 1950s. (Morris 1998)

An agenda to reject the conservatism of mainstream gay porn then informs the output of Treasure Island, producing pornography that is paradoxically about affirming existence through the depiction of activities defined as 'unsafe'. The deliberate strategy to provoke and outrage is symbolically made manifest through the company's skull and crossed cutlass logo.

The aesthetic strategies and stylistic features of Treasure Island productions – apparently 'impromptu' location shooting at well known cruising grounds and in almost self-consciously anonymous hotel rooms, jerky handheld camera movement, visible lighting set-ups and production personnel that all foreground the staged but simultaneously documentary nature of the process of recording the sexual encounters – are in stark contrast to the often orchestrated and choreographed sexual numbers frequently presented in the material previously discussed in this chapter. In Treasure Island productions, *vérité* style becomes the guarantee of the 'original heat' that Morris has referred to and takes precedence over the studied verisimilitude in the output of contemporary mainstream pornography.[5]

It is in the context of productions such as *What I Can't See* (1999), *Plowed* (2000), *Breeding Mike O'Neill* (2002) and *Riding Billy Wild* (2003) that the power bottom has emerged as the key figure of audience identification and desire, and it is with the Treasure Island exclusive performer Dawson that we see the most vivid and perhaps startling contemporary expression of the power bottom identity.

DAWSON: THE BAREBACK POWER BOTTOM

First seen in the eponymous *Dawson's 20 Load Weekend* (2004), the performer is exclusively contracted to appear in Treasure Island videos and is to a large extent presented as the studio's star. Whilst Dawson is athletically built in the natural and unselfconscious manner of a swimmer, and is conventionally though unremarkably handsome, he lacks either the overdetermined muscularity of the classic porn top, the androgynous physicality of the classic porn bottom, or the physical indexes of class position evident in performers such as Caesar. Indeed Dawson is distinguished by his very normality, by his appeal to mainstream taste, by his 'ordinary' appearance by the hyperbolic standards of mainstream gay pornography at least.

This sense is reiterated in the promotional copy that accompanies his videos and the anchoring text that contextualises the opening scenes of both *Dawson's 20 Load Weekend* and its sequel *Dawson's 50 Load Weekend* (2005). The audience for these texts is assured that his appearances are motivated by his own personal need to fulfil his fantasies, that he is in fact undergoing a process of self-realisation through this form of sexual performance. Dawson is presented as the archetypical 'guy-next-door' born in a small town in Maine: he starts his career in bareback pornography as a fan of Treasure Island material who contacts Paul Morris to suggest the idea of a video filmed over the course of a weekend in New York where he would be the sole receptive participant in a serial gangbang. The premise here is that Dawson would allow any man who showed up during the course of the shoot to have bareback anal sex with him.

To illustrate this, in the opening sequence of *Dawson's 20 Load Weekend*, the star is presented in mid-shot and nude from behind, gazing through a skyscraper window at a panoramic New York cityscape overlooking central park whilst titles that resemble tickertape set the scene. The audience is told that 'Dawson came to New York for a big city gang breeding [sic]' and 'he told us he wouldn't be satisfied until he took twenty loads'. The tone of the opening images and the text that accompanies them is paradoxically solemn given the two-hour bacchanalia that follows. The success and notoriety of the resulting video has been followed in fairly rapid succession by *Cumsloppy Buttholes* (2004), *Meat Rack* (2005), *Plantin' Seed* (2005), *Dawson's 50 Load Weekend*, *Meat Packing* (2006), and the ostensible star vehicles, *Loaded* (2007) and *Deeper* (2007). In all cases what distinguishes Dawson within these texts is not the specifics of his physicality but the performative qualities that he demonstrates.

As has been previously noted, the power bottom subverts the implicit dynamic of active and passive sexuality in gay pornographic performance by an 'active' performance of the supposedly 'passive' sexual role. However, in Dawson's case, this is emphasised almost to the point of excess by the sheer levels of gusto and abandon demonstrated in his performances. Demonstrable pleasure and a sense of euphoria are palpably evident in these scenes that are far removed from the often more self-consciously performed sex scenes in mainstream output. This hedonistic performance, combined with rhetorical strategies that reference fly-on-the-wall documentary realism and draw attention to the process of recording events, produces texts that are as powerful as they are problematic.[6]

In a notable sequence in *Meat Rack* set in a beach house location on Fire Island, following a lengthy orgy sequence around a swimming pool, an 'unscripted and unplanned' scene takes place between Dawson and three of the other performers who are due to leave the set. The urgency of this scene (illustrated by the variations in lighting quality and focus and camera men stumbling into frame) is further emphasised by the immediacy and raw quality of Dawson's sexual performance, his evident excitement (both in his performance and his commentary) about initiating and controlling this encounter, and its documentation and the evidence of its success revealed on his naked body. This 'unstaged' scene vividly illustrates through its absence of technical polish and subsequent impression of documenting the 'authentic' moment, the very normality that is key to Dawson's emblematic nature as the contemporary expression of the power bottom. His everyday quality enables his performance to suggest to some extent that he is living out the 'real' fantasies that many normal gay men have. His performance intimates that the desire for the sheer abandonment of responsibility and commitment, other than to the principle of sexual pleasure, to be fucked and to fuck without consequence, is a fundamental fantasy. Dawson then, as the contemporary expression of the power bottom, is simultaneously a powerful and problematic figure of identification and object of fantasy.

As a final postscript to this chapter, and as an indicator of the issues at stake in the changing face of the mainstream gay porn industry, I should point out that whilst this study was being researched *Boyz* magazine reported the story of three young performers (18, 21 and 26 years of age) who all contracted HIV during a bareback porn shoot from a fourth performer who had undergone HIV testing with a negative result only a few weeks before (see Riley 2007: 6). All of the performers had believed that their status was HIV negative whilst they were filming. Whilst this story has provoked some degree of controversy, it is notable that there is evidence in recent years of the erosion of mandatory safer sex practices in mainstream gay representation and this trend, it would appear, may continue. Changes in industry practice of this kind have potentially profound implications on the kinds of messages (positive or otherwise) that gay pornography communicates. This demonstrates the ways in which pornography can be seen to be both shaped by and, to some extent perhaps, shapes norms of behaviour and desires amongst its constituent audience.

NOTES

1. An extremely timely and useful article that discusses the relative absence of research into pornography in British universities published in the *Times Higher Education Supplement* in March 2007 summarised the various factors that inhibit scholarly enquiry in the area ranging from personal inhibitions and political, moral and ethical issues to the absence of sources of funding.
2. Gay pornography remains a significantly under-researched subject and, whilst Waugh's historical work is a major contribution to the understanding of the genre and its precedents, the period between the early 1970s to early 1980s during which Wakefield Poole's *Boys in the Sand* (1971) became the first gay pornographic film to ever be advertised in the *New York Times* and reviewed by *Variety* has still largely been overlooked. The 1970s was a particularly vibrant and diverse period in gay pornographic production ranging from Poole's experimental style in *Bijou* (1972), the elaborately stylised soft-core film *Pink Narcissus* (1971), and the semi-documentary *Adam and Yves*

(1974), to the hyper-macho road movies of Joe Gage – *Kansas City Trucking Company* (1976), *El Paso Wrecking Corp.* (1978), *L.A. Tool and Die* (1979).
3   These images are widely available at any number of websites that sell gay DVDs.
4   A considerable body of research into the barebacking phenomenon is beginning to emerge. Much of this material is web-based and the website devoted to HIV treatment and associated issues produced by University of California San Francisco (hivinsite.ucsf.edu/) is perhaps the most comprehensive and useful.
5   Controversy still courts Morris's work and Treasure Island output. Even whilst bareback porn has now established itself as a subgenre of contemporary pornography, Treasure Island productions continue to be widely vilified. When, in 2006, Treasure Island were awarded the 'Best American Studio' title at the European Porn Awards in Berlin, representatives from mainstream producers Titan and Channel 1 Releasing, refused to accept their own awards in protest. Previously, in 2005, The Eagle Bar in New York was criticised for holding a premiere and casting event for Treasure Island.
6   Whilst within a discussion of commercial gay pornography I would not wish to overstate the case, there are some parallels here between the strategies of these videos and the arguments suggested in Kristin Thompson's (2004) essay on the function of cinematic excess.

WORKS CITED

Jancovich, M. (2001) 'Naked Ambitions: Pornography, Taste and the Problem of the Middlebrow', *Scope*, June. On-line. Available: http://www.scope.nottingham.ac.uk/article.php?issue=jun2001&id=274&section=article (accessed 1 April 2009).

Kipnis, L. (1999) *Bound and Gagged: Pornography and the Politics of Fantasy in America*. Durham: Duke University Press.

Mercer, J. (2006) 'Seeing is Believing: Constructions of Stardom and the Gay Porn Star in U.S. Gay Video Pornography', in S. Holmes and S. Redmond (eds) *Framing Celebrity*. London: Routledge, 145–60.

Morris, P. (1998) 'No Limits: Necessary Danger in Male Porn'. On-line. Available: http://www.managingdesire.org/nolimits.html (accessed 1 April 2009).

Riley, K. (2007) 'Young Porn Actors Infected With HIV on Bareback Shoot', *Boyz Magazine*, 18 October, 6.

Sheon, N. (1999) 'Visual AIDS: Gay Male Porn and Safer Sex Pedagogy', *HIV InSite*, May. On-line. Available: http://hivinsite.ucsf.edu/InSite.jsp?page=au-00-00&doc=2098.4218 (accessed 1 April 2009).

Thompson, K. (2004 [1981]) 'The Concept of Cinematic Excess', in L. Braudy and M. Cohen (eds) *Film Theory and Criticism*. Oxford: Oxford University Press, 513–24.

Waugh, T. (1996) *Hard to Imagine: Gay Male Eroticism in Photography and Film from Their Beginnings to Stonewall*. New York: Columbia University Press.

Williams, L. (1990) *Hard Core: Power, Pleasure and the 'Frenzy of the Visible'*. London: Pandora Press.

CHAPTER FOURTEEN

INTERROGATING LESBIAN PORNOGRAPHY: GENDER, SEXUAL ICONOGRAPHY AND SPECTATORSHIP[1]

Rebecca Beirne

During the 1980s and 1990s, debate raged over whether it was politically and culturally acceptable for lesbians to produce pornography. This period of intense debate, known as the sex wars, prompted an outpouring of lesbian-produced screen pornography for lesbian audiences. Most of the critical discussion of such material has rested upon the political potentials and repercussions of such texts.[2] In contrast, textual approaches to these unique pornographic films have been relatively neglected, with the exception of work by Mary Conway (1997) on some early 1990s Blush/Fatale films, and a thorough history and analysis of 'cinematic lesbian sex acts and actual pornographic films from 1968 to 2000' by Heather Butler (2004: 167). This chapter in essence takes up where Butler left off, in its focus on lesbian pornographic cultural production. The contemporary lesbian hard-core pornographic films I will focus on here are *Sugar High Glitter City* (2001), produced by San Francisco-based S.I.R. Video, *Tick Tock* (2001) and *Madam and Eve* (2003), both produced by the UK-based Rusty Films and directed by Angie Dowling, and *The Crash Pad* (2005), the first pornographic film from Pink and White Productions. Each of these films resonates with the history of lesbian pornographic production, such as Blush/Fatale lesbian pornographic videos made in the 1980s and 1990s, including continuing the focus on 'the education of the lesbian porn spectator', questions of authenticity and the display of 'a diversity of body types' and the re-evaluation of the gaze (Conway 1997: 103).

THE FILMS

Sugar High Glitter City takes place in the fictional Glitter City (shot in San Francisco) where sugar is outlawed. This premise lends itself to scenarios involving prostitution for various forms of sugar, and includes such characters as police officers, a sugar madam, a reformed sugar addict and multiple young women who prostitute themselves for sugar. Openly classifying itself as within 'the dykesploitation genre' (DVD back cover), this film is very much in the realm of what Butler characterises as 'dyke porn' with its appropriation of the conventions of heterosexual and gay male pornography, extensive use of dildos, rough sex, role play and an urban setting (2004: 181–2; 185).

In contrast, *Tick Tock*, a UK film directed by Angie Dowling ('Rusty Cave'), appears more reminiscent of earlier models of lesbian pornography in its 'attempts to create a lesbian presence in pornography as *different*; that is, as distinctly non-heterosexual in its emphasis on the more erotic aspects of lesbian sexuality' (Butler 2004: 175). One extended scene, for example, simply shows a woman running her hand over her lover's body, and then doing the same with kisses. Likewise directed by Dowling and featuring as its cast 'members of a real-life sex commune' (Rowlson 2004), *Madam and Eve* is set in a 'hospital' named Eden whose purpose is 'sexual awakenings'. This latter film is more highly stylised, features more dildos and more elaborate, fetish-inspired costuming, and has higher production values than its predecessor. Comedy plays an important role in the interludes between sexual scenes, from the opening segments wherein Madam gazes into her crystal ball, to a wall of moving eyes under the sign 'ICU' (Eve tells a new nurse who is taken aback by them 'oh, don't mind them, they just like to watch'). This, together with the title, name of the hospital and 'treatment' of 'The Promised One', gives *Madam and Eve* a very camp tone, which is further reinforced by kitsch sets, music and acting style.

The most recent film under discussion, *The Crash Pad*, is made by San Franciscan director Shine Louise Houston, who has been prominent in the promotion of the film, including interviews in such publications as the US lesbian magazine *Curve* (see Lo 2006: 42–3). The ostensible narrative revolves around 'the crash pad', an apartment to which lesbian couples go to engage in sexual intercourse. One must be given the 'key' to the apartment, and various rules apply, including only using the apartment seven times before handing the key on to another. Houston's university training in film, and experience with several short experimental films, renders her pornography more thoughtful than other examples of the genre. This includes complex explorations of identity and metatextual gestures that will both be analysed later in this chapter. When asked in an interview given as an extra on the DVD edition as to her 'angle' as a pornographic filmmaker, Houston stated:

I'm sure as you can see from this cast I definitely wanna get some more diversity ... I think women-made porn just has a slightly different edge to it ... [and] being a person of colour, that brings a little bit [of a] different angle ... there's a big gap it seems like for women-made dyke porn.

During cast interviews, it becomes clear that several of the actors are real-life couples. This, together with Houston's assertion that 'pretty much anyone can come up to me and say "hey, I wanna be in your porn"' and that she expects to gain new participants from those who watch the video, emphasises both a certain authenticity of depicted lesbian desire and a potential community focus, in terms of viewers becoming participants.

SPECTATORSHIP

Lesbian and dyke pornography generally positions itself towards the lesbian spectator, particularly through its attempts to distinguish itself from straight-produced 'all girl' pornography that purports to display 'lesbians' and is directed toward a heterosexual male spectatorship. Some lesbian pornographic texts perform this through claiming lesbian authenticity extra-diegetically, as seen in S.I.R. Video's 'seal' sporting the guarantee '100% dyke produced' on its DVD covers, or Rusty Films' insistence on the covers of *Madam and Eve* and *Tick Tock* that they are '100% lesbian made' – a claim given further credence by having Red Hot Diva, a subsidiary of UK lesbian magazine *Diva*, as their co-distributors.

What of their context, however, within the adult entertainment industry, an industry largely catering to male spectators? Despite their often politically motivated efforts to challenge or create lesbian sexual cultures, these companies exist and survive within a very particular heteronormative and male-centric economic system. Looking from a purely economic standpoint, producers of video productions such as these may indeed wish to, or at least unintentionally succeed in, attracting a more general audience of male voyeurs attracted to 'lesbian' pornography. Indeed, *Madam and Eve*'s all femme cast, noted even on the back of the DVD as 'An all-stunning latex-clad femme cast of 7 luscious lesbians' could be argued to utilise the femininity and conventional beauty of its performers to market this commercial product to both lesbian and heterosexual male audiences alike. Such productions can thus be viewed as participants in commodifying lesbian sexuality in a manner which other, smaller scale cultural productions, such as lesbian women-only burlesque performances or independent lesbian sex magazines, can largely avoid.[3]

Tick Tock goes further than the other texts under consideration in its claims to lesbian authenticity by proclaiming on its cover that it features 'real lesbians enjoying real sex'. While this could be read as attempting to prove to a lesbian audience that it is not an example of male-centric faux-lesbian pornography, it could also be read as potentially appealing to an ethnographically curious gaze, a desire by males to 'know' lesbian sex. The latter fits into the traditional mode of hard-core pornography which 'obsessively seeks knowledge, through a voyeuristic record of confessional, involuntary paroxysm, of the 'thing' itself' (Williams 1989: 49). However, should the latter indeed be the case such viewers would seem to gain little extra knowledge from *Tick Tock*, which frustrates viewerly expectations in its inattention to the conventions of mainstream pornography (whether this is in deliberate appeal to a different form of pornographic spectatorship or due to inexperience on the part of the filmmaker is unclear). The goal-oriented nature of much pornography is structurally undermined in *Tick Tock* by cuts, at times in the middle of a sequence, to another couple, then back again, in a style more reminiscent of television narrative that wishes to portray its action as happening simultaneously, than of other pornography, where the journey to orgasm is usually visually depicted, in as much detail as possible.

These cuts provoke a disjointedness which is at odds with goal-oriented pornography, and decentralises the importance of orgasm, a decentralisation which is, as Butler has noted, a feature of other examples of lesbian pornography (2004: 187). Indeed, orgasms, or rather portrayals thereof, are infrequent in this video, with some scenes left still in process at the conclusion of *Tick Tock*. The 'very difficulty involved in the representation of lesbian sex acts' (2004: 177) that Butler identifies through *Erotic in Nature* (1985) is also highlighted in this video, where at times one can see little but the back of a cast member, or a tangle of limbs, shot in close up, with cuts to the faces and back again, often leaving the viewer quite perplexed as to what is actually happening between the couple. The cuts away from the 'action', together with the periodic difficulties in distinguishing exactly what the 'action' is, frustrates viewer expectations, and leaves a certain shroud of mystery around 'lesbian' sex. Cutting between various lesbian couples, however, also emphasises notions of community in terms of its evocation of the idea that multiple lesbian sex acts are going on at any given time, and offers its spectators the possibility of participating in a community of lesbian sex through their engagement with the film itself.

Tick Tock's claims as to the 'realness' of its sex scenes are somewhat undermined by the presence of a clearly staged 'storyline'; nonetheless, there are features that do highlight a certain lesbian authenticity, if not necessarily the enjoyment that is likewise touted on the cover. Firstly, the performers do not appear to be professionals; this is not only ascertained by the non-mainstream ideals of beauty they represent, but the decidedly amateurish nature of the film. The performers frequently burst into giggles in the midst of their scenes, supporting legs slip and the performers fall awkwardly, and there is communication between the performers followed by frequent changes in position when something doesn't 'work'. Such aspects, while positing a certain degree of not acting *lesbianism* (much of the ostensible narrative is indeed portrayed via cartoon-inspired 'thought bubbles') do however, at least in some cases, appear to undermine the 'realness' of the performers' enjoyment, and resituate the role of the spectator. Instead of being offered a narrative which requires a certain suspension of disbelief, but adheres to filmic conventions that situates the pleasure of the spectator at centre stage, viewers of *Tick Tock* are exposed to a pornographic film that, while clearly made with a lesbian viewer in mind (one performer even has posters of Ellen DeGeneres and Martina Navratilova behind her as if to 'prove' her lesbian credentials), does not appear to be explicitly focused on pleasing its viewership, but rather is more invested in the *creation* of lesbian pornography itself.

Theorists of lesbian sexual representation have long grappled with questions of spectatorship and address. This focus is often posited as a response to 'Feminist film and performance critics [who] argue that representation is addressed to the gaze of the male spectator' (Dolan 1989: 59). Looking through the perspective of a psychoanalytic discourse, which locks them into a dichotomy of men as bearer of the active 'look,' critics such as Laura Mulvey see little way out of women's entrapment as objects short of 'trans-sex identification' (1989: 33). Jill Dolan notes that 'Part of the problem with the psychoanalytic model of spectatorship is just this tendency to pose universal 'male' and 'female' spectators who respond only according to gender' (1989: 61). Lesbian critics have sought to problematise this tendency by introducing the lesbian gaze into the realm of debate – a gaze that both situates women as potential active bearers of 'the look', and dissolves 'The subject/object relations that trap women performers and spectators as commodities in a heterosexual context' (1989: 63).

Terralee Bensinger (1992) has also cited the potential of lesbian pornography to transcend 'the male gaze' through displacement – the simple removal of the male spectator from the viewing realm renders the problematic aspects thereof inconsequential. Although such a perspective is in some respects valid, it is also to a degree an oversimplification, through presenting both a universalistic model of lesbian desire and spectatorship, and representing 'the male gaze' in such monolithic and powerful terms. Perhaps power relations in specifically erotic spectatorship are more complicated than initially thought in discourses influenced by a highly rigidified gendering of power and desire.

Other writers question the very division between the active desiring gaze and the passive (narcissistic) identification with the objectified woman. Reina Lewis and Katrina Rolley (1996) for example discuss the consumption of mainstream fashion magazine images that are lesbian-coded, by virtue of displaying butch subjects, female couples or references to lesbian history, by both lesbian and heterosexual women readers. They suggest that 'the magazines themselves almost invite – indeed educate – the [heterosexual female] reader into something very close to a lesbian response in much of their imagery of women in general', implicating them into 'a paradigmatically lesbian viewing position in which women are induced to exercise a gaze that desires the represented woman, not just one that identifies with them' (1996: 181). Lesbian spectators are located by Lewis and Rolley as being positioned to simultaneously desire the woman in the fashion photograph and want to be that same woman being (presumably) desired by other readers. Having identified these dual capacities, they assert that

> this raises the question of whether/how far one can distinguish an overtly lesbian gaze, that self-consciously desires the represented woman, from a narcissistic one that identifies with the represented woman as an object of a presumed-to-be-male desire? ... either desiring for herself the represented woman or/and desiring to be the woman who is desired by other lesbian readers. (Ibid.)

Such readings complicate and potentially undermine the conception of split gazes (masculine-active-objectifying/feminine-passive-narcissistic) in lesbian visual pleasure by maintaining that the gaze can be (perhaps necessarily is) both one of distancing (understood as objectification) and narcissism: 'the double movement of a lesbian visual pleasure wherein the viewer wants both to be and *have* the object' (ibid).

What of the contemporary lesbian spectator? Lesbian cultures have certainly gone through periods where the spectatorship of pornography was considered a politically problematic internalisation of misogyny and male identification. Later, during the sex wars, with the cultural blossoming of lesbian-produced pornography and sex radical cultures, participating in and viewing lesbian porn was often viewed as a transgressively political gesture (see Healey 1996; Wilton 1996). Where are contemporary lesbian cultures positioned in terms of these histories? While the production of lesbian pornography has, as I have articulated above, continued into the present day, and indeed has branched out into new fields such as comics,[4] growing numbers of, and support for, politically and socially conservative platforms, the 'new homonormativity' as Lisa Duggan (2002) puts it, would seem to engender a culture more reluctant to embrace dyke porn.

Pondering these issues at the beginning of 2004, I attended a significant number of the lesbian-themed films screened during the Sydney Gay and Lesbian Mardi Gras Film Festival. While the majority of the lesbian films I attended screened to almost empty theatres, *Madam and Eve*, billed as 'lesbian cinema's sexiest and most visually exciting erotic film ever' (Queerscreen 2004: 13), played to a packed theatre. And yet, audience reception of *Madam and Eve* was certainly not uniformly positive. While this can be explained by either the film's own deficiencies or its promotion, which to some extent obscured the actual content of the film (it would be more honestly characterised as pornography than as an 'erotic film'), it would not seem to account for the extremity of the audience reaction. Audience members started leaving the theatre almost immediately, and by halfway through the film, there were less than half the initial audience numbers remaining. Many audience members who did remain either spent their time laughing or looking extremely uncomfortable, and continued to gradually leave throughout the screening.

This was, however, not the first time the Mardi Gras Film Festival had shown lesbian pornography as part of its programme. In 2001 they showed S.I.R. Video's *Hard Love/How to Fuck in High Heels* (2000), with *Sugar High Glitter City* being screened the following year. Had audience response to the previous two films been overwhelmingly negative, surely the festival organisers would not have chosen to once again programme a lesbian pornographic film.

EDUCATING THE LESBIAN PORN VIEWER

Perhaps this reaction simply points towards the necessity of the education of the lesbian porn viewer. Conway has discussed how a lesbian porn film can educate 'its intended emergent lesbian viewer on another subject: how to be a lesbian porn viewer … re-educat[ing] one sort of female viewer (previously absent, perverse, or punished), transforming her into a desiring lesbian spectator' (1997: 100). This is often achieved through bringing lesbian porn spectators into the frame of lesbian (video) pornography, who then 'serve as models for the education of lesbian-produced porn viewing' by performing 'spectatorship and voyeurism' (1997: 102). In the context of the Blush/Fatale film *Safe Is Desire* (1993) for example, the inclusion of intra-diegetic spectators complicates fixed economies of desire as 'The audience members model subject-status, but also are depicted as objects, for each other and for the extra-diegetic spectator [which] enables the dizzying, simultaneous occupation of both subject and object for nearly everyone in the video' (1997: 106–7).

The first sequence of *The Crash Pad* likewise utilises an intra-diegetic voyeur. As in Conway's discussion of *Safe Is Desire* in which the main characters 'serve as models for the education of lesbian produced porn viewing' (1997: 101), the presence of the voyeuristic Simone offers lesbian viewers unused to the consumption of pornography a desiring, voyeuristic subject on which to model themselves. Unlike in *Safe Is Desire* however, where the economies of desire are rather free-flowing, Simone is not positioned as an object of desire. Not only is she fully clothed, shots of her are apart from the pornographic 'action', and generally take the form of close-ups of her face in an eyeline match with the scene that is taking place, prompting the viewer to follow her gaze rather than gaze upon her.

It is significant that one of the participants in this scene (Jiz Lee) had initially come into the crash pad with Simone in order to have sex, and attempts to leave when noting that the venue is already in use. Simone stops Jiz, prompting her to engage in sexual intercourse with the two prior inhabitants (Dylan and Jo) for Simone's viewing pleasure. This narrative logic promotes the pleasurable possibilities of sexual voyeurism and is suggestive of sex-radical ideologies of non-monogamy. A flashback point-of-view sequence in black and white from Simone's perspective towards the end of the sequence further highlights her positioning with the viewer. This sequence shows Jiz kissing Dylan after her orgasm. That it is this gesture of intimacy that is recalled by Simone in a point-of-view flashback, and that it is then suggested as pleasurable for Simone via a close-up on her face, further offers to its viewers a cultural logic that discourages possessiveness in sexual partnerings.

A further level of intra-diegetic voyeurism takes the form of the metafilmic inclusion of the director, and the revelation at the ending that the crash pad itself is a 'set-up' by the director, filled with hidden cameras. *Tick Tock* also features a character who observes the other participants via hidden CCTV cameras, with frequent shots of the character masturbating to her screen – providing a model, like Simone, for the lesbian porn viewer. *The Crash Pad*, however, takes this trope further by highlighting the role of the filmmaker, generally absent from mainstream hard-core pornography, and indeed, film more generally. Early in *The Crash Pad*, we see the director give the key of the crash pad to another woman, outlining the 'rules' of the venue. During this scene, Houston is shot from a high angle, over the shoulder of the character to whom she is giving the key, thus positioning the viewer with this character as being given the metaphoric 'key' to the crash pad via the film itself.

During *The Crash Pad*'s final sexual sequence, a solo masturbation scene, the subject (Jo, who had previously been involved in the first threesome scene that Simone observed) gazes fixedly into the camera, with frequent cuts away to black and white footage, and shots from different angles. After Jo's orgasm, she looks directly at the camera, then laughs, turning away. The scene ends with a focus on Jo's face, zooming out in colour as Jo gives a little wave to the camera/viewer. A wipe of a water-ripple during the zoom-out transforms the colour image into a black and white image, which is revealed to be on a computer desktop with another shot of the scene, obviously part of an editing process, which it is then revealed is being presided over by

Fig. 27 *The Crash Pad*'s director Shine Louise Houston is revealed as 'behind' the hidden cameras.

Houston, who ends the film by turning to the camera, smiling and raising her eyebrow playfully before turning back to her work.

This segment not only reveals the narrative of hidden cameras, and a deliberate filmic voyeurism, but positions the viewer as complicit in Houston's secret watching of these women's sexual lives. This scene also, through Jo, demonstrates an exhibitionist willing to be watched, which acts to ethically authorise this device, and the viewer's voyeurism. This is quite unlike the positioning of the female voyeur in *Tick Tock*, who is 'caught' at the end by one of the women she has been observing, and is playfully told that she has been 'Busted. You know I could call the police and put you in jail for this. But you'd like it too much.' The – albeit playful – spectre of police in *Tick Tock* is nowhere present in *The Crash Pad*, as Houston is not only authorised by Jo's knowingness, but by her coy interrogation of the act of filmmaking itself as an act of voyeurism.

GENDERING

Another important feature of proving lesbian authenticity within lesbian pornography comes in the form of the character Conway describes as 'the most visibly deviant lesbian, the most serious contender for the male gaze, and as such the character absent from "All-Girl" mainstream porn: the butch dyke' (1997: 106). Such theorists of lesbian pornography as Butler see the butch as the figure who 'authenticates lesbian pornography, even if only superficially ... [w]ithout necessarily being convinced of 'real' pleasure or a real orgasm, the viewer may nevertheless acknowledge a lesbian authenticity through the figure of the butch' (2004: 169). The display of butch actresses, or those who otherwise do not fit within mainstream ideals of female beauty, within lesbian pornography can further be seen as bringing a specifically lesbian erotic economy to productions, as well as being indicative of a certain political intent that wishes to renegotiate accepted standards of which bodies are to be deemed attractive or erotic.

Sugar High Glitter City features a multiplicity of visual styles and body types. From co-producer and performer Jackie Strano's portrayal of a butch undercover detective, to a scene involving a drag king and a middle-aged boi engaging in sexual activity visually identifiable with gay male sex, to the high femme sugar 'Madam', who has a fuller figure than actresses generally seen in conventional pornography.[5] This 'diversity of body types' (Conway 1997: 95) is often a feature of lesbian pornography, and acts to authenticate the film and differentiate it from heterosexually-produced 'all-girl' pornography, in which the actresses are generally feminine, large breasted, and, quite disturbingly to many lesbian viewers, often have long fingernails.

Madam and Eve, conversely, does not display any butch actresses. Following Conway and Butler's perspectives, some may argue that the femininity of *Madam and Eve*'s actresses renders it less authentic, and more invested in catering to the male gaze. Indeed, with its fantastical scenario, and elaborate latex costumes, including the fetish-like nurse outfits, *Madam and Eve* could be said to be little different from heterosexual pornography. If we agree with Dolan's discussion of (live) sex performers in a lesbian environment claiming subjectivity through performing the butch role (1989: 63), these performers would be viewed as necessarily entrapped, due to their femininity, as objects in the realm of desire and spectatorship. But is feminine subjectivity, or at least agency, truly impossible within such a context? Within most examples of lesbian pornography that I have investigated, it is indeed the butch(er) one who is almost always the sexual top, furthering the ideological connections between masculinity and active sexuality. Where a masculine lesbian is topped, it is almost always by another masculine lesbian, which does not undermine this characterisation. Within *Madam and Eve*, however, perhaps due to this absence, there is room for the depiction of an active feminine sexual agency, most clearly articulated in the character of Eve.

The character of Eve is markedly feminine, and yet through her dominance and sexual prowess she displays an active feminine sexual agency. This occurs most distinctively in the *Madam and Eve* scene which depicts Eve having sex with two women simultaneously, utilising two dildos strapped to her thighs to pleasure the women. While entering into the phallic visual economy through the use of the dildos, the repositioning and doubling recontextualises this, so that within this sequence, the feminine woman is not only depicted as the

Fig. 28 Eve's active sexual agency in *Madam and Eve*.

sexual top, but is rendered as exceeding and thus potentially undermining the schema of super-virility usually associated with masculinity.

Unlike *Madam and Eve*, *The Crash Pad* offers a multiplicity of gendered styles. This includes an obviously butch-femme couple (who it is revealed, in an interview in the DVD extras, are a couple in real life), as well as a threesome involving a feminine woman and two more masculine women with a feminine intra-diegetic spectator. Each of these, however, do share the conventionalised schema of the butch(er) participant as necessarily the sexual top. The complication or difference of this from heterosexual pornography is that it is indeed the feminine, seemingly 'passive' character upon whose pleasure the activity is focused. Thus, she is not portrayed as a passive object as in much heterosexual pornography, but rather is an active, desiring subject.

Indeed, in the first sexual sequence of *The Crash Pad*, the feminine Dylan directs the actions of the two more masculine women who are ostensibly topping her, regularly switching positions to optimise her own pleasure. That the intra-diegetic voyeur is also on the feminine spectrum implies and encourages the viewerly identification with the one being penetrated, which encourages a different logic of spectatorship from much heterosexual pornography wherein the viewer is encouraged to identify with the (male) sexually 'active' participant. The conventions are also subverted in that the orgasmic culmination of the scene takes place via Dylan's digitally stimulating her own clitoris, while her two partners lie on each side of her, stimulating her nipples, rendering the 'active' sexual partner, if not superfluous, then at least foreplay to the 'main dish' of an empowered feminine sexuality that knows what it wants.

FEMALE EJACULATION

A later sexual sequence in *The Crash Pad* depicts a boi-boi couple. As Felice Newman observes 'Two bois enter the pad and proceed to wrestle for dominance – this is a visual reference to a standard in the canon of gay male pornography in which the loser's butt is the trophy of the victor' (2006). Despite such referents, and a certain level of adherence to these conventions, there is shortly some switching between the partners. The conventions of gay male and heterosexual pornography, and the power relations depicted therein, are further undermined by the female ejaculation scene. Butler proposes that

> Lacan's formula, and the subsequent feminist critique of its formulation, implies that the phallus belongs to the man, yet the lesbian with her object of penetration can perform all the same things that the penis/phallus can perform during the sex act, *except for one very important thing* – she, or rather her dildo, does not ejaculate … This stands in direct contrast to the end of a typical sex scene in heterosexual pornography, in which a man will ejaculate on some part of the female body … female protagonists in heterosexual pornography … turn, for the most part, into cum-catchers, and there is little attempt to represent female pleasure in any form other than a smiling or ecstatic face dripping with semen. (2004: 184–5)

Butler is using this discussion to argue that 'the strap-on dildo provides the kind of agency to a woman (or two women) that a man's penis simply does not' (2004: 185), noting but not positioning as central that while the strap-on itself may not ejaculate, the female partner of the woman wearing it may indeed do so.

Towards the end of this sexual sequence in *The Crash Pad*, the 'loser' of the initial wrestling match (Jiz Lee) who has been the primary bottom in this sequence, after much penetration, ejaculates copious amounts of fluid, to which her partner (Shawn) responds by positioning herself underneath Jiz and 'drinking' it. This is clearly a visual reference to the convention of 'ejaculation on the woman's face' or 'facial' (Butler 2004: 184) that Butler discusses, and yet it also undermines this convention through the reversal of power and sexual agency it performs. This scene in *The Crash Pad* repositions visually depictable erotic agency within the female body, subverting these conventions of ejaculation rather than simply removing them. This sexual sequence, which does not contain any dildos, empowers female sexuality, and recontextualises 'passive' female sexuality beyond the simple removal of the male or the male gaze, by rendering ejaculation the role of the penetrated partner, realigning notions of active and passive sexuality.

Linda Williams cites the work of Gertrud Koch, who asserts that

> all film pornography is a 'drive for knowledge' that takes place through a voyeurism structured as a cognitive urge. Invoking Foucault, Koch argues that film pornography can be viewed as an important mechanism in the wholesale restructuring of the experience of sexuality into a visual form. (1989: 48)

The principle of maximum visibility can be seen in the manner in which 'the genre has consistently maintained certain clinical-documentary qualities at the expense of other forms of realism or artistry that might actually be more arousing' (ibid.). With the principle of maximum visibility guiding the genre, difficulty arises in the restructuring of the experience of female sexuality into a visual form, for 'while it is possible, in a certain limited and reductive way, to "represent" the physical pleasure of the male by showing erection and ejaculation, this maximum visibility proves elusive in the parallel confession of female sexual pleasure' (1989: 49). Williams goes on to note that 'Hard core desires assurance that it is witnessing not the voluntary performance of feminine pleasure, but its involuntary confession' (1989: 50).

The abovementioned scene from *The Crash Pad* makes it possible to 'represent' the physical pleasure of the female, visibly depicting a 'confession' of sexual pleasure in much the same manner as it has been for males in the genre of hard core pornography. While the sheer volume of fluid that Jiz ejaculates may make the viewer question whether or not this indeed has been 'faked' in some way, the volume is also suggestive of a form of involuntary 'confession'. For if the filmmakers had wished to fake such a thing, they would undoubtedly have taken a more modest approach to the quantity of ejaculate in order to convince their viewers of the 'veracity' of the scene, as authenticity is clearly important in this video, as evidenced by the included interviews that are at pains to exposit that the women enjoyed the sex acts they engaged in for the making of the film.

The scene also takes on the 'educational' model Maureen Engel sees as a feature of such print forms of lesbian pornography as *On Our Backs* (2003: 80–8). As J. L. Sevely and J. W. Bennett observe, 'Culture and language tend to obscure knowledge that the human female has a prostate gland and is capable of ejaculation' (1978: 1). The question of whether women do indeed ejaculate, which Sevely and Bennett back in 1978 felt could not yet be answered conclusively, has since been determined by sex researchers through its being *made visible* to them via the anecdotes and testing of women who experience it (see Addiego *et al.*; Belzer 1981; Heath 1984), and indeed made further visible by such products as the Fanny Fatale (Debi Sundahl, co-founder of *On Our Backs*) sex educational video *How to Female Ejaculate* (1992). There is still, however, a great deal of ignorance about the possibility of female ejaculation, and visible depiction such as that seen in *The Crash Pad* demonstrates to women via visual representation sexual possibilities of the female body of which they may previously have been unaware.

Previous scholars have identified particular historical periods of lesbian pornography, and this chapter continues that project by analysing lesbian pornographic texts produced after the millennium. What can be witnessed in the post-millennial period is that elements of each of the earlier eras of lesbian-produced pornography coexist in contemporary lesbian pornographic films. The project of expanding the boundaries of pornographic film to create a specifically lesbian sexual iconography continues, and the genre is stretching and growing through the work of producers who thoughtfully consider such issues as the visual representation of female orgasm, and seek to subvert dominant gendered power dynamics.

NOTES

1 A longer version of this chapter has been previously been published as: Rebecca Beirne (2008) 'Dressing Up, Strapping On and Stripping Off: Contemporary Lesbian Pornographic Cultural Production', Chapter Five of *Lesbians in Television and Text after the Millennium*. New York: Palgrave Macmillan, 135–66.
2 See Henderson (1992), Bensinger (1992), Healey (1996) or Wilton (1996). The latter two monographs offer a fuller account of the political debates surrounding this issue.
3 For a discussion of the lesbian burlesque/striptease show Gurlesque please see Beirne (2008), 142-165.
4 Including such work as C. Coover's *Small Favors* (2002) or P. Waldron and J. Finch's *The Adventures of a Lesbian College Schoolgirl* (1998).
5 In lesbian culture, the identity of 'boi' refers to a masculine/androgynous woman.

WORKS CITED

Addiego, F., E. G. Belzer, J. Comolli, W. Moger, J. D. Perry and B. Whipple (1981) 'Female Ejaculation: A Case Study', *The Journal of Sex Research*, 17, 1, 13–21.

Beirne, R. (2008) *Lesbians in Television and Text after the Millennium*. New York: Palgrave Macmillan.

Belzer, E. G. (1981) 'Orgasmic Expulsions of Women: A Review and Heuristic Inquiry', *The*

Journal of Sex Research, 17, 1, 1–12.

Bensinger, T. (1992) 'Lesbian Pornography: The Re/Making of (a) Community', *Discourse*, 15, 1, 69–93.

Butler, H. (2004) 'What Do You Call a Lesbian with Long Fingers?: The Development of Dyke Pornography', in L. Williams (ed.) *Porn Studies*. Durham: Duke University Press, 167–97.

Conway, M. (1997) 'Spectatorship in Lesbian Porn: The Woman's Woman's Film', *Wide Angle*, 19, 3, 91–113.

Coover, C. (2002) *Small Favors Girly Porno Comic Collection: Book One*. Seattle: Eros Comix.

Dolan, J. (1989) 'Desire Cloaked in a Trenchcoat', *The Drama Review: A Journal of Performance Studies*, 31, 1, 59–67.

Duggan, L. (2002) 'The New Homonormativity: The Sexual Politics of Neoliberalism', in R. Castronovo and D. D. Nelson (eds) *Materializing Democracy: Toward a Revitalized Cultural Politics*. Durham: Duke University Press, 175–94.

Engel, M. (2003) 'Arousing Possibilities: The Cultural Work of Lesbian Pornography', unpublished Ph.D. thesis, University of Alberta.

Healey, E. (1996) *Lesbian Sex Wars*. London: Virago.

Heath, D. (1984) 'An Investigation Into the Origins of a Copious Vaginal Discharge During Intercourse: "enough to wet the bed"– that "is not urine"', *The Journal of Sex Research*, 20, 2, 194–215.

Henderson, L. (1992) 'Lesbian Pornography: Cultural Transgression and Sexual Demystification', in S. Munt (ed.) *New Lesbian Criticism: Literary and Cultural Readings*. New York: Columbia University Press, 173–91.

Lewis, R. & K. Rolley (1996) 'Ad(dressing) the dyke: Lesbian looks and lesbians looking', in P. Horne and R. Lewis (eds) *Outlooks: Lesbian and Gay Sexualities and Visual Cultures*. London and New York: Routledge, 178–90.

Lo, M. (2006) 'She's a Very Dirty Girl: The transformation from art student to pornographer was a simple one for queer auteur Shine Louise Houston', *Curve*, February, 42–3.

Mulvey, L. (1989) 'Afterthoughts on 'Visual Pleasure and Narrative Cinema' inspired by King Vidor's *Duel in the Sun* (1946)', in L. Mulvey, *Visual and Other Pleasures*. Basingstoke, Hampshire: The Macmillan Press, 29–38.

Newman, F. (2006) 'Don't Miss *The Crash Pad*', *San Francisco Bay Times*, 2 March. On-line. Available: http://www.sfbaytimes.com/?sec=article&article (accessed 8 April 2006).

Queerscreen (2004) 'Mardi Gras Film Festival Guide', liftout from *The Sydney Star Observer*, 15 January, QS01–20.

Rowlson, A. (2004) 'Gets Real', *Fab: The Gay Scene Magazine*. On-line. Available: http://www.fabmagazine.com/features/insideout2004/ (accessed 12 March 2006).

Sevely, J. L. and J. W. Bennett (1978) 'Concerning Female Ejaculation and the Female Prostate', *The Journal of Sex Research*, 14, 1, 1–20.

Waldron, P. & J. Finch (1998) *The Adventures of a Lesbian College Schoolgirl*. New York: Amerotica/NBM.

Williams, L. (1989) *Hard Core: Power, Pleasure and the 'Frenzy of the Visible'*. Berkeley and Los Angeles: University of California Press.

Wilton, T. (1996) *Finger-Licking Good: The Ins and Outs of Lesbian Sex*. London and New York: Cassell.

SELECTED FILMOGRAPHY

The following filmography is a select list of films relevant to the focus on hard-core pornography and explicit sex in this collection. This filmography is based on a variety of sources and is as accurate as possible.

9 Songs (Michael Winterbottom, 2004, UK)
Anatomy of Hell (Catherine Breillat, 2002 France)
Animal Trainer Series (Various, 1999–2009, USA)
Anonymous French Shorts (uncredited, n.d.)
Art School Sluts (Eon McKai, 2004, USA)
Auto Focus (Paul Schrader, 2002, USA)
Baise-Moi (Virginie Despentes, Coralie Trinh Thi, 2000, France)
Bare Tales (Daniel Bonneto, 1987, Germany/Czech Republic)
Behind the Green Door (Artie Mitchell, Jim Mitchell, 1972, USA)
Blacklight Beauty (Jack the Zipper, 2005, USA)
Big Guns (William Higgins, 1987, USA)
Breeding Mike O'Neill (Paul Morris, 2002, USA)
Bring 'em Back Nude (uncredited, c.1930s)
Butthole Pirates Series (Various, 2005–2006, USA)
The Casting Couch (uncredited, c.1920s)
Caught in the Barbed Wire (uncredited, n.d.)
Coed Devirginizations (David Luger, 2001, USA)
Confessions of a Co-ed (David Burton, 1931, USA)
A Country Stud Horse (uncredited, c.1920s)
The Crash Pad (Shine Louise Houston, 2005, USA)
Cumsloppy Buttholes (Paul Morris, 2004, USA)
Dawson's 20 Load Weekend (Max Stohl, 2004, USA)
Dawson's 50 Load Weekend (Max Sohl, 2005, USA)
Deep Throat (Gerard Damiano, 1972, USA)
Destricted (Marina Abramovic, Matthew Barney, Marco Brambilla, Larry Clark, Marilyn Minter, Gaspar Noé, Richard Prince, Sam Taylor-Wood, 2006, UK/USA)
The Devil In Miss Jones (Gerard Damiano, 1973, USA)
Do You Believe In Swedish Sin? (Gunnar Hoglund, 1972, Germany)

SELECTED FILMOGRAPHY

Dressage au Fouet (uncredited, n.d.)
E for Eva (Jonni Darkko, 2007, USA)
Emmanuelle (Just Jaekin, 1974, France)
Erotic Dreams a.k.a. *Wet Dreams* (Lasse Braun, Max Fishcer, Oscar Gigard, Hans Kanters, Geert Koolman, Lee Kraft, Dusan Makavajev, Nicholas Ray, Jens Jørgen Thorsen, Heathcote Williams, 1974, Nertherlands/Germany)
Erotic In Nature (Cristen L. Rothermund, 1985, USA)
Euro Domination Series (Christoph Clark, 2004–2006, USA)
Fashion Models Gone Bad (Hank Spain, 2005, USA)
Fashionably Laid (Jessica Dee, 2004, USA)
The Fashionistas (John Stagliano, 2002, USA)
Fashionistas Safado Series (John Stagliano, 2006–2007, USA)
Finnish Fuck Film (uncredited, 2007, Finland)
Flesh Hunter 3 (Jules Jordan, 2002, USA)
A Free Ride (uncredited, c.1923)
Fuck Team Five: The Afro Fuck (Bang Bros, 2008, USA)
Fucked in Finland (uncredited, 2004, Finland)
Getting His Goat a.k.a. *On the Beach* (uncredited, c.1925)
The Girl Next Door (Luke Greenfield, 2004, USA)
Girl Pirates Series (Various, 2005–2006, USA)
The Good Old Naughty Days (Michel Reilhac, 2002, France)
Hail Caesar (Chi Chi La Rue, 1999, USA)
Hardhat Gang Bang (Chi Chi La Rue, 2000, USA)
A Hole In My Heart (Lukas Moodysson, 2004, Sweden)
The Idiots (Lars von Trier, 1998, Spain/Denmark/Sweden/France/Netherlands/Italy)
In the Realm of the Senses (Nagisa Ôshima, 1976, Japan/France)
In Your Wildest Dreams (Bill Clayton, 1988, USA)
Initiations Series (Various, 1999–2006, USA)
Inside Deep Throat (Fenton Bailey, Randy Barbato, 2005, USA)
Intimacy (Patrice Chéreau, 2001, France/UK/Germany/Spain)
Intoxicated (Bunny Luv, 2005, USA)
Irreversible (Gaspar Noé, 2002, France)
Island Fever Series (Joone, 2001–2007, USA)
Jack's Playground Series (Robby D., 2003–, USA)
Jesse Jane Sexy Hot (Celeste, 2008, USA),
KKK Night Riders (uncredited, c.1930s)
Loaded (Max Sohl, 2007, USA)
Lord of the G-Strings: The Femaleship of the String (Terry West, 2002, USA)
Madam and Eve (Angie Dowling, 2003, UK)
The Magic Birds (Kullero Koivisto, 2008, Finland)
Max Extreme 4 (Max Steiner, 1998, USA)
Max Hardcore Extreme Schoolgirls 1 (Max Steiner, 2003, USA)
Max Hardcore Extreme Schoolgirls 6: Euro Version (Max Steiner, 2004, USA)
Max Hardcore Fists of Fury 3 (Max Steiner, 2004, USA)

Max Hardcore Golden Guzzlers 5 (Max Steiner, 2003, USA)
Max Hardcore Golden Guzzlers 6 (Max Steiner, 2003, USA)
Meat Packing (Max Sohl, 2006, USA)
Meat Rack (Max Sohl, 2005, USA)
Modern Pirates (uncredited, c.1930s)
The Moguls (Michael Traeger, 2005, USA/Germany)
Nasty Tails Series (Various, 2005–07, USA)
Nude Diversion (uncredited, n.d.)
The Opening of Misty Beethoven (Radley Metzger, 1975, USA)
Out of Bounds (Bill Clayton, 1987, USA)
The Passionate Farmhand (uncredited, c.1920s)
The Pay Off (uncredited, c.1950s)
Phoenix Rising (Chi Chi La Rue, 1999, USA)
The Piano Teacher (Michael Haneke, 2001, Austria/France/Germany)
Pirates (Joone, 2005, USA)
Pirates II: Stagnetti's Revenge (Joone, 2008, USA)
Plantin' Seed (Paul Morris, 2005, USA)
Plowed (Paul Morris, 2000, USA)
Pure Max 16: Euro Version (Max Steiner, 2004, USA)
Pussyman's Fashion Dolls (David Christopher, 2001–2005, USA)
Riding Billy Wild (Paul Morris, 2003, USA)
Roman Holiday (uncredited, n.d.)
Romance (Catherine Breillat, 1999, France)
Seymore Butts' Butt Pirates of the Caribbean (Seymore Butts, 2006, USA)
Sex: The Annabelle Chong Story (Gough Lewis, 1999, USA)
Shortbus (John Cameron Mitchell, 2006, USA)
Sleeping Around (Stormy Daniels, 2008, USA)
Smart Aleck (uncredited, c.1951–1953)
Specs Appeal Series (Andre Madness, 2001–2004, USA)
The Story of X (Chuck Workman, 1998, USA)
Sugar High Glitter City (Shar Rednour, 2001, USA)
Surrender the Booty Series (Various, 2005–2006, USA)
Taboo: The Beginning of Erotic Cinema (Brandon Christopher, 2004, USA)
Teenage Jailbait (Godfrey Daniels, 1973, USA)
Tera Patrick's Fashion Underground (Paul Thomas, 2006, USA)
Tick Tock (Angie Dowling, 2001, UK)
True Anal Stories (Various, 1998–2004, USA)
Uncle Si and the Sirens (uncredited, c.1938, USA)
Upload (Ellie Cross, 2006, USA)
Venus in Furs (Victor Nieuwenhuijs, Maartje Seyferth's 1995, Netherlands)
Virtual Sex Series (Joone, 2002–, USA)
What I Can't See (Paul Morris, 1999, USA)

INDEX

9 Songs (film) 24–5, 153, 196

Adam and Eve (production company) 129
agency 6–7, 51, 68, 73, 83, 86–90, 105, 118, 178, 191, 209–10, 238–40
AIDS; HIV 33, 36–7, 223–4
altporn 6, 42–54
amateur 20, 35, 44, 56, 68–9, 88–9, 103, 123, 131, 154, 180–1, 204, 209, 211, 232
Angelina, Eva 69, 194–200, 204–13
archive 81–99
arousal 3, 7, 11, 27, 34, 118, 148, 162–3, 183–4, 205, 207–8, 211
art-house; art cinema 22, 25, 153–4, 178, 196–7
Arthurs, Jane 27
barebacking 223–4, 228

Behind the Green Door (film) 6, 13–14, 101–12, 131
Belladonna 152–3, 159–60
Bella Vendetta 6, 43–4, 50–3
Biasin, Enrico 113, 124, 200, 212
Blacklight Beauty (film) 201, 213
body modification 43, 53
Boogie Nights (film) 13, 18–20
Braun, Lasse 178
Breillat, Catherine 23, 197
Butler, Heather 229–32, 237–8, 240
Caesar 221–3
Caesar's Hardhat Gangbang (film) 222

celebrity 3, 21, 32, 35, 41, 45, 63, 105, 161–2, 188, 228
censorship 13, 19, 35–6, 57–9, 61–2, 65, 75–8, 83

Chambers, Marilyn 101, 105
Church Gibson, Pamela 5, 7, 147
cinéma-vérité 154
coercion 70, 72, 83, 86, 91–4, 101, 104–5, 205
comedy 19, 24, 86, 166, 184, 214, 230
community 20, 53, 57, 59, 165–6, 175, 223, 231–2
consumption 11–16, 28, 48, 55, 65, 75, 95, 106, 110–11, 117, 150, 205, 209, 233
Conway, Mary 229, 235, 237–8
Crash Pad, The (film) 229–30, 235–42

Dark Side of Pornography, The (TV documentary series) 27–30, 33–4
Dawson 225–7
Dawson's 20 Load Weekend (film) 226
Deep Throat (film) 13–15, 18, 22, 25, 32, 65, 105, 131, 195
desire 5–6, 12, 16–18, 35, 56, 67, 71–2, 77, 86, 95, 99, 104, 106, 117–19, 123, 143, 147–9, 162, 166–7, 173, 175, 189, 197, 210, 221–2, 227, 231–6
Digital Playground (production company) 129–43
Dines, Gail 60
diversity 42, 47, 50, 176, 199, 223, 229, 238

documentary; docuporn 13, 18, 20–2, 27–8, 34–5, 37, 90–2, 105, 164, 169, 176, 178, 195, 225–7, 241
Dowling, Angie 210, 229–30
Dworkin, Andrea 61, 195, 205
dyke 230–1, 234, 237

E for Eva (film) 204–5
education 3, 6, 29, 57–8, 61–5, 69, 74, 97, 227, 235, 241–2
ejaculation 12, 24, 94, 109, 122–3, 136, 198, 202, 240–2
Elegant Angel (production company) 114
Evil Empire (production company) 152, 154, 157, 159
exploitation 5, 67, 92, 96, 105
Extreme Schoolgirls 1 (film) 119–21

fantasy 6, 23, 37, 47, 62, 70–2, 84, 101–12, 129, 150, 161, 180, 186, 203, 218–19, 227
Fashionistas, The (film) 7, 149, 152–4, 157–60
female sexuality 23, 37, 48–9, 104–5, 134, 207, 241
feminism 13–14, 49, 52, 102, 116–17
fetish 19, 43, 46, 48–50, 67, 71, 121, 156–9, 190, 223, 230
Finnish Fuck Film (film) 177, 182–5, 190
Foucault, Michel 5, 118, 241
Fuck Team 5: The Afro Fuck (film) 204, 207–8, 211

gay 7, 50, 83, 111, 134, 157–8, 215–30, 234, 238, 240
gaze 7, 48, 103, 109, 111, 118, 201–2, 230, 232–4, 236–8, 241
gonzo 37–8, 113, 118, 120, 154–5, 181, 184, 201–11
Good Old Naughty Days, The (film compilation) 12, 97

Hail Caesar (film) 221

Hardcore, Max 36–8, 113–25, 153
heterosexual 4, 7, 46, 72–3, 77, 82–3, 97, 104, 115–16, 119, 156–9, 189, 216–18, 230–4, 238–40
Hole in my Heart (film) 21–2, 24
homoerotic 83, 85, 99, 119, 134, 158
homosocial 83, 97, 199
Houston, Shine Louise 230–1, 236–7

In the Realm of the Senses (film) 173
Intimacy (film) 166, 196–7

Jacobs, Katrien 43–4, 52
Jameson, Jenna 47, 160
Jancovich, Mark 45, 216
Jeremy, Ron 47, 161, 199
Joone 130, 137, 141
Juffer, Jane 45

Kendrick, Walter 63, 95, 148
Kipnis, Laura 5, 46–7, 88, 148, 202
Krafft-Ebing, Richard von 159

Lehman, Peter 5, 68, 85–6, 141
lesbian 7, 49, 67–8, 161, 209, 229–42
Liekki, Rakel 178–80, 185
Lovelace, Linda 91, 105, 195–6, 210

McNair, Brian 5, 6, 11, 45
MacKinnon, Catherine 61, 102
McClintock, Anne 119, 121, 158
Madam and Eve (film) 229–35, 238–9
Magic Birds, The (film) 177, 182, 185–90
Meat Rack (film) 226
misogyny 104, 202, 234
Morris, Paul 224, 226, 228
Museum of Sex (MoSex) 1–5

neoliberal 114, 116–18, 122–3
No Fauxxx (website) 43–4, 47, 49–50, 53
non-nude porn 148, 156, 162

O'Toole, Laurence 5, 63, 131
objectification 14, 104, 155, 234
obscenity 57–61, 65, 102, 114, 153
Opening of Misty Beethoven, The (film) 105, 152

Paris, Tristan 219–20
Paasonen, Susanna 7, 28, 52, 177, 211
Penley, Constance 85–90, 93
perversion 156
Phoenix Rising (film) 220
pin-up 3, 46–50
Pirates (film) 7, 126–43
Playboy 49, 65, 90
pleasure 3, 5, 16–17, 32, 51–2, 56, 83–6, 92–3, 103–5, 113–26, 137, 163–4, 167, 171–5, 188–90, 194, 198, 206–10, 226–8, 234–41
Porn: A Family Business (TV series) 30–2, 36
porno-chic 3, 5, 13–23, 45, 101–2, 151–2
porn industry 13, 16–17, 19, 21–2, 37, 42, 47, 114, 122, 127, 131–3, 140, 190, 218, 222–3
Private (production company) 178

queer 7, 43, 53, 83, 223

realism 7, 47, 113, 119, 154, 177, 182–4, 190, 211, 226
'real' sex 29, 117, 163–4, 1904, 197–8, 204
Riot Grrrl 49
Romance (film) 23–5, 153, 164, 196–7, 211
Rubin, Gayle 63, 77

sadomasochism 23, 158
Schaefer, Eric 81, 91
sex industry 27–41, 50, 210
sex toys 46, 129, 189, 205
sexworker 53, 64, 81–98
Shortbus (film) 7, 24, 163–76

Siffredi, Rocco 23, 124, 152, 157, 159, 211
Sin, Allie 194, 200–1, 213
soft-core 7, 13–14, 27–8, 36, 60, 99, 156, 227
stag film 2–3, 6, 67, 81–99, 103, 119
Stagliano, John 149, 152, 154, 157–9
stereotypical 50, 71, 148, 160
subculture 43–4, 48–9, 52, 157, 224
subversion 45, 87, 115
Sugar High Glitter City (film) 229–30, 238
Suicide Girls 43–4, 46, 48–52, 54

tattoo 47–8, 51, 135, 149, 160, 196, 200, 204, 221
teaching porn 64
technology 3, 5, 11, 15, 17, 48, 77, 103, 109, 112, 115, 118, 127, 130–1, 133, 167, 173–4, 217
television 6, 22, 27–9, 33, 35–8, 40–1, 103, 161, 184, 232
Theroux, Louis 22, 199
Tick Tock (film) 229–32, 236–7
transgression 12, 18, 44–6, 68, 143
Treasure Island Media (Production Company) 223–4

video 3, 11, 15, 22, 45, 63, 72–3, 82–3, 87, 97, 100, 102, 108, 111, 115, 131–2, 140, 143, 150, 156, 169, 174, 176, 178, 181, 198, 203–4, 215, 217, 219–29, 231–2, 235, 241
violence 40, 51, 68, 102–4, 135, 205
Violet Blue 42, 53
Vivid (production company) 42, 53, 128
voyeurism 11–12, 171–3, 235–7, 241

Waugh, Thomas 83, 85, 87, 92, 98–9, 119, 216, 227
Williams, Linda 5–6, 11, 14, 61–3, 81, 96–7, 101, 103, 105, 113–14, 118–21, 136, 147, 152, 175, 187, 195–9, 241

Zecca, Frederico 113–14

GPSR Authorized Representative: Easy Access System Europe, Mustamäe tee 50, 10621 Tallinn, Estonia, gpsr.requests@easproject.com